Lead Us Into Temptation

Lead Us Into Temptation

The Triumph of American Materialism

James B. Twitchell

COLUMBIA UNIVERSITY PRESS

New York

Publishers Since 1893

New York   Chichester, West Sussex

Copyright © 1999 James B. Twitchell

All rights reserved

Library of Congress Cataloging-in-Publication Data

Twitchell, James B.

   Lead us into temptation : the triumph of American materialism /
James B. Twitchell.

      p. cm.

   Includes bibliographical references and index.

   ISBN 0–231–11518–0 (cloth)—ISBN 0–231–51919–9 (pbk.)

      1. Consumption (Economics)—United States.   2. Materialism—Social
aspects—United States.   I. Title.

   HC110.C6T89 1999

   339.4′7′0973—dc21   98–45385

Designed by Benjamin S. Farber

⊗

Casebound editions of Columbia University Press books are printed on permanent
and durable acid-free paper.

Printed in the United States of America

c 10 9 8 7 6 5 4 3 2 1

p 10 9 8 7 6 5 4 3 2 1

For Kate & Liz

They rage against materialism, as they call it,
forgetting that there has been no material
improvement that has not spiritualized the world....

—Oscar Wilde,
The Critic as Artist

Contents

Lead Us Into Temptation

Introduction

I don't care about losing the money, it's losing all this stuff.

—Mrs. Navin R. Johnson on filing for bankruptcy, *The Jerk*, 1979

ONE of the most helpful ways to understand modern American materialism is to watch Steve Martin in *The Jerk*. In this movie by Carl Reiner, Mr. Martin plays a kind of idiot savant named Navin R. Johnson. The story is held together by the running joke that when Navin is being the most idiotic, he is really being the most savant.

After a series of misadventures, Navin amasses a fortune by inventing a way to keep eyeglasses from slipping down the nose (the "Opti-grab"). He wins the hand of his sweetheart, buys incredibly gauche gold chains, swag lamps, outrageous golf carts, and ersatz Grecian mansions. Surrounded by things, he is finally happy. But then—curses!—he loses his possessions as google-eyed Carl Reiner wins a class-action suit because the Opti-grab has made many wearers cross-eyed. Navin's wife (Bernadette Peters) is distraught. She bursts into tears. "I don't care about losing the money, it's losing all this stuff."

Navin, as innocent as he is honest, says he doesn't really care about these things, he knows who he is without possessions. His sense of self is certainly not tied to the material world. "I don't want stuff . . . I don't need anything," he says to her as he starts to leave the room in his pajamas. He sees an old ashtray. "Except this ashtray, and that's the only thing I need is this," he says, as he leans over to pick it up. Navin walks to the door. "Well, and this paddle game and the ashtray is all I need. And this, this remote control; that's all I need, just the ashtray, paddle game, and this remote control."

Navin is growing progressively more frantic in vintage Steve Martin fashion. He is in the hall now, pajamas down around his knees and his arms full of stuff. "And these matches. Just the ashtray, paddle ball, remote control, and these matches . . . and this lamp, and that's all I need. I don't need one other thing. I need this [he picks up a kitchen chair], but I don't need one other thing . . . except this magazine." We hear him gathering more things as he disappears down the hall.

We next see Navin leaving the mansion, now under a mound of things, still repeating the litany of what he needs, and proclaiming he needs nothing more. He soon leaves our sight walking down the road and we hear him say, "I don't need anything except my dog [and we hear his dog growling], no, I don't need my dog, but I need this chair, but I don't need anything more than the ashtray, the paddle game, the remote control, the chair."

Navin, jerk enough to think he needs nothing, is sage enough not to leave home without a few of his favorite things. In doing so he opens up one of the central myths of consumerist culture: protestations of independence are loudest where things are paramount. Navin is Everyman for our times. No other culture spends so much time declaring things don't matter while saying "just charge it." The country with the highest per capita consumer debt and the greatest number of machine-made things is the same country in which Puritan ascetic principles are most pronounced and held in highest regard. In repeated Gallup polls, when respondents are asked to choose what is really important—family life, betterment of society, strict morals, and the like—"having nice things" comes in dead *last* (Schor, *The Overworked American* 126). On the way to Walden Pond, we pack the sport utility vehicle with the dish antenna, the cell phone, the bread maker, the ashtray, the paddle ball.

Such a paradox has traditionally (and logically) been interpreted as an indication of the basic instability of modern materialistic societies. To the enough-already crowd, it is a sure signal of imminent decline, coming right around the next corner. Study after study appears in the daily newspaper to the effect that in this age of plenty, in which capitalism seems to have won the day, Americans have loaded up on angst. Critics conclude that we are working more and enjoying the fruits less. We are gagging on goods.

As Eugene Linden has argued in *Affluence and Discontent: The Anatomy of Consumer Societies,* ironically (and perhaps illogically), a broad look at consumer societies leads to the conclusion that individual discontents and their larger manifestation in countercultural movements are a necessary part of a consumer society. Expressions of material discontent, far from being an indication of decline, are the way a consumer society balances conflicting demands and indulges different behaviors. Another paradox unique to our time and place is that many people are dispirited with materialism not because they have too little, but because they have too much.

This is the "complain about farmers with your mouth full" syndrome. One can see this characteristic contradiction in many places, but let's look at just two: our recent dread of garbage that is articulated in our passion to recycle regardless of costs; and our willingness to consume "self-help" programs that wean us from our willingness to consume.

✳ WASTE MATTERS: THE TERROR OF TRASH

A telling characteristic about our relationship to trash is that while it is viewed by the rest of the world as a sign of economic success and well-being, it is viewed by us with disgust bordering on reverence. How we now handle garbage has become a mark of our ability to be humble and contrite and, simultaneously, good and virtuous. So we separate the bottles from the paper, the plastic from the glass, the glossy paper from the cardboard in a weekly ritual of mild self-righteousness. Just as kids used to learn the three Rs of reading, 'riting, and 'rithmetic, they are now taught the modern version, Reduce, Reuse, Recycle.

If you don't think that these Rs have become serious, try tangling with a tot over McDonald's clamshell containers, or a teenager over how paper companies are raping the rain forest, or think of how you yourself feel when confronted by the modern riddle of the Sphinx: paper or plastic?

Trash is central to commercial culture. It is the remains of our incomplete love affair with stuff. While we claim to be wedded to responsible consumption, while we claim to abjure advertising, packaging, whimsical changes in fashion, and casual shopping, we spend a lot of our time philandering. Trash is lipstick on the collar, the telltale blond hair, cheek-smudge.

Shame is what humans feel when the disparity between do and ought occurs. We know what we should do, we don't do it, we feel ashamed, and shame makes us meek about ourselves, and often harsh on others. If you say you like the simple life, then why are you generating mounds of garbage? People who would never dream of telling you not to have children out of wedlock, or who would never criticize you for filing for bankruptcy, will express eye-rolling dismay if you use a plastic fork or get your smooth cardboard mixed in with your egg cartons.

Garbage has become mythic. Remember the strange national fascination with the "Islip garbage barge," which left Long Island in the spring of 1987, sailing for 55 days, searching in vain for a place to dump its pungent 3,168 tons of cargo? Or what of the "P.U. choo-choo," which rumbled out of New York City in the summer of 1992, chugging around the Midwest, searching unsuccessfully for a place to unload what Christopher S. Bond (R-Mo.) denounced on the Senate floor as "forty cars of rotting, maggot-filled trash." That's our culture, we say to each other. We filled up those boxcars. These stories made their way to the front pages because they seemed such apt images of our times. It was not Sierra Clubbers who expressed flagellating dismay, it was all of us.

We no longer seem able to discuss trash without invoking protective euphemisms and refrains. We call it waste, or solid waste, or municipal solid waste, or, better yet, MSW (which confers upon the lowly sack of garbage the exalted status of a Master of Social Work). We don't take this stuff to the dump, we go to the landfill. This landfill usually has a name like Shady Grove or Piney Woods. It is hard to imagine Bette Davis's famous line, "What a dump!" being rewritten, but that is the goal of landfill-think. The stuff we don't take to "Overlook Park" is called re-cyclable and you must *never* refer to it as trash. We will gladly drive across town to put it in a bin where, chances are, it will be carted off to Overlook Park if the aftermarket for glass, paper, or aluminum is not sufficiently profitable that week.

How many times have we been told that we throw out enough trash in a year to spread 30 stories high over a thousand football fields; enough to fill a bumper-to-bumper convoy of garbage trucks halfway to the moon; that we produce far more garbage than wheat or rice, nearly the same tonnage as corn; that we generate enough rubbish to fill the World Trade Center's twin towers 187 times over; enough to fill five million trucks, which would circle the globe twice if stood end to end? And . . . well, you get the point.

Like our Puritan ancestors, who enjoyed seeing themselves in the hands of an angry God and then went on to gleefully catalog the horrors, we entertain the suffocating vision of all the landfills being full, all the incinerators churning out toxic fumes, a nation engulfed by its own filth. Move over Commies, garbage has become the evil empire.

The key to such quasi-religious thinking is that it practices the economy of the closed mind. Orthodoxy will abide no stray interpretations. From time to time someone tries to confuse our shame of incomplete consumption with the facts. Most recently, John Tierney wrote the June 30, 1996 cover story of the *New York Times Magazine,* the *vade mecum* of the We Have a Serious Problem Here crowd. His title was "Recycling Is Garbage" and the subhead read, "Rinsing out tuna cans and tying up newspapers may make you feel virtuous, but recycling could be America's most wasteful activity." Reader response was vitriolic. This news was not fit to print![1]

Ironically, Tierney, the newspaper's staff science writer, said nothing new. He is not Rush Limbaugh, nor is he an "environmental whacko." But his thesis—much recycling "squanders money and goodwill, and doesn't do much for the environment either"—drew more mail than anything the magazine had ever published. How could this heretic have made his way into the sacred temple? reader after reader asked. Few questioned his facts.[2]

I'm not so much interested in those facts as I am in the outrage. If hypocrisy is the tribute that vice pays to virtue, then is our passion about recycling perhaps the tribute shame pays to desire? Instead of trying to understand the deep pull of the material world, instead of coming

---

1. This kind of demurrer has been written before. First, in the 1970s, William Rathje, an Arizona archaeologist, and Cullen Murphy, the essayist, wrote a sensible piece for *The Atlantic Monthly* and later expanded it into *Rubbish! The Archaeology of Garbage.* They argued that rumors of our impending asphyxiation by trash were a little exaggerated. A few years ago the *Wall Street Journal* published a comprehensive article under the comparatively mild headline, "Waste of a Sort: Curbside Recycling Comforts the Soul, but Benefits Are Scant" (Bailey A1).

2. The arguments presented were not particularly new. Recycling's costs generally outweigh its benefits; it is not always necessary for resource conservation; it attacks a nonexistent shortage of landfill space; and it may, in some cases, create environmental problems instead of solving them.

to grips with the allure of commercial culture, instead of trying to learn about why American marketing is so powerful, we focus on what we take to be the results of human yearning gone amok. We can't really want—ugh!—disposable things. We must have been tricked.

Or, to put it in slightly different terms, I'm not being tricked. I'm consuming sensibly. But *they* are so profligate, so wasteful, so careless. Someone should talk to them.

Our concern about garbage is really, as the psychologists might say, a displaced concern about consumption. We sort milk cartons and pop bottles, we put slick paper here and newsprint there, we step over dollars to pick up a dime, we indulge in fuzzy feel-good thinking because we live at a time when meaning and purpose are hard to come by, and much of what we have for meaning resides in manufactured objects. We want these objects and, if the price we have to pay is the ritual of sacramental separation, then so be it. While our Christian ancestors may have comforted themselves thinking they had dominion over the birds that fly and the fish that swim, we can find surcease consuming what we want as long as we are sure that the blue box—the eponymous Big Blue—is properly filled each week.

✳ *THE VOLUNTARY SIMPLICITY MOVEMENT*

If entering the recycling movement is possibly the penance we pay for the guilty pleasures of consuming, then alliance with the Voluntary Simplicity movement is the righteous renunciation of such sin. Both concerns represent a backhanded tribute to the power of materialism. Most of the world practices recycling and simplicity, but not voluntarily.

The Voluntary Simplicity (vs) movement is not to be confused with the back to nature, let's live off the land types, who tear up their social security cards, stop paying taxes, and pull the plug. The simplicity movement of today has no retrograde romance of nature about it, rather a passionate belief that we can live well for less . . . *if* we buy and use the right stuff. Let recyclers avoid styrofoam cups for their morning coffee, the simplicity people will tell you just put a cloth around the coffee grounds and squeeze hard.

VS proponents believe we suffer from a social disease. This disease is contracted by falling for the American dream. It is spread by advertising, packaging, fashion, branding, and all the base contagion of marketing. Its symptoms are swollen expectations, shopping fever, chronic stress, and broken-down families. The wretched malaise goes by any number of names: crass commercialism, blatant materialism, hollow consumption. The cure? Inoculate yourself by buying a how-to-stop-buying book, attend some meetings, practice meditation, buy other stuff.[3]

Recently, the movement received the ultimate accolade of Mother Jones culture. It was featured on two Public Broadcasting System specials. The disease, now sporting a new name—"affluenza"—was seriously discussed by a suitably dour Scott Simon from National Public Radio. We had the usual scolds, the usual psychologists, the usual reformed admen telling us what they know but what we haven't found out: Things Can't Buy Happiness, You Can't Have It All. If only the nasty marketers would lay off, if only greedy bankers would quit sending us those charge cards, if only Sears didn't have that softer side, if only . . . then we could quit being victimized by consumerism and get on with it.

But good news. Help is on the way. Go into any bookstore and you will see the booming industry of what in psychobabble is known as "de-cathection," the partial reversing of magnetic polarities from gathering things to refusing to gather things. These books are now the profit center of the flagging self-help industry. They adapt pop-addiction therapy to human desire—twelve baby steps to freedom.

What used to be a single shelf of self-help books by Dale Carnegie, Bishop Fulton J. Sheen, and Norman Vincent Peale has exploded into an entire subsection of books on building self-esteem. In the 1950s these books argued a variation of the Little Engine That Could. You can succeed. You can get to the top of the hill. Just keep at it. I think I can, I think I can, I can. The reason you wanted success was so you could buy a ton of stuff.

Now that we have so much stuff (and the debt that often comes with it) the modern version is dedicated to the concept of Recovery. Recovery is based on the romantic story of the Child Is Father of the Man. Want

---

3. Call it Voluntary Simplicity, Downshifting, or Simple Living, the Trends Research Institute of Rhinebeck, N.Y., claims it as one of its top ten trends of the 1990s and predicts that by the end of the decade, 15 percent of America's 77 million baby boomers will be part of a "simplicity" market (Brant 1995:6F). In a wonderfully mercantile term, the Trends Research Institute (holder of quite a name itself) calls this cashing out. Cha-ching.

success? Just relax. Let your inner child out. I don't think I can, I feel
I can. I feel okay. I am okay. I've just been trapped by advertising, fashion, packaging, and branding. I'll relax my way free.

What is interesting to the student of materialism is not the resurgence of object relinquishment but the profoundly commercial
nature of letting go. The male form of Voluntary Simplicity, as it
were, is more ancient than Ecclesiastes. It pops up in Marcus Aurelius,
St. Francis, the Puritans, Quakers, Shakers, Henry David Thoreau,
Gandhi, Ralph Nader, and even Jimmy Carter. The mantra of male asceticism is Thoreau's furiously famous advice in *Walden, or Life in the
Woods:*

> I went to the woods because I wished to live deliberately, to front only
> the essential facts of life, and see if I could not learn what it had to
> teach; and not, when I came to die, discover that I had not lived. I did
> not wish to live what was not life, living is so dear. I wanted to live deep
> and suck out all the marrow of life.

These males may have hectored their neighbors about consuming too
much, but they never offered to sell them advice, go on a lucrative lecture tour, hold seminars, produce videos, or merchandise their "unique
vision."

The current vs movement is the female form of asceticism. When a
woman feels overwhelmed by a flood of things, she really can't head out
to the woods. But she can buy a guide to help her stop consuming and
join a group.[4] These guides range from Duane Elgin's evangelical *Vol-*

---

4. Such books are not new but the mass audience is. Think only of Edith
   Wharton's *The Decoration of Houses* (1899), which argued for a less cluttered domestic existence, and Charles Wagner's *The Simple Life* (1901),
   which sold hundreds of thousands of copies in the New York area alone
   and made Wagner a celebrity. Both authors reprimanded their mainly
   upper-class female readers for reliance on material goods and abandon-
   ment of tradition. And both authors, of course, were deep in the material world—Wharton as a consumer and outfitter of sizable manses and
   Wagner as a fervent disciple and booster of the Philadelphia retailing
   baron John Wanamaker. The real shift in modern temper came in the mid-
   twentieth century with the publication of Anne Morrow Lindbergh's 1955
   book, *Gift from the Sea*. Lindbergh wondered why she was so busy when
   technology had given her so many new simplification tools. Her argument
   was an intellectual one, a proto-ecological one: step back, wonder, and
   reconsider.

untary Simplicity (first published in 1981 and rereleased in 1993); then the husband-wife Dominguez-Robin blockbuster, *Your Money or Your Life* (1992), which has sold almost half a million copies (despite their advice to save money by getting it from the library); and most recently Elaine St. James's *Simplify Your Life* (1994) and its many sequels like *Inner Simplicity* and *Living the Simple Life*.

Take the case of Sarah Ban Breathnach. In 1991 she was depressed. She had been hit on the head by a ceiling tile at a fast-food restaurant and was feeling punk. So she sat at her dining room table determined to write down one hundred things for which she could feel grateful. No problem with number one. She was still alive. She went on to continue the list until she found herself on another list: the *New York Times* Bestseller List. She had some help along the way. As is becoming customary for recovery books (or books in general, for that matter) she did a stint with Oprah. Millions of women in that audience resonated to her plight.

Breathnach has now become what is known in media culture as a profit center. Her initial inventory of blessings, *Simple Abundance* ($18.95!), a collection of 366 daily "meditations" for women ("I didn't know how men think," she has confessed) has become a cottage industry. In fact, Simple Abundance is now a corporation, a registered trademark, and a nonprofit foundation, all headquartered in a simple townhouse in suburban Washington. It is also an imprint of Warner Books—Simple Abundance Press—issuing four books a year on the importance of frugal living.

The ethos of the Voluntary Simplicity movement is, appropriately enough, simple. It is also as inadvertently deceptive as recycling. In the 1980s, it holds, much of America went astray, indulging in frivolous luxury consumption, frittering away time and money in wasteful habits and services, toiling in lucrative but ultimately unfulfilling jobs to pay for things we only thought we needed. (Does this sound like more yuppie shame, or what?) In the revered American tradition of sin, guilt, and merchandised redemption, we now can escape the cycle of consumption in the 1990s.

But how? Here's the kind of advice the simplify-your-life groups give to ward off the dreaded affluenza:

> ➤ Sell the boat
> ➤ Get rid of your car phone
> ➤ Pack your own lunch
> ➤ Buy only what you need

➢ Make your own entertainment
➢ Buy secondhand stuff
➢ Wear things out before replacing them
➢ Stop reading the newspaper
➢ Stop answering the door when the doorbell rings
➢ Cancel your magazine subscriptions
➢ Don't watch infomercials or the Home Shopping Network
➢ Dump household clutter
➢ Move to a smaller place
➢ Pay off your credit card balance
➢ Eliminate all but one credit card
➢ Opt out of holiday gift giving if it feels oppressive

As Dave Barry would say, "Honest, I am not making this up." My favorite: "Work less and enjoy it more." One is tempted to add, quit buying books to tell you how to quit buying, or, to turn the consumerist phrase a bit, Just Quit Doing It. Surely, it is a sign of our twelve-step times that one needs to consume a program before consuming less ("Today I will not buy another garment with a Ralph Lauren logo, even if it's at a factory outlet store.")

Admittedly, the Voluntary Simplicity movement seems appealing to those for whom simplicity is a preexisting mental condition. But it is part of a larger constellation that floats around the consumerist world. For instance, books like *Chicken Soup for the Soul, The Seven Spiritual Laws of Success,* or *Care of the Soul* have been atop the bestseller lists for well over a year and all repeat the same message: commercialism is suffocating your natural innocence and only I, Deepak Chopra (or whoever), can help (if you buy my book) return you to health (childhood).

✳ WHAT'S TO COME

I have (perhaps too harshly) calumniated the Recycling and Voluntary Simplicity movements not because they are not well-meaning and right-thinking, but because they distort common sense about consumerism in the name of helplessness. Why must we invoke social movements to describe individual responsibility? Recycling means, if I remember my mother's words, "Pick up after yourself," and vs means, to quote my father, "Don't buy what you can't afford."

But these movements say more—especially if you listen to those on their militant edges. What I hear goes like this: You have been led astray by the material world and those who champion it. Your innocence has been betrayed. You have been lead out of Eden into sin and waste, and you must struggle mightily to repent. You must promise to be good because the forces of evil are so powerful and tempting. You have been made materialistic. You have become addicted.

I also hear this: We are the solution and you who do not agree are still the problem. We are saving the world from you, for you.

Such movements are the civic religions of our times. In a way, recycling and downshifting are what we have for a modern potlatch. Potlatch, the voluntary dumping of personal goods, was once a sign of dominance and prestige for Indian tribes in the Northwest. When the chief divested himself he was delivering the double whammy: I got it, but I don't need it. Now potlatch is practiced as a way of middle-class coping: I can't really afford it, but I could have it if I wanted. You, however, shouldn't even want it.

✳ A DIFFERENT VIEW

What is overlooked in our hand-wringing about commercialism is what Navin R. Johnson, the jerk, seems to know. Consumerism is not forced on us. It is not against our better judgment. It is (at least for much of our lives) our better judgment. We are powerfully attracted to the world of goods. Navin knows what we may forget: we call them goods, not bads. He also knows that our passion to amass is as perplexing as our confusion about what to do next.

American culture is often criticized for being too materialistic, for taking too much from the general store. We are forever reciting the mea culpa of capitalism that, although we are only 10 percent of the world's population, we consume 90 percent of its resources. While the percents may change, the shame remains. We are continually being told our bloated consumption comes from greed, and that greed results from our making wants into needs, and then making false needs into real ones.

I think there are no false needs. Once we are fed, clothed, and sexually functioning, needs are cultural. Furthermore, I will contend that we are not too materialistic; if anything, we are not materialistic enough. If we craved objects *and* knew what they meant, there would be no signifying systems like advertising, packaging, fashion, and branding to get in the way. We would gather, use, toss out, or hoard based on some *inner* sense of value.

It is that inner sense of value that we don't have. Rousseau, Wordsworth, Shelley, Thoreau, Emerson, and the Romantics notwithstanding, we have never had it. No one has. What sets American culture of the late twentieth century apart is not avarice, but a surfeit of machine-made things. What is clear is that most of these things in and of themselves simply do not mean enough. So we have developed very powerful ways to add meaning to goods. This is a chicken-and-egg situation, to be sure. For it is American production and marketing techniques (advertising, packaging, branding, fashion, and the like) *and* our eagerness to embrace them that have produced surplus. Consumption of things and their meanings is how most Western young people cope in a world that science has pretty much bled of traditional religious meanings.

➤ Be what you can buy: Visa Platinum Card. (*New York Times,* September 30, 1997, A21)

And here we come to the nubbin of what makes the way we live now so interesting, what makes recycling and downsizing so relevant. We currently live in a culture in which *almost everyone can have almost everything.* What used to be "Use It Up, Wear It Out, Make It Do" or "Do Without" has become "Use It or Lose It." Thanks to the credit card and installment debt, you can get your hands on almost anything, and you can use it before middle age.

GenXers' whining notwithstanding, numerous studies show that if you just play by a few rules you'll have more things—if that's what you want—than any generation before. What are these rules? Simple. Finish high school, get a job, don't get pregnant or get someone pregnant before you finish high school, don't become addicted to drugs, and you can make it in America (Bennett). No "morning again in America" Panglossian promise, that's reality.

Here, in 1969, was Peter Drucker, who saw what managerial enterprise was doing to the old politics of depressive restraint:

> A universal appetite for small luxuries has emerged. They signify a little independence, a little control over economic destiny. They are a badge of freedom. Where the means are very limited—among the poor or among teenagers without much income of their own—the small luxury may be a soft drink, a lipstick, a movie magazine or a candy bar. For the emerging middle class, it may be the appliance in the kitchen.

> For the truly affluent it may be the advanced degree. That one can do without it makes the small luxury into a psychological necessity. (97)

In the past thirty years, for the first time in Western culture, lower economic classes have had access to objects previously in the domain of the well-to-do. To be sure, we can't all have the same brands. We can't all have '57 T-birds, we can't all go off hiking in Nepal; we can't all afford to send our kids to Princeton. But play by these rules and chances are you can have a car, weeks of leisure time as well as a five-day work week, and access to good education and medical care.

✳ HOW GOOD DO WE HAVE IT?

In earlier cultures, sumptuary laws were often enacted to remove specific objects from circulation. Certain kinds of meats like the king's deer, beverages like exotic teas and coffee, styles of fashionable livery and particular fabrics, rare spices and sweeteners, styles of wigs, places to live, and the like were placed off limits to the hoi polloi. These laws against consuming what was called luxury were administered by the ecclesiastical courts. This was because luxury was defined as living above one's station, a form of insubordination against the concept of *copia*— the idea that God's world is already full and complete. Until the nineteenth century it was customary in England for such laws to be read from every pulpit once a year, a daunting task that took more than an hour.

While the proffered sins behind such laws were gluttony and greed— luxury objects were by definition *sumptuous*—in truth the prohibitions were social. Sumptuary laws were part of an elaborate symbolic system designed to keep class demarcations in place. We now use excise taxes on cigarettes, expensive automobiles, yachts, liquor, and gasoline; the purpose is not to separate groups, but to make consuming certain materials a burden.

Absent sumptuary laws, from a historical perspective, if you can play by these few rules you will have access to about the same number of objects (and two decades longer life) and degree of easy living as was had by the courtiers surrounding Louis XIV, the Sun King. Achieve a bit more—go to college and keep your family small and intact—and you will have more objects and physical comfort than were had by those in the inner circle of Versailles. Go to a professional school like law, business, or medicine, don't get a Ph.D. in English, and—move over Louis—you can live like a king.

But watch out! Deviate from these rules by just a hair and you can fall over the edge. Drop out of school, do some jail time, stay unemployed in the inner city, take a drug stronger than marijuana for longer than a week, or attempt to raise a child by yourself, and you will have the life of a peasant. The invisible hand of the modern market will administer its own, often brutal and occasionally terrible, version of sumptuary law. Even the basics of life will become luxuries.

✳ *A NOTE ON THE TITLE*

What you hold in your hand is the last of three books I have written about the business of popular culture. In the earlier two, *Carnival Culture: The Trashing of Taste in America* and *Adcult USA: The Triumph of Advertising in American Culture,* I tried to correct what I saw as the lamentable, but entirely understandable, drift to the left in Cultural Studies. I have used bits and pieces of these earlier books about the nature of carnival and commercial speech to help make the case here that modern consumption has become a never-ending, two-handed game. The main focus of this project, however, is the argument that such matters as branding, packaging, fashion, and even the act of shopping itself are now the central meaning-making acts in our postmodern world.

I can distinguish my general approach from most of my colleagues with a quick trip to the barnyard. The usual academic critic sees the consumer as a dumb ox. The producer is the scheming farmer who forces the ox to both plow furrows and then consume the mediocre harvest of its labor. The critic, meanwhile, sees himself as the village priest taking time off from Really Important Studies to come out to the countryside to save the day. I, on the other hand, see the consumer as the wily fox leading the flabby squire on one wild chase after another. Round and round they go. I tend to see the academic critic as a cross between the village idiot and the schoolmarm, wildly gesticulating but unnoticed by either fox or farmer.

In the spirit of our recycling times, I have lifted the first part of my title from the last lines of a prescient short story by Mark Twain, "The Man That Corrupted Hadleyburg." In this story Twain imagines a Puritan village utterly debased by the simple intrusion of a stranger bearing a sack of gold. The town's biblical creed, at the tale's end, is amended to: "Lead Us Into Temptation."

While it is alluring to think that Twain was comparing the onset of materialism to the serpent in the garden of American innocence, such was hardly the case. While the Lord's Prayer may implore: "Lead us *not* into Temptation," Twain knew better. Temptation is exactly what human beings—especially self-righteous ones—crave. Or, as in the title of a recent country song by Lari White, "Lead Me Not Into Temptation (I Already Know the Way)." Temptation is, after all, the patron saint of the marketplace and both the farmer and the fox know it. Evil though it may be, the alternative boredom is far worse. Let Oscar Wilde, the last great Puritan, make Hadleyburg's motto thoroughly modern: "The only way to get rid of a temptation is to yield to it." For better and for worse, in the last century, we pretty much have. Tallyho.

1

Attention Kmart Shoppers

A Brief Consumer Guide to Consumption, Commercialism, and the Meaning of Stuff

To speak of American "materialism" is . . . both an understatement and a mis-statement. The material goods that historically have been the symbols which elsewhere separated men from one another have become, under American conditions, symbols which hold men together. From the moment of our rising in the morning, the breakfast food we eat, the coffee we drink, the automobile we drive to work—all these and nearly all the things we consume become thin, but not negligible, bonds with thousands of other Americans.

—Daniel J. Boorstin, *The Decline of Radicalism: Reflections on America Today*

OF all the "-isms" of the twentieth century none has been more misunderstood, more criticized, and more important than materialism. Who but fools, toadies, hacks, and occasional loopy Libertarians have ever risen to its defense? Yet the fact remains that while materialism may be the most shallow of the twentieth century's various -isms, it has been the one to ultimately triumph. The world of commodities seems so antithetical to the world of ideas that it seems almost heresy to point out the obvious: most of the world most of the time spends most of its energy producing and consuming more and more stuff.

The really interesting question may be not Why are we so materialistic? but Why are we so unwilling to acknowledge and explore what seems to be the central characteristic of modern life?

When the French wished to disparage the English in the nineteenth century, they called them a nation of shopkeepers. When the rest of the world now wishes to disparage Americans, they call us a nation of consumers. And they are right. Almost all mature American cities have a Market Street and almost all of us have been there. No longer. We are developing and rapidly exporting a new material culture, a "mallcondo" culture.

The bus lines today terminate not at Market Street but at the Mall, the heart of our new modern urbia. All around mallcondoville is a vast continuum of interconnected structures and modes of organizing work, shopping, and living, all based on principles of enclosure, control, and consumption.

Most of us have not entered the mallcondo cocoon . . . yet. But we are on our way. We have the industrial "park," the "gated" community, the corporate "campus," the "domed" stadium, all of which play on the same conception of Xanadu's pleasure dome. Get inside. In the modern world the Kubla Khan down at the bank or over at the insurance company is not building a mallcondo dome around the natural world, but around a commercial one. Few are willing or able to live outside except, of course, the poor. "If you lived here, you'd be home by now" is no idle billboard; it is the goal of middle-class life.

To the rest of the world we do indeed seem not just born to shop, but alive to shop. We spend more time tooling around the mallcondo—three to four times as many hours as our European counterparts—and we have more stuff to show for it. According to some estimates we have about four times as many things as Middle Europeans, and who knows how much more than the less developed parts of the world (Schor, *The Overworked American* 107). The quantity and disparity is increasing daily, even though, as we see in Russia and China, the "emerging nations" are playing a frantic game of catch up.

✳ *THE IMPACT OF THE BABY BOOM*

This burst of mallcondo commercialism has happened recently—in my lifetime—and it is moving outward around the world at the speed of television. The average American consumes twice as many goods and services as in 1950; in fact, the poorest fifth of the current population buys more than the average fifth did in 1955. Little wonder that the average new home of today is twice as large as the average house constructed after World War II (Bennett). We have to put that stuff somewhere—quick!—before it turns to junk.

Manufacturing both things *and* their meanings is what mallcondo culture is all about, especially for the baby boomers. If Greece gave the world philosophy, Britain gave drama, Austria gave music, Germany gave politics, and Italy gave art, then America has recently contributed mass-produced and mass-consumed objects. "We bring good things to life" is no offhand claim but the contribution of the last century. Think about it: did anyone before the 1950s—except the rich—ever shop just for fun? Now the whole world wants to do it.

Sooner or later we are going to have to acknowledge the uncomfortable fact that this amoral commercial culture has proved potent because human beings *love* things. In fact, to a considerable degree, we live for things. Humans like to exchange things. In all cultures we buy things, steal things, and hoard things. From time to time, some of us collect vast amounts of things such as tulip bulbs, paint drippings on canvases, bits of minerals. Others collect such stuff as thimbles, shoes, even libraries of videocassettes. Often these objects have no observable use.

We live through things. We create ourselves through things. And we change ourselves by changing our things. We often depend on such material for meaning. In the West, we have even developed the elaborate algebra of commercial law to decide how things are exchanged, divested, and recaptured. Remember, we call these things goods as in "goods and services." Academics aside, we do not call them bads. This sounds simplistic, but it is crucial to understanding the powerful allure of materialism, consumption, mallcondo culture, and all that it carries with it.

Things are in the saddle, no doubt about it. We put them there. If some of us want to think that things are riding us, that's fine. The rest of us know better.

✳ THE COMPLEXITY OF CONSUMING COMMERCIALISM

That consumption gives meaning to life seems to be rearranging the terms, getting things backwards. But think about it: do we work in order to have the leisure to buy things, or is the leisure to buy things how we make work necessary? We forever talk about how work gives meaning—*labore est orare*—but it may be consumption that we are referring to. Give a banana to a monkey and he eats it right away. Give him a bundle and he gets confused. He has no idea what to do with surplus. Should he hoard, should he gorge himself, should he share? This used to be a problem only for the rich; now the rest of us can share the perplexity.

I never want to imply that, in creating order in our lives, consumption is *doing* something to us that we are not covertly responsible for. We are not victims of consumption. Just as we make our media, our media make us. Again, commercialism is not making us behave against our "better judgment." Commercialism *is* our better judgment. Not only are we willing to consume, and not only does consuming make us happy, "getting and spending" is what gives our lives order and purpose. We have a deluding tendency to consider advertising, packaging, fashion, branding, and the rest of the movement of goods in the way we consider many other cultural sequences, like politics and religion, as somehow "out there" beyond our control. Not so.

Our desire to individualize experience causes us to forget that there is a continual interaction between forces—between people and their leaders, between males and females, between readers and writers, between young and old, even between producers and consumers—in which there is a struggle not for dominance, but for expansion. In the language of William Blake, the endeavor is not to separate the Prolific and the Devourers, not to blame one for the condition of the other, but to realize that in the shifting of forces is the excitement and the danger of change. In this sense, commercialism is just another site in which the sometimes opposing forces of a culture are brought to bear on each other. The resulting friction is often quite hot.

I make this point now because commercial speech—how we talk about manufactured things—has become one of the primary hotspots of modern culture. It has been blamed for the rise of eating disorders, the spreading of affluenza, the epidemic of depression, the despoiling of cultural icons, the corruption of politics, the carnivalization of holy times like Christmas, and the gnat-life attention span of our youth. All of this is true. Commercialism contributes. But it is by no means the whole truth. Commercialism is more a mirror than a lamp. That we demonize it, that we see ourselves as helpless and innocent victims of its overpowering force, that it has become scapegoat du jour, tells far more about our eagerness to be passive in the face of complexity than about our understanding of how it does its work.

20   Anthropologists tell us that consumption habits are gender specific. Men seem to want stuff in early adolescence and post-midlife. That's when the male collecting impulse seems to be felt. Boys gather playing

marbles first, Elgin marbles later. Women seem to gain potency as consumers after childbirth, almost as if getting and spending is a nesting impulse. There are no women stamp collectors of note. They do save letters, however, far more often then men do.

Historians, however, tell us to be careful about such stereotyping. While it is clear that women are the primary consumers of commercial objects today, this has only been the case since the Industrial Revolution. Certainly in the pre-industrial world, men were the chief hunter-gatherers. If we can trust works of art to accurately portray how booty was split (and art historians like John Berger and Simon Schama think we can), then males were the prime consumers of fine clothes, heavily decorated furniture, gold and silver articles and, of course, paintings in which they could be shown displaying their stuff.[1]

Once a surplus was created, as happened in the nineteenth century, women joined the fray in earnest. They were not duped. The hegemonic, phallocentric patriarchy did not brainwash them into thinking goods mattered. The Industrial Revolution produced more and more things not because production is what machines do, and not because nasty producers twisted their handlebar mustaches and whispered, "We can talk women into buying anything," but because both sexes are powerfully attracted to the world of things. Stuff is not nonsense. The material world magnetizes us and we focus much energy on our relationship with it.

Marx himself knew this better than anyone else. In the *Communist Manifesto* he writes:

> The bourgeoisie, by the rapid improvement of all instruments of production, by the immensely facilitated means of communication, draws

---

1. An occasional gentleman would admit what he was up to as did John Harrington, Queen Elizabeth I's favorite godson:

   We go brave in apparel that we may be taken for better men than we be, we use much bombastings and quiltings to seem better framed, better shouldered, smaller waisted, and fuller thighed than we are, we barb and shave off to seem younger than we are, we use perfumes both inward and outward to seem sweeter, wear corked shoes to seem taller, use courteous salutations to seem kinder, lowly obeisance to seem humbler, and grave and godly communication to seem wiser and devouter than we be. (in Harrison 38) all, even the most barbarian nations into civilization. The cheap prices of its commodities are the heavy artillery with which it batters down all Chinese walls. . . . It compels all nations, on pain of extinction, to adopt the bourgeois mode of production; it compels them to introduce what it calls civilization into their midst, i.e., to become bourgeois themselves. In one word, it creates a world after its own image. (9)

Marx uses this insight to motivate the heroic struggle against capitalism. But as we have seen, especially in the last few decades, it proved feckless. The struggle should not be to deter capitalism and its mad consumptive ways, but to appreciate how it works so its furious energy may be understood and exploited.

✹ MY ARGUMENT IN A NUTSHELL

I am going to put forward a seemingly naïve thesis to understand the triumph of our commodity culture: (1) Humans are consumers by nature. We are tool users because we like to use what tool using can produce. In other words, tools are not the ends but the means. Further, materialism does not crowd out spiritualism; spiritualism is more likely a substitute when objects are scarce. When we have few things, we make the next world holy. When we have plenty, we enchant the objects around us. The hereafter becomes the here and now. You deserve a break *today*, not in the next life. (2) Consumers are rational. They are often fully aware that they are more interested in consuming aura than objects, sizzle than steak, meaning than material, packaging than product. In fact, if you ask them—as academic critics are usually loath to do—they are quite candid in explaining that the Nike swoosh, the Polo pony, the Guess? label, the DKNY logo are what they are after. They are not duped by advertising, packaging, branding, fashion, or merchandising. They actively seek and enjoy what surrounds the object, especially when they are young. (3) We need to question the criticism that consumption almost always leads to "buyer's remorse." Admittedly the circular route from desire to purchase to disappointment to renewed desire is never-ending, but it may be followed because the other route from melancholy to angst is worse. In other words, in a world emptied of external values, consuming what looks to be overpriced kitsch may be preferable to consuming nothing. And (4) we need to rethink the separation between production and consumption, for they are more alike than separate, and occur not at different times and places but simultaneously.

Ironically the middle-aged critic, driving about in his well-designated Volvo (unattractive and built to stay that way), is unable to provide much insight into his own consumption practices, although he can certainly criticize the bourgeois afflictions of others. Ask him to explain the difference between "Hilfiger" inscribed on the oversize shirts worn outside pants slopped down to the thighs, and his rear window university decal (My child goes to Yale, sorry about yours), and you will be met with a blank stare. If you were to then suggest that what that decal and automotive nameplate represent is as overpriced as Calvin Klein's initials on a plain white T-shirt, he would pout that you can't compare apples and whatevers. If you were to say next that aspiration and affiliation is at the heart of both displays, he would say that you just don't get it, just don't get it at all.

But don't talk to critics if you want to understand the potency of American consumer culture. Ask any group of teenagers what democracy means to them and you will hear an extraordinary response. Democracy is the right to buy anything you want. Freedom's just another word for lots of things to buy. Appalling perhaps, but there is something to their answer. Being able to buy what you want when and where you want it was, after all, the right that made 1989 a watershed year in Eastern Europe.

Recall as well that freedom to shop was another way to describe the right to be served in a restaurant that provided a focus for the early civil rights movement. Go back farther. It was the right to consume freely that sparked the fires of separation of this country from England. The freedom to buy what you want (even if you can't pay for it) is what most foreigners immediately spot as what they like about our culture, even though in the next breath they will understandably criticize it.

Paradoxically, buying stuff is not just our current popular culture, it is how we understand the world. High culture has pretty much disappeared, desperately needing such infusions of life-preserving monies from taxpayer-supported endowments and tax-free foundations to keep it from gasping away. One might well wonder if there is anything more to American life than shopping. After all, we are all consumers now, consumers of everything—consumers of health services, consumers of things and ideas, consumers of political representation, even consumers of what high culture there is left.

The new model citizen wearing his Calvins and eating his Paul Newman popcorn while applying his Michael Jordan cologne, described by both Left and Right, is the citizen consumer, the one who makes rational choices based on assimilating all the available information. Thinking ends in action and that action is buying. W. H. Auden may have lampooned this creature as the drone of the modern state (*The Unknown Citizen*), but it seems it is not the state that makes the drone, but the drone that makes the state.

✳ THE CASE OF SEVEN-YEAR-OLD MOLLIE

We learn early that shopping around is the way to organize experience. Enid Nemy reports in my favorite part of the *New York Times*, "Metropolitan Diary," this passing tidbit: "Seven-year-old Mollie Kurshan of Ridgewood, N.J., recently attended *The Nutcracker* with her grandmother at the New York State Theater at Lincoln Center. There was a Sugar Plum Fairy and beautiful costumes, Mollie told her mother, and, best of all 'They stopped in the middle so you could go shopping.' The Kurshans now have a cute little wooden nutcracker, bought at the gift shop during intermission" (A27).[2]

By the time she gets to school, Mollie may see her education as something to purchase. Many of my students think of themselves as buyers of a degree. They can even tell you how much a credit hour *costs*. In addition, when we talk about how much a credit hour is *worth*, we mean in dollars and cents. A diploma is valued for how much it improves your starting wage.

Just look at the admission process, complete with competition for financial assistance. Schools live and die by what *US News & World Report* or *Money* magazine says about them. You make a deal with one school. You show the deal to other schools. They make counteroffers. It's just like car shopping.

---

2. Lincoln Center is not alone in realizing that shopping and entertainment mix. Movies longer than two hours were once frowned on because they tied up the seats for too long. But now theaters, which can afford curio shopping during a long intermission, find they can make more money with smaller audiences. Moviemakers like Disney have long since realized that the movie is just a way to sell trinkets anyway.

Why go to a prestigious school? Not for good teaching—you are al-most assured of being treated poorly in the full professor/teaching as-sistant configuration. No, you go because the school name improves the relative worth of the line on the vita, the certificate. The assumption is that you pay your money, you get your degree.[3]

Mollie will also learn that what she experienced in Lincoln Center is the norm for what was once called High Culture. Art today is almost always commodified. Juliet B. Schor, a Harvard economist who wrote *The Overworked American* and then *The Overspent American*, quotes a museum curator sheepishly explaining why his museum had to be combined with a shopping mall: "The fact is that shopping is the chief cultural activity in the United States" (1991:108). He is right, as the endless catalogs from the Metropolitan or the Museum of Modern Art attest. Not only are all major museum shows sponsored by corporate in-terests, but they all end in the same spot: the gift shop.

Mollie may discover that shopping for stuff is so powerful that it sets not just mallcondo culture but our biological clocks. The weekend developed so that shopping day—Saturday—would be set aside and formalized for consuming. Blue laws were passed because clearly Sat-urday was not enough, and the desire was spilling over to the Sabbath. The year is punctuated by shopping extravaganzas from Christmas to Valentine's Day to Mother's Day to Halloween. By the age of ten, we all know what Mollie Kurshan is learning: what to buy and when. We even know when prices fall: Washington's birthday, Labor Day, after Christmas.

Mollie even knows that objects themselves have seasons. Take candy, for instance. She knows exactly what kind of candy to expect as these days pass by: candy canes, sugar hearts, chocolate, candy corn. As she grows up she will even know what to buy during the day. Take fluids; we have coffee breaks, teatime, cocktail hour, and nightcap. The night be-longs to Michelob. One of the biggest marketing problems Coca-Cola had was being thought of only as a hot weather drink. It created the im-age of Santa Claus, the one recognized by Mollie—a construction of ad-man Haddon Sundbloom—in order to show Santa drinking a summer-time beverage in the dead of winter.

---

3. One of the reasons administrations have not cracked down on grade infla-tion is that an unhappy student/consumer is as bad as a defective product. Bad word-of-mouth can be devastating, especially to private colleges.

Shopping is so powerful that it even generates our urban architecture. Since the 1950s, towns and cities have grown in grids around not office buildings or schools but malls. Look at Atlanta or Los Angeles. The city of the future is spoked outward from a shopping hub. What of transportation? Every fifth time Mollie's mom gets in the car it is to go buy something. Why do people go to New York City? The third most important reason is to go shopping. Shopping—as Mollie will learn—is not just how we organize our life at various times. It *is* our life, especially when we are young.

Is this hyperbole? Is it possible for any of us to take a trip and not buy a souvenir? Getting there may be half the fun, but when you return home the experience may be forgotten without the aide memoire. The anxiety of returning empty-handed means we may lose the event. Kodak used this as a way to sell cameras. Show pictures of faraway places and people will travel to faraway places and take pictures of exactly what the ad showed. They were not duped or tricked by this process. We were there, we saw the picture, we "took" a picture just like it. We brought it home. Of course perception is reality, as the ad says. Is there any other kind?[4]

✳ *THE CARNIVALIZATION OF SHOPPING*

"Fill 'er up," we say as we motor through life from one defining purchase to another. On our journeying juggernauts we tape tributes onto our bumpers so all can see that we have been there, done that. Sometimes what we memorialize is not the trip but the purchase, not the thing but the image of it. On the bumpers of self we slap stickers: "Shop 'til you drop," "He who dies with the most toys wins," "People who say money can't buy happiness, don't know where to shop," "When the going gets tough, the tough go shopping," "But I can't be overdrawn! I still have some checks left!," "I'm spending my grandchildren's inheritance," "Nouveau riche is better than no riche at all," "A woman's place is in the mall." For those who want a thought larger than what fits on a car bumper, here is a greeting card. It says, "Work to Live,

---

4. Or ponder this: before Kodak ads there was no universal blowing out of candles on a frosted cake. That image resulted from the need to show what you can do with fast Kodak film and the Kodak flashmatic attachment on your Kodak camera.

Live to Love, Love to Shop, so you see . . . if I buy enough things I'll never have to work at love again." Wink wink, we say, but under the irony is truth.

Let me reiterate what is central to my thesis and so overlooked in much academic cultural criticism. We were not suddenly transformed from customers to consumers by wily manufacturers eager to unload a surplus of crapular products. We are many things, but what we are not are victims of capitalism. With few exceptions (food, shelter, sex), our needs are cultural, not natural. We have created a surfeit of things because we enjoy the process of getting and spending. The consumption ethic may have started in the early 1900s and hit full tilt after the mid-century, but the desire is ancient. Whereas kings and princes once thought they could solve problems by possessing and amassing things, we now say, "Count us in." Whereas the Duchess of Windsor once said, "All my friends know that I'd rather shop than eat," we now say, "Hey, wait for me."

Generations ago, consumption played out its Saturnalian excesses alongside the church, literally, at the carnival. Mardi Gras and Lent were connected. Consumption, then denial. It was the world turned upside down, then right side up. We used to go into the dark cathedral looking for life's meaning and then do a little shopping on the side. Now we just go straight to the mall. If you travel about the globe, you will find that millions are quietly queuing up waiting their turn to start shopping. Woe to that government or church that tries to turn them back.

By standards of stuff, the last half century of our national life has been wildly successful. We have achieved unprecedented prosperity and personal freedom. We are healthier, we work at less exhausting jobs, and we live longer than ever. Most of this has been made possible by consuming things, ironically spending more and more time at the carnival, less and less in church.

❋ THE MIXED BLESSING

"Wanting," "desiring," "needing" are the gerunds that lubricated this strain of capitalism and made our culture so compelling for have-nots around the world. In the last generation we have almost completely reversed the poles of shame so that where we were once ashamed of consuming too much (religious shame), we are now often ashamed of consuming the wrong brands (shoppers' shame).

Was it worth it? Are we happier for it? Was it fair? Did some of us suffer inordinately for the excesses of others? What are we going to do when all this stuff we have shopped for becomes junk? How close is the connection between the accumulation of goods and the fact that America also leads the industrialized world in rates of murder, violent crime, juvenile violent crime, imprisonment, divorce, abortion, single-parent households, obesity, teen suicide, cocaine consumption, per capita consumption of all drugs, pornography production, and pornography consumption?

These are important questions and we need to continually talk about them. I'm not going to. However, there is a mixed aspect of the material world that I will have to confront. The cornucopia of stuff—which I will address under the rubrics of advertising, fashion, branding, and marketing—is to a considerable number of people an experience that is not just boring but banal, almost obscene. The fact is that the carnival is a world of brazen excess, full of sound and excitement but signifying little in the way of philosophical depth. Most critics of mallcondo culture usually feel this antipathy toward commercialism in midlife, after they have chased the meaning of objects and have settled into a routine of low and simplified consumption. In advertising lingo, they no longer change brands because they have made their affiliations. For them the carnival is over and the church is beckoning.

✳ *WHERE THE GENERATION GAP BEGINS*

Yeats forecast this split between wanting and no longer interested via a sexual metaphor. In *Sailing to Byzantium* he wrote of the world of youthful urges from which the speaker is now alien:

> That is no country for old men. The young
> In one another's arms, birds in trees
> —Those dying generations—at their song,
> The salmon-falls, the mackerel-crowded seas,
> Fish, flesh, or fowl, commend all summer long
> Whatever is begotten, born, and dies.
> Caught in that sensual music all neglect
> Monuments of unaging intellect. (1–8)

To translate this "sensual music" into a consumerist apology: once you have passed through "prime-branding time" you are almost impossible to sell to. The mall carnival is not for you. You become in our culture, "a paltry thing,/ A tattered coat upon a stick" . . . forgotten. Very little entertainment, let alone information, flows your way because no one is willing to pay the freight to send it. You better find your own Byzantium in far off High Aesthetica because you are not going to find it here in Lower Vulgaria. No one really makes movies for you (blockbusters are for the kids), programs television for you (check who watches prime-time), publishes books and magazines for you (look at the bestseller lists or the flood of magazines like *Details, Rolling Stone, Wired*) because, although you have the money, your kids spend it. No wonder you become a critic of a culture that has made you a pariah.

There was no generation gap two generations ago. Fashions, like moral and ethical values, flowed down from above, from old to young, rich to poor. But the money in materialism is to be made from tapping those with excess disposable time and money—the young. Ironically, the only way to return to a culture that served the mature would be if everyone over forty made it a habit to change brands of everything every week or so just like the kids.[5]

This generation gap and the hostility it has engendered is part of the reason we have recently been so passionate about condemning commercialism, and yet so unwilling to examine its workings. These are our kids. We have raised them. They have (gasp!) our values. Clearly we are perplexed about how they act, and just as clearly we have selectively forgotten how important consumption was for us. Their excitement in consumption has been little studied, perhaps because while it is so unfocused, so common, so usual, it is also so youthful.

✳ A FEW WORDS—JUST TWO FOR NOW—FROM THE SPONSOR

While consumerism is the water in which we have all swum, we seem as eager to criticize the aquarium as we are casual about how the tank is filled, cleaned, and drained. Let's look at the words we use. Consumerism is defined by *The American Heritage Dictionary* as the "theory that

---

5. In a revealing study published in 1997, "Kids These Days: What Americans Really Think About the Next Generation," the hostility between adults and the nation's teenagers came into public view. Two thirds of adults surveyed came up with words like "rude," "wild," and "irresponsible" to describe kids—their own kids. Nearly half of the polled adults called children "spoiled" and nearly a third called them "lazy." The research organization, Public Agenda, was itself startled by the hostility (Applebrome A25).

a progressively greater consumption of goods is economically beneficial," but the base word "consume" tells a different story, more frightening. To consume means to "ingest, use up, to waste, squander, or to
destroy totally."

In consuming we become omophagic—creating ourselves by eating
ourselves up. Not by happenstance did the disease that decimated so
much of the Victorian world become known as consumption. Tubercu-
losis, the AIDS of our grandparents, carried the cultural censure of exactly what high-Victorian critics like Matthew Arnold and John Ruskin
claimed was occurring in the marketplace. We were going to be consumed by consumption.

Here's another word, a modernization of consumption: commercialization. This is another loaded (and usually negative) term. Essentially
it involves two processes: *commodification,* or stripping an object of all
other values except its value for sale to someone else, and *marketing,* the
insertion of the object into a network of exchanges only some of which
involve money. Until the 1900s, commercialization was pretty well limited to commodification since large-volume market networks scarcely
existed throughout much of Christian Europe. But with the creation of
the first European colonial empires, and even more with the creation of
mass industrial production, cheap transportation, and communications, the marketing of commodities took on a relentless life of its own.

Marketing should not be a nasty word. Religions have been doing
it for generations. If you like it, it is called saving souls; if you don't,
it is called proselytizing. But, whatever it is called, marketing depends
on branding, packaging, and distribution and it evolved from organized
religion.

The pressure to commercialize—to turn things into commodities
and then market them as charms—has always been particularly Western. As Max Weber first argued in *The Protestant Ethic and the Spirit
of Capitalism* (1905), much of the Protestant Reformation was geared
toward denying the holiness of many things that the Catholic Church
had endowed with meanings. From the inviolable priesthood to the
sacrificial holy water, this deconstructive movement systematically unloaded meaning. Soon the marketplace would capture this offloaded
meaning and apply it to secular things. Buy this, you'll be saved. You deserve a break today. You, you're the one. We are the company that cares
about you. You're worth it. You're in good hands. We care. Trust in us.
We are here for you.

We have grown not weaker but stronger by accepting these self-evidently ridiculous myths that sacralize mass-produced objects; we have not wasted away but have proved inordinately powerful; have not devolved and been rebarbarized, but seem to have marginally improved. Dreaded affluenza notwithstanding, commercialism has lessened pain. Most of us have more pleasure and less discomfort in our lives than most of the people most of the time in all of history.

✻ WHAT DO WOMEN WANT? WHAT WE ALL WANT: MEANING

An important reason for benign neglect, or a halfhearted indictment of consumerism, is that shopping seems to be women's work. Men make, women buy. Men construct, women consume. Men add, women subtract. This is absolutely wrongheaded, of course, but powerful. The academic field of study is not how we know what to buy, when to buy, and, most important, how and what to think about what we're buying. Instead, we study what we might call the masculine side: how we know what to produce, what is the return on investment, what is the marginal utility of production, how it can be sold, what are the costs of land, labor, capital.

This is a curious dichotomy because for most of us in the Western world, the act of shopping has very little to do with the necessities of life. We shop to satisfy desires, not needs, and in this act we help produce meanings for objects and, by extension, for ourselves.

The act of gratifying desire by shopping has a great deal to do with the creation of state, community, family, and especially self. Thanks to advertising, packaging, branding, and fashion, even the simplest of things have taken on meaning well in excess of their material life. This tectonic shift in where meaning is located is not the province of the well-to-do as it was a generation ago. Meaning does not trickle down as classical economics claimed; it just as likely trickles up as postmodern aesthetics contends.

Knowing this, we can appreciate how poverty can be so crippling in the modern Western world. For the penalty of intractable, transgenerational destitution is not just the absence of things; it is also the absence of meaning, the exclusion from participating in the essential socializing events of modern life. It is an irony worthy of note that while much fashion now flows up from the 'hood, little *information* flows back down. When you hear that some ghetto kid has killed for a pair of branded sneakers or a monogrammed athletic jacket, you can realize how chronically poor, unemployed youth are indeed living the absurdist life proclaimed by existentialists. The poor are the truly selfless ones in commercial culture.

Clearly what the poor are after is what we all want: association, affili-ation, inclusion, magical purpose. While they are bombarded, as we all are, by the commercial promise of being cool, of experimenting with various presentations of disposable self, they lack the wherewithal to even enter the loop. Hence the suggestion by some social reformers that affirmative action may make more sense applied to poor youths than to members of gender and racial groups.

Wordsworth said at the beginning of the Industrial Revolution that in "getting and spending, we lay waste our powers." He implied that we are losing life's natural meaning when we give ourselves over to ma-terialism. He would rather be a "pagan suckled in a creed outworn" than think that value and meaning could ever be even associated with machine-made objects. How do we find this natural meaning? Go out to nature:

> One impulse from a vernal wood
> May teach you more of man,
> Of moral evil and of good,
> Than all the sages can. (*The Tables Turned,* lines 21–24)

In the modern world it is precisely the process that Wordsworth (and Thoreau, Emerson, Whitman) abhorred by which most of us gener-ate our power and make meaning out of life. As Professor Stanley Lebergott, an economist at Wesleyan University, has recently argued in *Pursuing Happiness: American Consumers in the Twentieth Century,* most Americans have "spent their way to happiness."

Lest this sound overly Panglossian, what Lebergott means is that while consumption by the rich has remained relatively steady, the rest of us—again the intractable poor (about 4 percent of the population) are the exception—have now had a go of it. If we think that the rich are different from you and me, and that the difference is that they have longer shopping lists and are happier for it, then we have, in the last two generations, substantially caught up. To slightly rephrase the old saw that given a choice between riches and poverty, one would be wise to choose riches, given a choice between surrounding oneself with mate-rial stuff or living in Wordsworth's "vernal wood," take the stuff. Life in the vernal wood, as Darwin made clear, is not very pleasant. It is a little too "red in tooth and claw" for most of us. In fact, the closest approximation of the vernal wood in the post-Darwinian world is the urban slum.

The most interesting part of *Pursuing Happiness* is the second half. Here Lebergott unloads reams of government statistics and calculations to chart the path that American consumption has taken across a wide range of products and services: food, tobacco, clothing, fuel, domestic service, and medicine, to name only a few. Two themes emerge

Luxuries No More
Average number of hours' labor needed to purchase various products

EARLY YEAR	PRODUCT	EARLY COST	1970 COST	1997 COST
1908	Automobile	4,696	1,397	1,365
1915	Refrigerator	3,162	112	68
1915	Long-distance call	90	0.4	0.03
1917	Movie ticket	0.48	0.47	0.32
1919	Air travel, 1,000 mi.	221	18	11
1919	Chicken, 3 lb. fryer	2.6	0.4	0.2
1947	Microwave oven	2,467	176	15
1954	Color television	562	174	23
1971	Soft contact lenses	95	n/a	4
1972	VCR	365	n/a	15
1984	Cellular phone	456	n/a	9
1984	Computing*	57	n/a	0.4

*Million instructions per second
Source: Federal Reserve Bank of Dallas

➤ The Low Cost of Living. (W. Michael Cox, *Wall Street Journal*, April 9, 1988, A22)

strongly from this data. The first, not surprisingly, is that Americans were far better off by 1990 than they were in 1900.[6] And second is that academic critics from Robert Heilbroner, Tibor Scitovsky, Robert and Helen Lynd, and Christopher Lasch to Juliet Schor, Robert Frank, and legions of others now teaching American Studies, who have censured the waste and tastelessness of much of American consumerism, have simply missed the point. Okay, okay, money can't buy happiness, but with it you stand a better chance than with penury.

Lebergott poses a simple question for such critics: would they want to return to 1900? Even if they say yes, would they be justified in forc-

---

6. For example, real consumer spending rose in 70 of the 84 years between 1900 and 1984. In 1990 an hour's work earned six times as much as in 1900. Most Americans walked to work at the start of the century, but by 1990 very few did and nearly 90 percent of families had a car. By 1987 most households had a fridge and a radio, nearly all had a TV, and about three quarters had a washing machine. Per capita spending on food rose by more than 75 percent between 1900 and 1990, with a marked increase in meat consumption.

ing their aesthetic and moral judgments on other consumers as they do now on us?

Okay, counter the cultural pessimists, while it may be true that materialism offers a temporary palliative for the anxiety of emptiness, we still must burst joy's grape. Consumption will turn sour because so much of it is based on the chimera of debt. Easy credit = overbuying = disappointment = increased anxiety. Sooner or later the piper must be paid, and we are doing everyone a service to sound the warning.

This is not just patronizing, it is wrongheaded. As another economist, Lendol Calder, has argued in *Financing the American Dream: A Cultural History of Consumer Credit in America,* debt has been an important part of families' financial planning since the time of Washington and Jefferson. Not by happenstance does it occur concurrent with the hand-wringing headlines of DEBT THREATENS DEMOCRACY and NEVER HAVE SO MANY OWED SO MUCH. This tension between work ethic and consumerist hedonism seems to have dynamic overtones in an entrepreneurial culture. While installment credit does seem to be irrational to the haves, the have-nots are willing to run risk not to postpone desire and to enter the loop right now.

Although consumer debt has consistently risen, the default rate has remained remarkably stable. In fact, the increased availability of credit to a growing share of the population, particularly to lower-income individuals and families, has allowed many more have-nots to enter the economic mainstream. It may be risky to the borrower, but not to the lender. Given a chance to extend credit to consumers or to commercial interests, go with the consumers. More than 95.5 percent of consumer debt gets paid, usually on time. True, a small percent—less than 5 percent—will become delinquent and default. But note: only a small percent of those in default are led astray by the oxymoronic "easy payments." Most people know installment buying is "hard payment" and act accordingly. The bumper sticker, "I owe, I owe; it's off to work I go" doesn't just acknowledge this, but also implies that the trade-off has been worth it. For a few it is not. For the many it is.

We should be eternally suspicious of those fully tenured economists of the John Kenneth Galbraith school with their summer houses in Vermont. Think carefully when they criticize the size, waste, indebtedness, and cultural depravity of what they take to be tailfin culture. The butt end of the 1958 Cadillac is now considered a work of industrial art, not a sign of outrageous profligacy. Furthermore, remember: well-paid academic critics are often more than happy to zip over to Switzerland for a week or two of skiing, writing part of it off on their tax forms for attending a kaffeeklatsch on the excesses of American commercialism. Just whose "affluent society" are they talking about?

Often the melancholy Eeyores condemning your consumption are confusing what you buy with what they buy. They can spend thousands of dollars hiking in Provence, but don't you even think of gambling away a sawbuck in Las Vegas. Questions of morality often are really matters of taste. Barbarian display for one is Elysian fields for another. Their is is passed off as your ought.

A more perceptive economist, Charles Dickens may have understood the laws of simple gratification better. Mr. Micawber opines in *David Copperfield:* "Annual income twenty pounds, annual expenditure nineteen six, result: happiness. Annual income twenty pounds, annual expenditure twenty pounds ought and six, result: misery." Why, rather than maintain our checkbooks in the happiness balance, we should choose to run the risk of debt and unhappiness may be a tribute not only to aspirations but to the pull of the meaning of goods and the palpable reward of their consumption.

✳ WHY TRADITIONAL ECONOMICS IS DOWNRIGHT DISMAL IN DEALING WITH CONSUMPTION

One of the casualties of looking at the world from the shopper's point of view is Econ 101. Producer-centered interpretations are as dismal as Carlyle claimed. Since such economists think males do most of the object production (most of the real "work"), they naturally grab for the same side of the elephant. The elephant is called supply, production, running the machine, putting stuff in the stores.

So we hear a great deal about monopolistic practices, money supply, finite resources, labor costs, allocation of capital, interest rates, return on equity, and the like. When traditional economists talk about the presence of consumer sovereignty or consumer desire/need, it is almost as an afterthought. Consumers are along for the ride. They just take stuff out of the stores. Captains of industry run the show.

Classical economics has tended to be at best patronizing to the consumer, at worst a downright scold. From time to time a practitioner thrashes his way out of the groves of academe and ministers to the unwashed. The four most famous of this evangelical clergy are Thorstein Veblen, John Kenneth Galbraith, Vance Packard, and, in his own way, Ralph Nader. Each preached the same gospel: you have sinned by following the demands of your flesh, you have fallen from grace, you have bought the wrong stuff, you have been gulled. Quit shopping so much. Get serious.

Of these scolds Thorstein Veblen, an eccentric Minnesotan who coined the phrase "conspicuous consumption," has become almost a cult figure among critics of consumption. All his books (save his translation of the Lexdaela Saga) are still in print; his most famous, *The Theory of the Leisure Class,* has never been out of print since it was first published in 1899. His ideas inspired a school of thought that publishes a professional journal, and international organizations exist to discuss the relevance of his ideas. Veblen's intellectual stock is still strong because he coined some great phrases, and he spent his career railing against industrial waste and the attendant environmental problems—a greenie before his time.[7]

Veblen claimed that the leisure class set the standards for conspicuous consumption. Without sumptuary laws to protect their markers of distinction, the rest of us could soon make their styles our own. The Industrial Revolution saw to that. Through this trickle-*down* effect, objects lose their status distinctions when consumed by the hoi polloi, so the leisure class must eternally be finding newer and more wasteful

---

7. Ironically, at the same time Veblen was writing, the first ideological champion of American consumption was hard at work on the other side of the fence. The economist Simon Nelson Patten is a peculiar and neglected figure in American social thought primarily because he argued the obvious, and the academically unpopular. While conservative critics fretted that excessive spending would destroy the work ethic, the family, and the ideal of character, Patten applauded the urge to consume and acknowledged the pleasures and meaning of exchange. Consumption provided initial purpose to life, but it was not an end in itself. It was just the first step up the ladder to transcending desire and accepting asceticism. Patten's social gospel was a potent blend of Victorian uplift and post-Victorian pleasures, harmonizing work and leisure, acquisition and toil, spending and spirit. While Veblen became part of the curriculum, Patten helped found the classroom. He was responsible for the creation of a separate division of the University of Pennsylvania dedicated to supporting business—the Wharton School of Economics.

markers. Waste is not just inevitable; it is always increasing as the mindless wannabes chase the wily gentry.

But there is more. First, there is the snob effect—that false pride of having status goods—which is related to the eternally changing criteria of what constitutes the bugaboo of good taste. Second, there is the band-wagon effect, which is based on emulating that good taste as it works its way down the social scale.

Veblen lumped conspicuous consumption with sports and games, "devout observances," and aesthetic display. They were all reducible, he insisted, to "pecuniary emulation," his characteristically bloated term for getting in with the "in" crowd. Veblen fancied himself a socialist looking forward to the day when "the discipline of the machine" would be turned around to promote stringent rationality among the entire population instead of wasted dispersion. If only we had fewer choices we would be happier, there would be less waste, and we would accept each other as equals.[8]

The key to Veblen's argumentative power is that, like Hercules clean-ing the Augean stables, he felt no responsibility to explain what hap-pens next. True, if we all purchased the same toothpaste things would be more efficient and less wasteful. Logically we should all read *Consumer Reports,* find out the best brand, and then all be happy using the same product. But we don't. Procter & Gamble markets thirty-six sizes and shapes of Crest. There are forty-one versions of Tylenol. Is this be-cause we are dolts afflicted with "pecuniary emulation," obsessed with making "invidious distinctions," or is the answer more complex? No matter, Veblen made his points: individuals' needs are manipulated by producers; production is inevitably wasteful; individuals compete with and relate to each other mainly through consumption. He never con-sidered that consumers might have other reasons for exercising choice in the marketplace. He never even considered that along with "keeping up with the Joneses" runs "keeping away from the Joneses."

---

8. Rather like those who currently tout the simple life exempt from public haunt, Veblen juxtaposed the homely practices of his rural Minnesota life to the practices of an increasingly urban, industrial, consumer society. Al-though it may seem churlish to speculate, one wonders how Veblen would have reacted had he been able to find a job. For both St. Olaf and Carleton Colleges passed on employing the desperate academic—with a Ph.D. from Yale, no less—because, although he was a Norwegian and should have fit in, he was extremely hard to get along with.

✳ SO WHY "NEEDLESSLY" CONSUME IF NOT TO SHOW OFF?

Remember in *King Lear* when the two nasty daughters want to strip Lear of his last remaining trappings of majesty? He has moved in with them, and they don't think he needs so many expensive guards. He has feasted enough, they say, let him eat salad for awhile. They convince themselves by saying that their dad, used to having everything he has ever wanted, doesn't need a hundred or even a dozen soldiers around him. They whittle away at his guards until only one is left. And you don't even need that one, they say.

Rather like governments attempting to redistribute wealth or like academics criticizing consumption, they conclude that his needs are excessive. They are false needs. Lear, however, knows otherwise. Terrified and suddenly bereft of purpose, he bellows from his innermost soul, "Reason not the need."

True, Lear doesn't need these soldiers any more than Scrooge needed silver, or Midas needed gold, or I need a sports car, but it doesn't stop the desiring. If the speed limit is sixty-five M.P.H., a Ford goes as fast as a Ferrari. Lear knows that possessions are definitions—superficial meanings perhaps, but meanings nonetheless. Without soldiers he is no king. Without a BMW there can be no yuppie, without tattoos no adolescent rebel, without big hair no Southwestern glamourpuss, without Volvos no academic intellectuals, and, well, you know the rest.

Let me reiterate these central points because they so strain our usual academic interpretation of materialism. Then I promise I'll give them a rest. First, the opposition between real and false needs or desires is preposterous on the face of it. There are no false needs. Once we are fed, clothed, and sexually functioning, our needs (really, wants) are cultural. Second, we are not too materialistic; if anything we are not materialistic enough. Meaning is added to objects by advertising, branding, packaging, and fashion because that meaning—derisively called status—is what we are after, what we need, especially when we are young.

✳ THE ANALOGY OF TELEVISION AS MODERN MARKETPLACE

For an analogy, take watching television. In academic circles, we assume that youngsters are being retarded from healthy growth, robotized, by passively consuming pixels in the dark. Meaning supposedly resides in the shows and is transferred to the spongelike viewers. So boys, for example, see flickering scenes of violence, internalize these scenes, and willy-nilly are soon out jimmying open your car. In nonscientific language, monkey see, monkey do. Consumption of images of danger is a priori dangerous to your kids' health and your possessions.

This is the famous Twinkie interpretation of human behavior—consuming too much sugar leads to violent actions. Would listening to Barry Manilow five hours a day make adolescents into loving, caring people? No one has ever done such a study, but the results would be interesting. If it works, we should be reading Hallmark cards more seriously.[9]

Watch kids watching television and you see something quite different from what is seen by the critics. Most consumption, whether of entertainment or of what's in the grocery store, is active. We are engaged. In fact, observe yourself watching and you will see that unlike reading, which really is passive, watching television is almost frantic with creative activity.

Here is how I watch television. I almost never turn the set on to see a show. I am near the machine and think I'll see what's happening. I know all the "dayparts" by heart and so have a good idea what to expect from first thing in the morning to last thing at night. I know all the channels; any eight-year-old does. I am not a passive viewer. I use the remote control to pass through various programs, not searching for a final destination but making up a shopping basket, as it were, of entertainment.

In the evening, for instance, I'll start off with the local news, then go over to the national news, flip to the weather, then check on the stock market, run up to the movie channel to see what's there, over to Nickelodeon for a shot of nostalgia, then on to movies, which I watch two at a time. I have my own repertoire of favorite images. The ones I like most have to do with scenes of sex and violence. Car chases and décolletage stop me in my tracks. I even use the picture-within-a-picture

---

9. In studies of the effects of television violence, researchers show the test audience a concussive program and then test for increased kinetic behavior afterward. These studies, called Joe Palookas in the trade, count the number of times a kid hits an inflatable, knockover balloon doll. Not very sophisticated, but such "scientific tests" are the basis of much academic criticism of television and movies.

device so I can have my nesting show on most of the screen while prospecting for these images of interest.

I'll watch with other family members, but usually the image salad they toss leaves me antsy so I'll get up and either go prospecting on another television, or do something else. Often I enjoy watching them make up their entertainment. My wife and two daughters watch much the same way I do, except in slower motion. They shop for meaningful glances, not action sequences. They seem to like watching people looking intently at each other. If you were to ask them why they click on to a different show, it is almost never because they are interested in plot resolution—they know all the plots by now and have known them since early adolescence. What they like is repetition and slight variation.[10]

✳ TELEVISION AND THE PROBLEMS OF VULGAR MARXISM

If you ask most academics to describe how the medium of television works and to characterize its viewing, they would say that a passive observer sits quietly in front of the set letting the phosphorescent glow of mindless "infotainment" pour over his consciousness. The video consumer is narcotized. This is a passive medium programmed for the LCD (lowest common denominator) as a means of inserting commercials that manipulate the drowsy viewers into buying worthless stuff they certainly never desired, let alone needed. In the hypodermic analogy beloved by critics, the potent dope of desire is pumped into the bleary dupe. Another favorite trope is the couch potato vegetating in the cush-

---

10. I don't know how I lived before cable and the remote control, but I do remember I used to have to go to the cellar where my father had put the set to get it out of the way. I would sit real close so I could work the channel changer by hand. In the old days scientists used to fit viewers with the Mackworth headcamera to see what they were seeing, and they were amazed by how much eye movement viewers were producing—much more than in REM sleep. As Nielsen has replaced the old-style diary with the electronic peoplemeters, they have learned (much to advertisers' distress) that my style is not unique. These passive scanners not only keep track of all the channels visited but periodically check the couch to see who is watching. While the young and the males actively consume violent entertainment, women are not far behind in at least stopping to have a quick look. Only the elderly and dedicated sports viewers stay put.

ion cracks of the sofa. Better yet might be the couch mushroom, for the viewer just sits in the dark and is fed crap.

This paradigm of passive observer and active supplier, of receptive moron and smart manipulator, is easily transported to the marketplace. One can see why such a system would appeal to the critic. After all, since the critic is not being duped, he should be empowered to protect the young, the female, the foreign, the uneducated, and the helpless from the onslaught of *dreck*. If you are a gatekeeper you need more than a gate. You need some bogey on the other side and that bogey is/was dangerous images, empty calories, unnecessary products, too many soldiers—even for King Lear.

✳ *THE FRANKFURT INTERPRETATION*

To a degree this patronizing view comes from the modern academy's need to find a purpose. As the canon has evaporated, the purpose of many professors who grew up in the 1960s has become creating and then exploiting cultural politics. Nine times out of ten, if you take a course in anything described as Cultural Studies, you will find that individuals are invariably seen as victims, while your instructor is the sage protector. There are forces abroad in the entertainment/advertising complex that seek to control your every desire and we must resist them. Hence, the attraction of the so-called Frankfurt theorists (and later, the Center for Contemporary Cultural Studies at the University of Birmingham) of the 1950s and 1960s, who essentially argued that what we see in popular culture is the result of the manipulation of the many for the profit of the few.

Here is the argument in all its jargon. The manipulators, aka "the culture industry," attempt to enlarge their "hegemony," establish their "ideological base" in the hearts and pocketbooks of the innocent. The masters of the media strive to "infantilize" the audience, to make it both docile and anxious, and consumptive with "reified desire." The predominantly male media lords are predators, and what they do in no way reflects or resolves genuine audience concerns. Just the opposite. While we may think advertising is "just selling a product," this is not so; it is selling the oppression of consumption. The weak and marginalized, especially the young and female, are trapped into a commodifying system, a "false consciousness" and a "fetishism" that only we, the enlightened, can correct.

In this context, we might well recall George Orwell's quip that some ideas are so preposterous that only intellectuals could believe them. The key to the currency of these ideas is that the academics who held them so confidently never observed, let alone actually asked, the objects of their criticism to explain what was going on. Hence their conclusions more nearly describe the biases of the cosseted commentators than the behavior of the observed.[11]

✳ THE NEWER ACADEMIC VIEW

In the last decade, scholars in various fields of the humanities and the social sciences have been reviewing these assumptions and, as is typical in higher education, are now saying just the opposite. This shift to the right has occurred for a number of reasons. First, of course, you

---

11. However, a few striking aspects of the Frankfurt school: (1) Until the 1980s their influence was profound in academic circles—hardly a day went by when one did not hear in the halls of academe such jargon as Antonio Gramsci's "ideological hegemony," Theodor Adorno and Max Horkheimer's "culture industry," Hans Magnus Enzensberger's "consciousness industry," Friedrich Schiller's "mind managers," Michael Real's "mass-mediated culture," Fredric Jameson's "use value overcoming exchange value," and the old standby, Herbert Marcuse's "systematic moronization" and best yet, "repressive tolerance." (2) Their intellectual descendants produced a disproportionate amount of university-based criticism—mostly at the better schools where publishing is rewarded and graduate students can participate—and dominated the lists of such presses as Routledge and Pantheon, as well as many university presses. Generations of students grew up believing this interpretation of the market was the result of some scientific process of hypothesis, observation, and conclusion. (3) Most of the explanations and predictions of the Frankfurt school are now having to be reconsidered not because the old guard has stopped to reconsider, but because world politics has shown the rest of us how wrong they were. In retrospect, given the political transformation of Eastern Europe and the Pacific mainland, fewer books were needed on the necessity of cultural socialism and more were needed on how to transform controlled cultures into less restricted ones. And (4) this leftward-leaning Germanic interpretation of the material world is vanishing as the French, who have been so influential in semiotics and deconstruction, start to make their way over to discussing the commercial world.

cannot publish if all you are saying is "count me in." Second, because
today's scholars were in graduate school when the Frankfurters were
holding sway, they have started to reconsider the accepted dogmas of
the fathers—the "anxiety of influence." And third, there is the hobgob-
lin of reality. It simply became clear that when the Frankfurt sieve was
applied to reality almost everything slipped through.[12]

At the risk of oversimplification, let me give the gist of the more
modern view of consumption. As we have seen, the assumption of the
old-style interpretation was that the machine-made world is divided
into twos: producer and consumer, male and female, supply and demand, make and use. The male producer fires up the machine, makes
the product, sells it to the female consumer by creating a culture of desires where none previously existed, and then soon controls not just the
market but the mentality of consumption. He makes, she shops; phallo-

12. The reconsideration is now occurring in many academic disciplines, especially anthropology. The central text is *The World of Goods: Towards an
Anthropology of Consumption* (1979) by Mary Douglas and Baron Isherwood. These anthropologists show how various domains of consumption, such as food, clothing, and shelter, become highly symbolic contexts
invested with meanings derived from commercial frames. Store-bought
goods convey messages between individuals and between groups of individuals. In the last few years we have been learning more and more
about the dynamics of consumption as audience-inspired, not producer-
induced. Social scientists have attempted to understand the meaning of
things by actually observing consumption and then asking end users
what happened. This view has spread into communication studies (William Leiss), sociology (Dick Hebdige), history (Jackson Lears), anthropology (Daniel Miller), cultural studies (David Morley), advertising (Michael
Schudson), consumer research (Sidney Levy), economics (Tyler Cowan),
fashion (Grant McCracken) and even art history (Simon Schama). One of
the more interesting recent shows (May–August 1997) at the Museum of
Modern Art, titled "Objects of Desire: The Modern Still Life," actually
focused on the salutary influence of consumer culture on high culture.
In addition, this shift to studying consumer influence has even resulted
in new journals—most importantly *The Journal of Consumer Research* and
even a special issue in 1991 of the *Journal of Social Behavior and Personality*. A three-year-long (1988–1991) symposium on consumption (held
in southern California, naturally) resulted in the publication of a three-
volume set. The most relevant for our purposes is a massive compen-
dium of articles published in 1993, *Consumption and the World of Goods*.

centric production, ovarian consumption; he profits, she is perpetually disappointed.

Although this would never be admitted, these dichotomies really stand for smart and stupid: produce = smart, consume = stupid. And, even though the list becomes more complex as it is applied to the nonmaterial world—culture/nature, Occident/Orient, high/low—the value judgments remain. Each pair represents a difference, and usually the first term is given a superior status over the second term. Right away you can see why this appealed to male-dominated graduate education. Little wonder that capitalism, so described, is a frightening world. Little wonder we need professional gatekeepers from Veblen to Nader to protect us from it.

In the modern interpretation the scholar has left the comfy cubicle to actually observe and question. Just one example: In the 1980s Mihaly Csikszentmihalyi, a psychology professor at the University of Chicago, interviewed 315 Chicagoans from 82 families asking them what objects in the home they cherished most. He then compared the five families who described themselves as the happiest with the five who were most dissatisfied. The adult members of the happiest families picked things that reminded them of other people and good times they'd had together. They mentioned a memento (such as an old toy) from their childhood 30 percent of the time. The other group cited such objects only 6 percent of the time.

In explaining why they liked something, happy family members often described the times their family had spent on a favorite couch, rather than its style or color. Although objects might change, it was clear that both happy and unhappy families found great meaning and sense from the consumption and interchange of manufactured things. The thesis, reflected in the title of his 1981 book, *The Meaning of Things*, is that most of the "work" of consumption occurs after the act of purchase. Things do not come complete; they are forever being assembled.[13]

Perhaps we need to rework Tolstoy's famous first line of *Anna Karenina:* "Happy families are all alike; every unhappy family is unhappy

---

13. A quick way to see how rapidly the pendulum is shifting from production to consumption is to check the titles of other more recent scholarship: *The Social Life of Things, The World of Consumption, Consumption and the World of Goods, The Romantic Ethic and the Spirit of Modern Consumerism, Consumer Culture and Postmodernism, Culture and Consumption,* and *From Graven Images: Patterns of Modern Materialism.*

in its own way" into something like "Happy families find and exchange meaning through objects; unhappy families think they are dealing with just things."

The weary dichotomies of machine-made materialism are being questioned, or in the jargon, are being "decentered." Why should male/producer/intellect be automatically ranked over female/consumer/emotion? Why is consumption denigrated when it is, after all, the spark plug of the machine? We denigrate the "end user" as if she is somehow responsible for the process going awry. But is this the truth? Why are her choices always called foolish? And why is she the one who causes waste?

Just as likely it is the male producer who is flummoxed. If the producers are so smart, why do 80 percent of new products fail? The waste may be in advertising, packaging, and marketing, not in incomplete use of the frivolous object. And isn't it more logical to assume that some meaning is added to products by the shopper even though the producer usually gets the credit? In fact, the happy consumer seems to be the one who makes objects come alive, while the unhappy one lets the producer generate meaning. The compulsion to consume is not reducible to the power of manipulation, or emulation, or conspicuous display. Consumption is not just desire–purchase–disappointment–rekindled desire. When consumption leads to the generation of meaning, as it almost always does, it is an active and creative imaginative endeavor.

So why not turn the searchlight from the work of making to the work of using, from the factory to the store, from the planting of crops to the eating of food? In fact, eating may be the appropriate trope. Social identity created via consumption may be summarized in the catchphrase, "you are what you eat." So too you are what you wear, what you drive, where you holiday, where you live, and even what you decide to video-graze on. In fact, the aphorism about being what we eat is a distortion of the more palatable claim of the nineteenth-century French gourmet, Brillat-Savarin: "Tell me what you eat and I will tell you what you are." Tell me what you buy and I'll tell you who you are, and who you want to be.

✴ OH LÀ LÀ, THE ROLE OF THE FRENCH

Twentieth-century French sociologists have taken the argument even further. Consumption for many of them is, if not the equal to production, then inseparable from it. Two of the most important French sociologists are Pierre Bourdieu and Jean Baudrillard. Their recent books on consumption (Bourdieu's *Distinction: A Social Critique of the Judgment of Taste*, and Baudrillard's *The Mirror of Production* and *Simulacra and Simulation*) have been influential in acknowledging that most of the meaning in the way we live now is derived from commercial transactions. Essentially, they admitted the inevitable: commercialism is driving popular culture, and popular culture is driving almost everything else.[14]

Although they have many differences, both sociologists attempted to account for social classes by positioning themselves with consumers as they struggled to make distinctions and derive meaning from purchasing decisions. Consumption is negotiation, a never-ending conversation held in the languages of advertising, packaging, branding, fashion, and entertainment. Consumers are not passive. Like television viewers, they only *look* mildly lobotomized. And they are certainly not wax figures formed by producers and portrayed in Hollywood as Doris Day in Filene's basement. If they were, we would all be driving Edsels, listening to eight-track stereo, and drinking New Coke. Rather, *consumers* are the ones with the power, continually negotiating new sites for meaning. In fact, if anyone is being manipulated it is the M.B.A.s reading the *Wall Street Journal* and filing Chapter 11 as they continually misinterpret the audience they supposedly control.

The French sociologists see consumer culture as multiple and interpenetrating discourses or fields, rather than as a singular dominant ideology that can be accepted or resisted. In the spirit of reader-response theory in literary criticism, they see meaning not rigidly superapplied to consumer goods by producers who hold the meaning stable, but rather supplied by the user who jumbles various interpretations simul-

---

14. This interest in consumption also spilled over into literary studies. Taking a turn on existentialists like Gabriel Marcel who, in *Being and Having*, toyed with the concept of "being as having," George Perec published a fascinating novel called *Things*. The story is told not in terms of consciousness, but in terms of acquisition, use, and disposal of store-bought objects. The French even have an ephemeral genre called *chosisme*, which is vaguely analogous to what Tom Wolfe calls "Kmart fiction." You read character via brand choice. If character is action, then action is consumption.

taneously. Consumers are just another interpretive community. They are readers. For them, consumer goods should be considered as "polysemous cultural resources" (aargh!) that can be interpreted in a variety of ways by different groups of consumers. Goods are poems, paintings, texts.

Essentially, beneath the jargon, this means that the Budweiser you drink is not the same as the one I drink. The meaning tastes different. The fashion you consider stylish, I think is ugly. If we buy the package not the contents, it is because the package means more. That little Polo pony is on the cotton T-shirt for a reason; that winged woman is flying from the prow of a Rolls Royce for a reason; Absolut vodka is in that bottle for a reason. Filter, flavor, (and especially) flip-top box. What is being packaged is not the goods as much as the buyer of the goods.

The process of consumption, therefore, is creative and even emancipating. In an open market we consume the real and the imaginary meanings, fusing objects, symbols, and images together to end up with John Donne's "little world made cunningly." Rather than lives, individuals since mid-century have *lifestyles*. For better or worse, lifestyles are secular religions, coherent patterns of valued things. Your lifestyle is not related to what you make but to what you buy. It is what the French call *mentalité* except that it is almost totally unrelated to the individual's identity as a laborer. One of the chief aims of the way we live now is the enjoyment of clustering with those who share the same clusters of objects as do we.

✳ BIRDS OF A FEATHER FLOCK TOGETHER

Once consumption is separated from concerns of class and oppression/ exploitation and made part of a lifelong attempt at creating meaning, we can finally appreciate why mallcondo culture is so powerful. The object of self-realization via consumption is no longer preordained by class but results from a never-ending shifting of individual choice. No one wants to be middle class, for instance. You want to be cool, hip, with it, with the "in" crowd, instead.

As you mature in this culture you move through consumption clusters of cool until finally finding stability in middle age. You consume progressively less in the way of new products and brands, and can finally turn your attention to criticizing others as they create their own thing-based selves and lifestyles. "My, my, how materialistic teenagers are today," we say to each other, forgetting our own getting and spending experiences.

One of the reasons terms like "yuppie," "baby boomer," and "GenX" have elbowed aside such older designations as "upper-middle class" is that we can't understand class as well as we can understand lifestyle. Even if no one knows exactly how much money it takes to be a yuppie, or how young you have to be, or how upwardly aspiring, everybody knows where yuppies gather, how they dress, what they play, what they drive, what they eat, and how they hate to be called yuppies. They are instantly recognizable in movies. Everybody knows that they were the first ones to serve goat cheese, that they tend to drink spritzers, and that they populate 90 percent of all ads. "Die Yuppie Scum" is immediately understood because our knowledge of consumption communities is so complete, as is our own conflicted response.

As one might imagine, the keenest knowledge about these consumption communities comes from those who have the most to gain by understanding and selling such information, namely marketing specialists. Tell a savvy marketing analyst your most recent purchase and he will tell you with amazing detail what you'll buy next. Dr. Johnson said you could tell a man by his library; now just a peek at his running shoes will do.

Take zip codes, for instance. Marketing firms have separated neighborhoods into some forty or so designations complete with snappy names called prizm (Potential Rating Index For zip Markets) clusters. So at one end of the residential microgeography are consumption communities like Blue Blood Estates, Money and Brains, Furs and Station Wagons that buy predictably expensive stuff. Then in the middle are clusters like Pools and Patios, Two More Rungs, Black Enterprise, New Beginnings, New Melting Pot, Towns and Gowns, Rank and File, Old Yankee Rows, Bohemian Mix, Gray Power, Young Influentials, Young Suburbia, and Blue-Chip Blues. Off to the side are Shotguns and Pickups, Levittown, U.S.A., Public Assistance, and the newest category, Old-Old.

Each of the forty clusters is defined by detailed demographic, lifestyle, and consumption information, often including brand-level data. For example, the Shotguns and Pickups cluster is partly defined by high usage of chain saws, snuff, canning jars, frozen potato products, and whipped toppings. Members of this cluster are exceptionally unlikely to use car rental services, belong to country clubs, read *Gourmet* magazine, and drink Irish whiskey. By contrast, in the Furs and Station Wagons cluster members are much more likely than the typical consumer to have a second mortgage, buy wine by the case, read *Architectural Digest*, drive BMW 5-series cars, eat natural cold cereal and pumpernickel bread, and watch *The Tonight Show*. Members of this cluster are unlikely to chew tobacco, hunt, drive a Chevette, use non-dairy creamers, eat canned stews, or watch *Wheel of Fortune*.

You immediately get the point of this data because observing stuff is the way we understand each other. What you may not appreciate is that each of these groups has more in common with a ZIP code thousands of miles away than with one a few digits off. For instance, parts of Palo Alto, California can be exchanged with parts of Princeton, New Jersey (both are dominant in the Money and Brains category) and no one would know the difference. Marketers can predict not just the kind of automobile, but the specific brands of camera, television set, toilet paper, and deodorant for specific ZIP codes in Beverly Hills in California, Scarsdale in New York, Bloomfield Hills in Michigan, McLean in Virginia, and Lake Forest in Illinois with eerie accuracy.

Marketers can also chart your passage through life by using not ZIP codes but shifting purchases. Give a consumer specialist an optical reader, a computer, and all your bar-coded purchases for the past week and he will tell you not only what you bought last year but what you will consume next week. Taking this into consideration, "tribe" would be a better descriptive term than "class" to describe the way we live now, and the tribe you affiliate yourself with probably has more to do with the brand of refrigerator you just bought last Tuesday than with your income, age, education, job, bloodline, religion, or country club.

In becoming the central register of selfhood, commercial culture is now playing out what was the historic role of organized religion. The brands you once applied on Saturday or Sunday at the church of your choice are now being applied daily down at the mallcondo. That the House of Worship has become the Marketplace of Commerce is a melancholy transformation, to be sure. Much has been lost. A sense of missionary purpose, for example. But in many ways it is also a far more equitable and democratic process to trust pocketbooks over prayerbooks. Whereas the minister/rabbi/priest/shaman once spoke from on high, ex cathedra, the dominant conversation is now between consumers and their goods, from aisle to aisle. The language of community and shared values is now on the package, in the brand, from fashion, and, as we will now see, most especially through a most peculiar language—advertising.

2

The Language of Things

Advertising and the Rhetoric of Salvation

Advertising ministers to the spiritual side of trade. It is a great power that has been entrusted to your keeping which charges you with the high responsibility of inspiring and ennobling the commercial world. It is all part of the greater work of the regeneration and redemption of mankind.

—Calvin Coolidge, speech to the American Association of Advertising Agencies, 1926

IF religion is how we talk about the world beyond, then advertising is how we talk about the machine-made world of the right here and now. True, we have other languages—political speak, psychobabble, geekspeak, jive, babytalk, litcrit, the language of love, medical and legal jargon—but advertising is the primary language, the lingua franca, of commercial culture. What separates it from other tongues is that "adspeak" is language always on the take. As Jay Gatsby says of Daisy Buchanan's laugh, this language is "full of money."

You cannot *not* hear it, and when you do hear it you probably are not even listening. Your kids do listen intently and so does much of the rest of the world. Although the language of yearning for things is ancient, its fluency has increased dramatically in the last two generations thanks primarily to television. The numbers are astonishing. In 1997 more than $200 billion was spent on advertising; in 1915 that figure was about one billion dollars. The A. C. Nielsen company reports that two- to five-year-olds average more than 28 hours of television a week, which is

40 school days a year, in front of the flickering screen. Assuming they reach maturity with consciousness intact, the current crop of teenagers will have spent years of their lives watching and listening to commercials. No one has done the numbers on what happens if you factor in radio, magazines, newspaper advertisements, and billboards, but it would not be surprising if a decade of their lives was spent being bombarded by bits of adspeak. In 1915 it was perfectly possible to go entire weeks without observing an ad. The average adult today sees some 3,000 ads each day.

Like the Blob of science fiction fame, advertising is all over our lives, a wafer-thin coating of the way we live now. Cock an ear anywhere and you can hear its plaintive appeals. Not only has it saturated print and electronic media, it is colonizing the furthest regions of our everyday experience. In schools there is Channel One; in movies there is product placement; ads are in urinals, played on telephone hold, in alphanumeric displays in taxis, on the endless belt carrying your groceries past the optical scanner, sent unannounced to fax machines, inside catalogs, on the video in front of the StairMaster at the gym, on T-shirts, on golf tees, on golf balls, at the bottom of golf holes, at the doctor's office, on grocery carts, stuck on labels that are slapped on apples and bananas, on college athletes' uniforms, on parking meters, on inner-city basketball backboards, on the backs of Metrocards, piped in along with Muzak, ad nauseum (and yes, even on airsick bags).

You can't get free of it. You have to shake magazines like a rag doll to free up the pages from the "blown-in" inserts and then wrestle out the sewn-in ones before reading can begin. In GenX talk this is called boning the magazine, literally pulling out what is attached to the spine. You have to fast-forward through some five minutes of advertising on rental videotapes. In President Clinton's first inaugural parade was a Budweiser float. For his second inauguration he allowed $15 T-shirts and $690 gold medals with his likeness to be sold alongside exercise equipment and costume jewelry on the QVC shopping channel. At the Smithsonian, the Orkin Pest Control Company sponsored an exhibit on exactly what it advertises it kills: insects. Is there a blockbuster museum show not decorated with corporate logos? Public Broadcasting is littered with "underwriting announcements" that look and sound almost exactly like what PBS claims they are not: commercials. Professional athletes look like Indy 500 cars, which look like billboards, which themselves are looking more and more like television, eternally blinking on and off. You can't "surf the Net" without drowning in banner ads. With interactive technology advertisers are going to know not just where you live, but *how* you live. The interesting question is: Where is commercial speech *not* "heard" every minute of every day?

In the last decade this boom box noise has crossed over into hitherto protected space. From the heavens, threatened with being covered with blimp billboards, to the linoleum tiles on the supermarket floor, the ancient concept of *copia* has been fulfilled. The world may have been "charged with the grandeur of God" for earlier generations, but for us it is chock full of commercials.

Public space is going fast. This is the modern "tragedy of the commons," as countless billboards beside state highways attest. Some admen have seriously suggested that ads might appear embedded in highways. Or on stamps. After all, what was good enough for Elvis should be good enough for General Motors. And what of the currency? Why not replace that anachronistic eyeball atop the pyramid on the dollar bill with the Golden Arches? The state of Iowa has already sold space in the state income tax booklet for $38,225 a page with a guaranteed circulation of 1.3 million motivated close readers. The big battle on university campuses is not interleague rivalries, but who will get "pouring rights" for athletic games, Coke or Pepsi? Who will outfit the athletic teams, Nike or Reebok?

Little wonder that advertising is the favorite scapegoat of the way we live now. Has there ever been an institution so reviled as modern advertising, so hectored, so blamed for the ills of society? Who but industry flacks has ever come to its defense? Arnold Toynbee summed up the view of many residents of Upper Aesthetica when he dourly commented, "I cannot think of any circumstances in which advertising would *not* be an evil." Yet has there ever been an institution so responsible for conveying not the best that has been thought and said, but the most alluring, the most sensitive, and the most filled with human yearning?

As I will argue later in this chapter, the only institution comparable in scope and magnitude was the Holy Roman Catholic Church of the early Renaissance. Long before Philip Morris, Procter & Gamble, and General Motors, long before N.W. Ayer, J. Walter Thompson, and Young & Rubicam, the most effective advertiser and carrier of culture was the Church. While it has often been remarked that this institution was neither holy, roman, nor catholic, it has never been denied that as a social force, which directed the attention and faith of a mass audience toward a specific pattern of consciousness *and* consumption, the Church was without equal, at least until the industrial age.

Leaving aside its efficacy, one of the most interesting aspects of the modern material world is that we now cannot understand it without the advertising. Case in point: One of the most popular games in the 1980s was called Adverteasing. To play you matched the jingle or slogan with the branded product. Why was it so popular? It was one of the few games the whole family could play.

Ads have become so much the vocabulary of our times that they themselves are layered over other ads like so much alluvial sediment. So the Pepsi ad in which Shaquille O'Neal walks over to a youngster drinking a Pepsi only to have the kid refuse the star's request for a swallow is built over a Mean Joe Green Coke ad in which the same interaction occurred, only this time the kid shared. Clearly, the point is that Pepsi is more valuable than Coke. The only way to know this is to have consumed not the drinks but the ads.

When the Energizer Bunny walks across the literal turf of other ads, only those who know the other ads can appreciate the trek. What was it T. S. Eliot said? "Artists borrow, amateurs steal." But there is a more profound epistemological point here: ads are what we know about the world around us.

✳ ONE INTERPRETATION OF ADVERTISING: OLD STYLE

Here is the supply-side explanation of why advertising has pushed other languages aside. We know how this explanation goes because it is the basis of Econ 101.

Machines do two things with amazing ease. They produce identical objects and they tend to produce them in mass quantities. As a way to work off those surpluses, as well as differentiating what are essentially interchangeable objects, capitalists had to create a new signifying system or they would glut themselves on their own overproduction. Advertising was that system.

There need be nothing nefarious about this. The "masters of capital" did not intend to create a surfeit—from time to time it just happens. It happened in this country first after the Civil War and then again after each of the two World Wars. As one wag has asserted, if surplus is the mother of advertising, then war is the mother of surplus. This statement is as simple-minded as it is true, for what it takes to fight a war is to produce certain otherwise needless objects in such quantities that you can last longer than your opponent. Alas, when the conflict is over, the market for these products is predictably glutted. Now the Battle of the Bulge begins as industry needs to disgorge this surplus or suffocate. Producers may not want to advertise; they *have* to advertise or drown in their own overproduction.

Look at history. The Civil War produced a surplus of what are now ordinary items of underwear, canned food, and utensils. The First World War produced a surplus of technical things like gears, bearings, binoculars, engines, gunpowder, and radio receivers. World War II produced a surplus of almost everything, especially new customers: wage-earning women. When the story of modern economics is told it centers on how companies set about to turn customers into consumers, riveters into housewives, warriors into wage-earners. Industry needed new markets and advertising could make them.

This interpretation is true enough. Think only of how consumer debt was merchandised until it became an accepted habit, not an ab-horred practice. Think only of how shame was transformed from consuming too much to consuming too little. Think only of how the concept of shine and "new and improved" replaced the previous value of patina and heirloom. Naming something differently was often a prima facie case for renewed consumption. You never questioned whether this merited buying more, just as you supposedly never questioned if Jumbo was larger than Giant, or exactly what Premium or Super meant. Creating a massive consumer class with semantic aphasia was the necessary accomplishment of supply-side capitalism.

✳ *ANOTHER INTERPRETATION: NEW AND IMPROVED*

But seeing commercial speech from the producers' point of view tells only half the story. Here's the rest. Consumers have not been victims in this process. In fact, we have eagerly participated. The balderdash of cloistered academics aside, human beings did not suddenly become materialistic, nor were they made so by conniving producers. We have always been desirous of things. We have just not had many of them until quite recently and, if the eco-doomsayers are correct, in a few generations we may return to having fewer and fewer.

Our love of things is the *cause* of the Industrial Revolution, not the consequence. Producers conspired, to be sure, but consumers were already eager to buy. "Gimmie, gimmie, gimmie" comes before "You gotta have one of these." Mankind is not only *homo sapiens*, or *homo ludens*, or *homo faber*, but also—if there are surpluses—*homo emptor*.

John Kenneth Galbraith's famous patronizing statement that "Few people at the beginning of the nineteenth century needed an adman to tell them what they wanted" is true only because there was no extra stuff around to want. Recall that the word "shopping" only entered common parlance in mid-century as stores in London had a regular restockable inventory. But we have always been browsers.

The best approach to understanding advertising is to realize that, like religion, it is an organizing system of meaning for surpluses. Both sell peace of mind either in this world or in the next. In both cases, the system appears to be coming from the top down, from the priests to the parishioners, from the producers to the consumers. In truth, however, it works just as well the other way around. To a considerable degree the parishioners/consumers set the agenda and the priests/producers are forever scurrying around attempting to predict where demand will next appear.[1]

---

1. The process occurs wherever selling takes place. Take my job, for instance. I teach school. You would think that what I sell/teach comes from what my colleagues and I have cooked up as a curriculum—a supply-side marketplace if ever there was one. After all, I choose the books, I make the syllabus, and—most important—I grade the exams. But let the composition of my class change just a bit and I will start rearranging my produce. I want to succeed, I want to teach well, I want to be seen as effective. I want to make the sale, close the deal. Let women into my class and I will want to provide them with a learning experience they appreciate and enjoy. Let African Americans in, and I will try to find texts that they will respond to. It is really quite unconscious, but I want to have the hour of instruction interesting for me and beneficial to them. I will even make up literature— after all, that's my job as gatekeeper—so the experience will succeed. I'll include Victorian cookbooks, slave narratives, and whatever, and I will call it literature because the alternative—a class bored and boring—is demoralizing for both sides. Have a look at *The Heath Anthology of American Literature* and you can see this process in slow motion. The changes in the curriculum are unnerving to many because they are usually considered the result of instructor/producer shifts. However, they are better understood as changes in demand. Multiculturalism, diversity studies, or whatever it is called is not a change resulting from shifting supply but from changing demand. Had schools not become coeducational and had affirmative action not accepted hitherto-excluded students, the canon would have stayed very much the way it was in the 1950s.

Organizing systems, be they religion, art, commercialism, politics, or the law, are founded on magical thinking. Although the analogy seems sacrilegious, the marketplace of belief is rather like a magic show. The magician does indeed perform the trick, but it works only if the audience cooperates. If you turn aside and refuse to look, then there is no show, no magic, no meaning.

✳ *THE FUNCTION OF MAGIC IN THE WAY WE LIVE NOW: THE ENCHANTMENT OF GOODS*

Magic is indeed the appropriate trope of all human life for all times in all cultures. Never more so than now. Not to put too fine a point on it, but the alternative demands it. Take just Western culture, for instance. The intellectual history of the last few hundred years has shown that we are not the center of the universe (thanks, Galileo), not the center of God's creative nature (thanks, Darwin), not the center of a coherent self (ditto, Freud), and so, rather than cast our lot with the moody existentialists and admit we are but mites on dust bunnies skittering around the universe, we prefer a touch of order.

In commercial culture, this order comes from talking about things in this world. Two hundred years ago we did the same thing with angels on the heads of pins and had categories like seraphim, cherubim, archangels, and even entire casts of ordinary angels to prove it. Whereas the Heavenly Host organized the world of our ancestors, the Marketplace of Objects does it for us. They both promise redemption: one through faith, the other through purchase.

Of all the characteristics of advertising, therefore, nothing is more important than generating magical order. Advertisers have always known this. It's second nature to the best of them. In addressing his colleagues at a convention of advertising agencies, Leo Burnett, the creator of the Marlboro man, Tony the Tiger, and the Jolly Green Giant— to name just a few—explains the job:

> After all the meetings are over, the phones have stopped ringing and the vocalizing has died down, somebody finally has to get out an ad, often after hours. Somebody has to stare at a blank piece of paper. This is probably the very height of lonesomeness. Out of the recesses of his mind must come words which interest, words which persuade, words which inspire, words which sell. Magic words. I regard him as the man of the hour in our business today. (in Simpson 83)

Advertising is a magical culture not because it is forced on us by sorcerers, but because we are understandably eager to believe the trick if only to avoid the alternatives.

Said another way: in a strictly formal sense, if objects (works of art, literature, cars, rocks, whatever) carried value, we would not need much in the way of language. To paraphrase Archibald MacLeish, things would mean, not be. Clearly, however, objects around us don't have such value. They have attributed value and that process of attribution is continually shifting. It is magical. Gold sells for $250 an ounce not because the miners set the price, but because consumers do.

I am hardly the first to recognize that advertising is the gospel of redemption in the fallen world of capitalism, that advertising has become the vulgate of the secular belief in the redemption of commerce. In a most profound sense, advertising and religion are part of the same meaning-making process. They attempt to breach the gap between us and objects by providing a systematic order *and* a promise of salvation. They deliver the goods.

But how is this order and salvation effectuated? By magical promise, pure and simple. The most magical power of magic is that it is so resolutely denied as the major organizer of meaning. We acknowledge all manner of nefarious magic and have special names for it: black magic, sorcery, voodoo, witchcraft, and necromancy. What we overlook is that until modern times our ancestors also believed in theurgy, or white magic.

The ability to coax beneficent spirits from their habitations was very much a part of classical beliefs of theurgy. These spirits, be they gods, dryads, nymphs, or mythic personages with names like Zeus, Hera, Jupiter, or Ajax became the saints, cherubs, and seraphim of the Christian heavens. The Jolly Green Giant, the Michelin man, the Man from Glad, Mother Nature, Aunt Jemima, Speedy Alka Seltzer, the White Knight, the Energizer Bunny, and all the otherworldly kin are descendants of these earlier gods. They now reside in manufactured products not in the natural world and while earlier gods were invoked by fasting, prayer, rituals, and penance, their modern ilk are called forth by the prospect of purchase.

The magi, plural of "magus," were the ancient Zoroastrian theurgists whose actions animated the universe. They were the ones who knew the buried codes. Little wonder then that it was members of this caste who traveled to Jerusalem to bear witness to one of their own— the Christ child, the new and improved magus. And little wonder that the modern magi are in advertising all around the globe, adding "value" to interchangeable objects. They make disposable goods into long-lasting charms.

No matter that the value added to most objects is simply the advertising. Admen are the ones who produce Budweiser beer trucks in the middle of the desert, transform monsters into gentlemen hulks with a spray of Right Guard, activate those cute scrubbing brushes for Dow Cleanser, put the smile on the pitcher of Kool-Aid, change a deep-swimming shark into a Chevrolet Baretta, and make millions of pimples disappear in the mirror—like magic. When the harried housewife tells Madge the manicurist that soaking her hands in Palmolive has made them feel so great that "It's black magic," Madge corrects her. Madge says, "It's real magic." And she is right. Only in a magical world could the phrases "Nationally Advertised" and "As Seen on TV" be transformed into a recommendation.

How do we think things work if not through the powers of the magi? Why should we think that ours is an age of reason, an age of scientific observation, an age devoid of wishful thinking? The days of the Inquisition, Ponzi schemes, the South Sea Bubble, witchcraft, the Compagnie d'Occident, and Dutch Tulip mania are hardly over. In their place we have new improved Tide, diamond rings, Land Rovers in the city, designer clothing, Great Big Bertha golf clubs, bottled water from glaciers, credit cards, filter tips, premium gas, lotteries, vitamin supplements, Amway, baldness creams, breast enlargers, installment buying, the sex appeal of cigarettes, the socializing power of liquor, and hair conditioners.[2]

---

2. The incurably romantic John Kenneth Galbraith may comment that "We live surrounded by a systematic appeal to a dream world which all mature, scientific people really would reject. We quite literally advertise our commitment to immaturity, mendacity and profound gullibility" (*Economics, Peace, and Laughter*), but Galbraith forgets that without the magic of this dream world we would not have "reality." He also forgets that his specialty, economics, is one of the most magical of all human organizing systems. Consider the magical thinking that gives paper money its value. Even better, consider gold. But then again, it is an irony worth noting that modern science, now the vastest repository of magical thinking, has given magic such a bad name.

✳ THE KINDS OF MAGIC

In one of the best books ever on advertising, *The Golden Bough,* the anthropologist James Frazer outlines the two kinds of magic that make up human reality: theoretical and practical. The theoretical has to do with heavens, weather, tides, cycles of planets, and is the province of religion. It governs our far-off concerns such as what we see when we look up, or how we feel when we think about death. The practical kind of magic, however, is when we cast our eyes downward and contemplate ourselves and the objects around us.

The practical, or nearby, magic is divided into the contagious and the imitative. The contagious is the basis of all testimonial advertising— the explanation of the importance of celebrity endorsement—and has its religious counterparts in such matters as the hagiography of the saints or the relics of Christ. If you use this product, if you touch this stone, if you go to this holy place, if you repeat this word, you will be empowered because the product, stone, place, word has been used by one more powerful in what you want than you. Michael Jordan wears Nikes. He jumps high. I'll buy Nikes. I'll get there too.

Imitative magic, on the other hand, is a variation of *post hoc ergo propter hoc* thinking. It is metonymical thinking—the part becomes the whole. Because the product is made of something, you will be likewise if you consume it. So Africans use the powder of rhino horns to increase sexual potency, the Japanese crave certain mollusks, and we deodorize our bodies and then apply musk (from Sanskrit for "testicle") perfume. Then, all over the world, we get into a car with an animal name (yet more imitative magic) and go on the prowl for mates. Magic is such second nature that even when we see it right before our noses in advertising, we are not stupefied. We expect it.

Traveling with the magical totem is the tabooed. The magical power concocted to transform objects into salvation is the same power that can exile them. Where did such currently widespread afflictions as BO, halitosis, iron-poor blood, gray hair, water spots, vaginal odor, dishpan hands, and split ends come from? Where were they two generations ago? Clearly, magical thinking is at work or we would expose this charade for the protection racket that it is. If one wants to observe the push-pull of magic, the conflict between totem and taboo, a trip to the perfume counter will suffice. How to explain such names as Tabu, Forbidden Fruit, Vampire, Scandale, Obsession, My Sin, Shocking, Poison,

> Magical thinking is the reality of materialism (as well as of religion).

Voodoo, Sorcery, Love Potion, or Black Magic, other than as a kind of unrequited tension between the desired and the forbidden? Since the tension was magically created, it is magically resolved. Good thing, too, as perfume names are losing their magical charm, now often named for glorified tailors like Vanderbilt, Miss Dior, Lauren, Donna Karan, Armani, Coco, Perry Ellis, and Calvin Klein.[3]

Once we realize that magical thinking is at the heart of both religion and advertising, it will become clear why semiotics has become such a productive approach of study. Once we realize, as Mark Poster has argued, that "the consumption of an object—almost any object—has more semiological than material significance" (in Lears, "Some Versions of Fantasy" 383), we will appreciate the vast power of the amulets, icons, images, statues, relics, and all the assorted stuff of organized systems of transcendental barter. Advertising fetishizes objects in exactly the same manner that religion does: it charms objects giving them an aura of added value. An Archbishop of Canterbury supposedly said, "I do not read advertisements—I would spend all my time wanting things," quite forgetting that indeed he does "read advertisements" and that he does spend much time "wanting things" as well as exchanging them.

✳ THE PROTESTANT-INDUSTRIAL COMPLEX

What makes Christian materialism so powerful a precursor to commercial culture is that in both Catholic and Protestant teachings it is so fiercely denigrated. The Protestant may condemn the Catholic love of

---

3. In this context, how naive is the complaint that advertising is suffused with sexual innuendo. Of course it is. Naturally enough, the advertising directed at the adolescent is invariably the most drenched in libidinous oil. Look at any magazine from *Details* to *Detour* and you will see more adolescent hands in other people's pockets and down their trouser fronts; more faux-intercourse with motorcycles, automobiles, and cigarettes; and more simply lewd positioning of the human form than in any porno store. What do we expect? In adolescence we lather our bodies in unguents, slither into the most uncomfortable clothing, perform ritualistic dances that often include slamming into immovable objects, drive hunks of pig iron at breakneck speed, and ingest poisons, until finally we exchange amulets, recite mystical vows, and finally get on with it. All the time we are quite unaware of the authority of such behavior, and later when our children start to consume the same magical mumbo jumbo we say, "My, my, isn't this advertising dreadful. It's making Missy and Junior behave so badly."

icons, and the Catholic may counter that ill-gotten indulgences had by the captains of industry are sacrilegious. But neither system makes any effort to resolve the paradox, let alone divest itself of treasures. Just the opposite. Bring it on, evil though it may be.

At the heart of Christian orthodoxy is a fierce condemnation of the material world. We all know this litany of condemnation by heart. Here is just a bit of how it goes. In the Bible Jesus tells the rich ruler to sell everything he has in order to qualify for eternal life. When the well-meaning man is saddened by the severity of the prescription, Jesus makes his famous remark about rich people, camels, and needles (Luke 18:18–25).[4]

Lest we be in doubt, there is the flat pronouncement: "You cannot serve God and mammon" (Luke 16:13b). If you ask most people today, they will tell you that mammon is the name of an ancient god. It is not; "mammon" is the ancient Aramaic word for money. Can there be any doubt about the Christian view of commercialism? The poor are blessed, the rich cannot pass through the eye of a needle, and no one can worship God and mammon. Class dismissed.

It is no happenstance that the advertising men, or "ministers of commerce," who helped bring about the rise of Consumer Culture were steeped in exactly this Christian teaching. They understood both the forbidden nature of yearning for objects and how to franchise it. They knew the seven deadly sins were full of life. They knew the language of sincerity. They knew the power of promise, large promise. They knew how to make the sale and close the deal. Better yet, they knew how to create and overcome inhibition.

---

4. While the prosperous can be comfortable with Matthew's version of the Sermon on the Mount ("Blessed are the poor in spirit"), Luke leaves no room for complacency: "Blessed are you who are poor, for yours is the Kingdom of God." We know Luke's version. To make sure we don't miss the point: "But woe to you who are rich, for you have received your consolation. Woe to you who are full now, for you will be hungry." As if this were not enough, Jesus continues: "From anyone who takes away your coat do not withhold even your shirt. Give to everyone who begs from you; and if anyone takes away your goods, do not ask for them again" (Luke 6:20ff.). Or what of this from Timothy: "The love of money is the root of all evil," and from Proverbs, "Labor not to be rich," and from James, "Ye rich men, weep and howl for your miseries that shall come upon you."

Advertising was a white upper middle-class *Christian* endeavor, in part because most of the educated population was Protestant, and in part because the procedures for selling therapeutic resolution to life's problems were so similar to what Western religion had developed over the centuries. Let's just look at one of the sellers, Bruce Barton.[5]

✳ BRUCE BARTON: MAN OF THE HOUR

Of all the evangelical confidence men, none was more influential in translating the zeal of magical thinking to sectarian matters than Bruce

---

5. Barton was not the exception, he was the rule. Among the most important early "attention engineers" with deep evangelical roots were: Artemas Ward, son of an Episcopal minister, whose slogans for Sapolio soap were almost as well known as the Songs of Solomon; John Wanamaker, a staunch Presbyterian who considered the ministry and whose marketing genius helped make both the modern department store and the holidays like Mother's Day that give us time to use it; Claude C. Hopkins, who came from a long line of impoverished preachers, preached himself at seventeen, and translated his talent into copywriting for beer, carpet sweepers, lard, and canned meats; James Webb Young, who sold Bibles door-to-door as a true believer until he went to work at J. Walter Thompson where he did much the same job; Helen Lansdowne, the daughter of a Presbyterian minister, who studied three years at Princeton Theological Seminary before applying her talents to selling all manner of products to women; Theodore MacManus, one of the few devout Catholics in early advertising, who held honorary degrees from three Catholic colleges and was the master of the "soft sell" until he quit, disgusted with advertising, especially its huckstering of cigarettes as health foods; Rosser Reeves, son of a Methodist minister, who mastered the "hard sell" and left as his legacy the Anacin ads with all the hammers pounding their anvils; Marion Harper, Jr., the president of his Methodist Sunday school class, who went on to manage McCann-Erickson; and F. W. Ayer, a devout Baptist and Sunday school superintendent, who gave his own agency his father's name, N. W. Ayer & Son, because it sounded more established, and then coined the motto "Keeping everlastingly at it" to make sure the point was made. These are only a few of the anonymous priesthood of advertising, but the list shows that the vast majority of early advertisers came by their theological zeal honestly.

Barton (1886–1967). And none was more typical. As did so many of his colleagues, he came from the heartland (Oak Park, Illinois) and moved East for a blue-ribbon education at Amherst. With no intention of going into advertising, he did graduate work at University of Wisconsin and spent time writing and editing at *Every Week* magazine—a Sunday supplement. Then quite by happenstance Barton met someone equally at loose ends (Roy Durstine), and they decided, rather in the manner that musical comedies are staged, to go into advertising. Barton had two other attributes common to early advertising men: his father was a powerful Baptist minister and young Bruce was subject to spells of nervous exhaustion, or nervous prostration, as it was called.

When you read the lives of the first and second generation of advertising impresarios, this configuration occurs with such startling regularity that it is hard to believe the combination was haphazard. Almost as if he has to shove aside the old father (the church) in order to get to the new text (commercialism), the youthful copywriter proceeds to apply what he has been taught about ecclesiastical hermeneutics to create a new parochial gospel of salvation. The transition was not easily made; hence the neurasthenic crisis.

Moving the merchandise of mammon was not without compensation, however. Batten, Barton, Durstine & Osborne soon became a powerhouse of advertising, doing the selling for such American institutions as General Motors and General Electric. The agency's name itself—which Fred Allen quipped sounded like "a trunk falling downstairs"—became synonymous with the aspirational advertising of the 1920s. While building BBDO into acronymic success (it would become the fourth largest agency by the 1920s, later consumed by Omnicom, the agency holding company), Barton felt it was time to pay back his debt and perhaps relieve a guilty conscience. He did this in a characteristically American Protestant way. He wrote a book of instruction for others less fortunate on the way to success.

In the context of literary history Barton's book, *The Man Nobody Knows*, fits into a robust genre of "What if Jesus were alive today: how would He act?" Best-selling books like *In His Steps*, in which we are encouraged to imagine what life would be like if we were to respond to day-to-day problems by consulting the Lord, were as popular with our grandparents as "how to be your own best friend" books are today. Barton's Jesus was an advertising executive busy at "my father's business," selling redemption by the newly named but ancient devices of advertising. So Barton imagines a dapper Jesus at a cocktail party or a ballgame with the rest of us, a man among men who knows well what his people need and struggles to explain how to get it. So what if his explanation sounds a little like BBDO advertising copy?

In *The Man Nobody Knows*, Jesus and his little band of twelve entrepreneurs are shown carrying the Word to the modern world. He is no passive "lamb of God," but a full-fledged salesman going about his business. The omniscient narrator, the voice of advertising, often glosses the text with up-to-date information, but essentially the chapters represent a quasi-religious musing on American business. Here's a bit of how it reads:

> I am not a doctor, or a lawyer or critic but an advertising man. As a profession advertising is young; as a force it is as old as the world. The first four words ever uttered, "Let there be light," constitute its charter. All Nature is vibrant with its impulse. The brilliant plumage of the bird is color advertising addressed to the emotions of its mate. Plants deck themselves with blossoms, not for beauty only, but to attract the patronage of the bee and so by spreading pollen on its wings, to insure the perpetuation of their kind.
>
> It has been remarked that "no astronomer can be an atheist," which is only another way of saying that no man can look up at the first and greatest electric sign—the evening stars—and refuse to believe its message: "There is a Cause: A God." I propose to speak of the advertisements of Jesus which have survived for twenty centuries and are still the most potent influence in the world.
>
> Let us begin by asking why he was so successful in mastering public attention and why, in contrast, his churches are less so? The answer is twofold. In the first place he recognized the basic principle that all good advertising is news. He was never trite or commonplace; he had no routine. [In the second place] he was advertised by his service, not by his sermons. Nowhere in the Gospels do you find it announced that:
>
> **Jesus of Nazareth Will Denounce**
> **The Scribes and Pharisees in the**
> **Central Synagogue**
> **To-Night at Eight O'Clock**
> **Special Music**
>
> If he were to live again, in these modern days he would find a way to make his works known—to be advertised by his service, not merely by his sermons. One thing is certain: he would not neglect the marketplace. Few of his sermons were delivered in synagogues. For the most

part he was in the crowded places, the Temple Court, the city squares, the centers where goods were bought and sold. . . . Where will you find such a market-place in these modern days? A corner of Fifth Avenue? A block on Broadway? Only a tiny fraction of the city's people pass any given point in the down-town district on any given day. No; the present day market-place is the newspaper and the magazine. Printed columns are the modern thoroughfares; published advertisements are the cross-roads where the sellers and the buyers meet. Any issue of a national magazine is a world's fair, a bazaar filled with the products of the world's work. . . . Jesus would be a national advertiser today. I am sure, as he was the great advertiser of his own day. (125, 126, 136, 138, 139, 140)

Jesus was a businessman; advertising is a business. Jesus spoke in parables; advertising speaks in parables. Christianity sells a product; advertising sells products. Jesus did miracles; advertising works magic. The similarities are too powerful to overlook. As Barton once said to a meeting of advertising agencies, "If advertising speaks to a thousand in order to influence one, so does the church." He glossed the text "And Pharaoh died, and there arose a new king in Egypt which knew not Joseph" as a need for building brand awareness for Christianity.

Barton's charm, as well as his slightly unnerving danger, was that he was absolutely sincere. "Without sincerity," he once wrote, "an advertisement is no more contagious than a sprained ankle." Communicating that sincerity by offering access to the supernatural worlds above or to a used car out in the lot was Barton's stock in trade. He was a fearless Republican who never forgave FDR, and who represented the "silk-stocking" district of Manhattan in the U.S. Congress for a number of terms. Perhaps of more lasting importance, in 1952 he helped Rosser Reeves to develop the first coherent advertising campaign for a presidential candidate—Dwight Eisenhower. Ike claimed that this was a "hell of a way to get elected," but for Barton religion and politics and refrigerators were part of the same culture, a culture based on a kind of providential realism in which the powers of advertising could only spread the good word and re-enchant the world.

The powerful allure of religion and advertising is the same: we will be rescued. This act of rescue, be it effectuated by the Man from Glad or the Man from Galilee, transports us to the promised land of resolution. We will find the peace that passeth understanding. We will find the garbage bag certified by the American Association of Sanitary Engineers. The stigmata will be removed. Ring around the collar will disappear. Sin, guilt, redemption: problem, anxiety, resolution—the process of transformation is clear. The more powerful the redemption/ resolution, the more otherworldly becomes the final site of salvation.

If you wish to see the similarities between religious and advertising pitches, turn on your television set. The television commercial is an almost perfect mimic of a religious parable. It is a microtext of drama, an epitome of ecclesiastical exemplum, a morality play for our time, a simulacrum of the Christian worldview. We sit meditatively in front of the electronic altar, absorbing sermons from corporations on how to get "the most out of" your detergent, your cold remedy, your floor wax, your family, your love life. In the television commercials we all know by heart someone—a young female if the sponsor is a household product, or a middle-aged male if it is for a cold remedy—is in distress. This Everyperson is middle class and usually white. Everyperson needs rescue and consults some other figure who promises relief. This other person testifies, gives witness; the product somehow appears, is tried, and poof!— resolution. From on high, the disembodied voice of the male announcer then makes the parable unambiguous by reiterating the curative powers of the product. Our Everyperson is well on the way to Valhalla.

✳ *WHEN WORLDS DON'T COLLIDE*

Along the way to this Happy Valley runs a parallel universe peopled with emissaries from the eternal Beyond. In the Christian scheme this is the world of the Apostolic Church consisting of pope, bishops, priests, nuns, and functionaries inside holy orders, all variously tied to the "other world." In addition, slightly above the Church Triumphant is a mythic world of all those who have migrated between "here" and "there" like the various seraphim, cherubim, archangels, and saints. Below the world is yet another hierarchy, this time of malevolent spirits surrounding Satan, made up of fallen angels like Beelzebub, Mephistopheles, and all manner of demons, fiends, succubi, ghouls, vampires, and ogres who reverse the force fields of supernatural powers. Perhaps Christianity was built on the classical template since these chains of command resemble the Greco-Roman orders, descending from Zeus to the likes of Apollo and Hermes, then to the levels of Poseidon, and then to the netherworld. Between are all manner of dryads, nymphs, sprites, gnomes, and the host of natural spirits.

While we may have lost the superhuman beings and regions of classical and Christian mythologies, we have not lost our desire to link with this parallel world. It is, after all, a source of abiding comfort to think we are not alone. Just on the far side of the margin are others who care about us. Furthermore, it is a powerful belief that we, by the powers of prayer and devotion, can encourage these forces beyond our ken to enter our world. Once invoked they do more than give aid and succor; they give our world meaning and purpose. What characterizes commercial culture is that this parallel world, our utopian otherland, has been populated by new beneficent spirits, spirits magically residing not in nature, holy books, magical signs, or chants but in objects as mundane as automobile tires, rolled-up tobacco leaves, meat patties, green beans, and sugar water. The Man with a Thousand Faces simply has a few more, and he spends most of his time inside containers on shelves down at the A&P.

In our empire of things we have all manner of creatures vying for our companionship. Here are just a few:

➤ From Greek mythology: Hermes carrying flowers for FTD, Ajax, the white knight with that magical lance, Pegasus at the Mobil station

➤ From folklore: the Keebler elves living in the Hollow Tree, Snap, Crackle, and Pop residing in Rice Krispies, the Jolly Green Giant inhabiting Happy Valley

➤ From cartoon town: Elsie the Cow, Bibindendum (or Mr. Bib, the Michelin tire man), Poppin' Fresh (the Pillsbury Doughboy), Mr. Peanut, E. B. (the Energizer Bunny), Reddy Kilowatt, Tony the Tiger, Cracker Jack, the Underwood devil

➤ From crossover land, characters from the world of half human/ half cartoon: Ronald McDonald, Johnnie Walker, the Quaker Oats Quaker, the Smith Brothers (Trade and Mark), Mr. Clean

➤ From our human world: the Philip Morris bellhop, the Morton Salt Girl, the Marlboro man, Aunt Jemima, Betty Crocker, Mrs. Olsen, Mr. Whipple, Little Debbie, Madge the manicurist, Josephine the plumber

➤ From our world who have gone into some other world and returned: Robert Young who became Marcus Welby to return as "I am not a doctor" Dr. Robert Young, and some who never come back like Colonel Harlan Sanders, the Hathaway shirt man, the man from Schweppes, Duncan Hines

➤ From animals made human: Charlie the Tuna, Spuds Mackenzie (the party animal), Morris the Cat, the Playboy bunny, the Taco Bell chihuahua, Smokey Bear

➤ From cartoon characters who have been pressed into commercial service: Bugs Bunny gone to work for Nike, Yogi Bear, spokesman for Arby's, Bart Simpson hawking Butterfingers, Rocky and Bullwinkle peddling tacos for Taco Bell

➤ From the natural world: Nipper the dog, White Owl, the John Deere leaping deer

➤ From the once-with-us-but-now-no-more land: the Uneeda biscuit boy, the Gold Dust Twins, Yaller kid, Sunny Jim, the Clicquot Club Eskimo

➤ From bizarre-mutation world: Joe Camel, a dromedary on the cigarette pack and in the cartoon world as Smokin' Joe, super-cool musician. Joe has entered the highest pantheon of the enchanted world of advertising, having proven so popular that he is on all manner of clothing, beach towels, baseball caps, etc., as well as on the hit list of the FTC as a public nuisance

Starting decades ago with Sunny Jim for Force Food, the bent-over washerwoman for Dutch Cleanser, and the Campbell kids for the soup company, the creation of imaginative characters and the lining up of these characters with commodities has shown that we have not lost the deep desire to animate the world around things with the stuff of meaning. Objects must be made to "mean" and we willingly suspend disbelief to make it happen. Like the gods that we create to give us creation, in thinking about machine-made objects we externalize the magic in order to make the profoundly unmagical world have meaning. The process is so powerful that it even extends to geometric forms, such as the Golden Arches, the checkerboard square, the Nike swoosh, or the Heinz keystone.

✳ *THE POWER OF COMMERCIALIZED PRAYER*

It is as simplistic to say, "Here are the nasty advertisers leading us into temptation for their own profit" as it is to say, "Here are the nasty churchmen capturing our imaginations and manipulating them for their own aggrandizement." These transformations are not imposed on us any more than Zeus really terrorized the ancients. We need the gods more than the gods need us. That our gods are now in the hands of commercial manipulators, that folklore has become "fakelore" and "folklure," that holy grails have become spot removers, and that the magic of the Eucharist has been stolen by liquor campaigns, is possible only because the yearnings of humans and the power of institutions to direct those yearnings has remained in place. However much we may feel comforted by thinking "they are doing *this* to *us*," in truth we are doing it to ourselves.

So we find advertising loaded down with the rhetoric of religious thanksgiving: "Thank you, Paine-Webber." "Thank you, Tastykakes." "I love what you do for me." "Thanks, Delco." "Thanks, Crest." "Thank goodness for Chef Boyardee." Conversely the sense of self-worth and salvation is also apparent: "I'm worth it." "Master the moment." "Be all you can be." "I found it!" "Looking good makes us feel good." "You deserve a break today." "You, you're the one." "You've come a long way, baby." Our companies are godlike in their concern for us: "Ford wants to be your car company." "You asked for it, you got it—Toyota." "Have it your way." "Something to believe in." "We bring good things to life." "It's the right thing." With the product you have a constant friend. "You're in good hands." Jesus has entered your life. It's "me and my R.C.," "me and my Arrow." Advertising does not create these relationships; they had already been established long before Christianity. Advertising exploits the hell out of them.

Although it is comforting to contend that *they* are doing this to *us,* such is almost never the case. You may not like what is happening when you go to church, or watch television, or read the newspaper, or even are hauled into court, but each of these cultures is programmed with exacting care to cater to specific demands of specific audiences. People choose denominations as they change channels to find what they want. While the institution may pretend to receive their programming decisions from on high (God's word, "All the News That's Fit to Print," the Constitution), in truth they are listening first to their audience. If history shows us anything it is that the most successful institutions are those that claim to lead while following some abstract code, but, in fact, are those most sensitive to audience concerns. The most powerful institutions over time are those whose membranes give the impression they are impermeable, but are the most porous.

What makes organized Christianity the appropriate precursor of modern materialism is that it does indeed trade a surplus product—redemption of some sort, which can be branded as Calvinism, Anglicanism, Catholicism, or whatever—for the attention of a willing populace. The relief of audience anxiety, albeit created by the institution that resolves it, is effectuated by membership, and membership depends on contributions of some sort, be they made in coin or sweat. You contribute to the church, you receive comfort in return. *You* will be saved (others won't be). In the material world of capitalism the exchange is effectuated through things. Buy this. Be someone special. Advertising has been rightly called the church art of capitalism because it continuously reiterates this deep desire for meaning.

Scholars have long noted that the medieval peasant could not move far from the iconography of Catholicism. It was hung around his neck, carved into his bedstead, painted over his doorway, engraved on his flatware, hung on his walls, the subject of his songs, the plot of his morality plays, and, of course, imaged in every inch of his holy places. Modern culture, a culture centered around the production, distribution, and consumption of machine-made objects, is equally inundated with the iconography of capitalism. Just as we may recognize the difference between Coca-Cola red and Marlboro red, the medieval audience knew well that Christ's robe was a distinct shade of red. Commercial speech is here for the same reason Christian iconography was there. It is how we sort through things. It is how we know where we are. As with our medieval counterparts, there is almost no private space left, for the first commandment of both institutions is: Where empty space is, there iconography/advertising shall be.

✳ HOW ADVERTISING WORKS

If you ask the ordinary man on the street (a character created by advertising in the 1940s, incidentally, along with Brand X) to tell you how advertising works, you will probably hear the actual word, or at least the concept of, "subliminal." Most people believe that advertising sneaks some foreign matter under the surface, slides some message under the margin of consciousness that stimulates us to feel some anxiety capable of relief only by the consumption of a product we would ordinarily not buy. This is utter nonsense, but utterly powerful nonsense.

The idea that "they" are tampering with "my" natural desires is a comforting thought in the modern world. How else to explain the polyester bell-bottom jump suit? In fact, to many Americans the notion that advertising manufactures anxieties, creates desire, and thwarts resolution by literally speaking to us under our own protective consciousness goes without question. By far the most popular books on advertising are written by Wilson Brian Key with tell-all titles like *Media Sexploitation* and *Subliminal Seduction.* Mr. Key (he used to be Professor but was untenured by his Canadian university) looks at ads and sees the word "fuck" written all over crackers, vaginas on the forearms of little children, and penises in pictures of ice cubes. Although subliminal seduction has been thoroughly discredited, even mocked in countless advertisements (notably for Seagram's Gin), the books clearly appeal by applying Occam's razor to cut through the thorniest issue: why is a supposedly rational culture interested in consuming so much of what it doesn't seem to really need?[6]

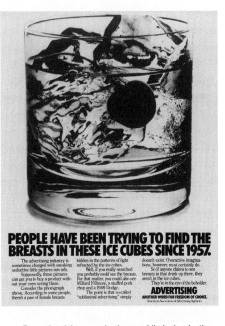

PEOPLE HAVE BEEN TRYING TO FIND THE BREASTS IN THESE ICE CUBES SINCE 1957.

The advertising industry is sometimes charged with sneaking seductive little pictures into ads. Supposedly, these pictures can get you to buy a product without your even seeing them. Consider the photograph above. According to some people, there's a pair of female breasts hidden in the patterns of light refracted by the ice cubes. Well, if you really searched you probably *could* see the breasts. For that matter, you could also see Millard Fillmore, a stuffed pork chop and a 1946 Dodge. The point is that so-called "subliminal advertising" simply doesn't exist. Overactive imaginations, however, most certainly do. So if anyone claims to see breasts in that drink up there, they aren't in the ice cubes. They're in the eye of the beholder.

ADVERTISING
ANOTHER WORD FOR FREEDOM OF CHOICE.
American Association of Advertising Agencies, Inc.

➤ Even advertising agencies know subliminal seduction is a joke. They don't want to sell you gin, they want to sell you a *brand* of gin. (American Association of Advertising Agencies)

---

6. This interpretation of advertising starts with the invention of the Tachistoscope by the Eastman Kodak Company in the early 1950s. A superfast strobe light—it could flash at 1/60,000th of a second—was the reason we saw all those photographs of bullets caught in mid-air and open-winged hummingbirds in the pages of the *National Geographic* and *Life.* It was also the reason that an unemployed market researcher named James M. Vicary made a lot of money and mischief. Vicary contacted marketing directors and advertising managers in New York offering to instruct them (on plump retainers) in a new selling technique based on the Tachistoscope. He called his technique "subliminal advertising." He even made up a story, now part of commercial folklore. He claimed that experiments had been done at an unidentified motion picture theater on 45,699 unidentified persons at some unspecified but recent time. While watching a movie, the audience had been exposed to two messages. One said "Eat Popcorn," the other, "Drink Coke." Vicary swore that the invisible advertising had

Two matters are important. First, the subliminal thesis would be derided on Madison Avenue were it not so preposterous. They don't want you to buy crackers, or beer, or cars. They want you to buy Ritz, Schlitz, and Studebakers. What they sell is brands, not products. And second, it is not that they wouldn't love to sneak selling messages at you under the surface; it is just that the process hasn't proved effective. They've tried it.

Subliminal seduction is tripe, but the real work of advertising *is* subliminal. Not in the sense of messages slid below the threshold, but subliminal in the sense that we aren't aware of what commercial speech is saying. We rarely really listen to it. What advertising does is add meaning to otherwise interchangeable and often unnecessary products by the dull hum of background noise. It is a delicious irony that not only do we participate in creating our own advertising/meaning (in the sense that we create our own literature or politics) but that we then proceed to buy not the product but the aura around it. So if we buy the sizzle not the steak, is there any possibility that it is the sizzle that we want? Which do we thirst for: Evian advertising or water? What do we want to wear: the T-shirt or the initials CK? We might consider that the

---

increased sales of popcorn an average of 57.5 percent and increased the sales of Coca-Cola an average of 18.1 percent (Rogers 4). No explanation was offered for the difference in size of the percentages, no allowance was made for variations in attendance, and no other details were provided as to how or under what conditions the purported tests had been conducted. The Federal Communication Commission was suspicious and ordered Vicary's firm, The Subliminal Projection Company, to conduct a closed-circuit demonstration in Washington, D.C. During January 1958, before an audience of congressmen, bureaucrats from appropriate agencies, members of the press, and broadcasters, Vicary flashed his "Eat Popcorn." *Printers' Ink*, the advertising trade journal, commented, "Having gone to see something that is not supposed to be seen, and having not seen it, as forecast, the FCC and congressmen seemed satisfied." After the show, Senator Charles E. Potter waggishly said, "I think I want a hot dog" (Rogers 6). The story of subliminal manipulation lives on along with such immortal tales as the vanishing hitchhikers, sewer alligators, eyelids superglued shut, rat tails in soft drinks, and microwaved pets, becoming part of what Jan Harold Brunvand (author of *The Choking Doberman* and *The Vanishing Hitchhiker*) calls "urban legends." If they are not true, they ought to be.

customer often drinks the advertising, not the beer; drives the name-plate, not the car; or smokes the advertising, not the cigarette.

✳ HOW WELL ADVERTISING WORKS

What advertising does and how it does it has little to do with the movement of specific goods. Rather like religion, which has little to do with the actual delivery of salvation in the next world but everything to do with the ordering of life in this world, so commercialism in all its manifold forms has little to do with material objects per se, but everything to do with how we perceive them. What is ultimately branded in advertising is not objects but consumers. If religion serves as Milton said to "justify the ways of God to man," then advertising serves to "justify the ways of things to man."

If advertising doesn't really sell specific goods, then why do companies spend so much money on it? From the microcosmic view, with reference to moving specific products, the answer must be that no one really knows. First, of course, although the numbers are huge, the percents are not. Procter & Gamble may spend billions to advertise but this accounts for less than 5 percent of total expenditures. Second, businessmen have always known most advertising is a waste. Lord Leverhume (of Lever Brothers) and John Wanamaker (of the Philadelphia department store) are both credited with the quip that each knew half his advertising budget was wasted, but couldn't figure out which half. There is no meter, no dial, no needle that can be placed on an individual ad. Advertising is like grass. You never see it grow, but every once in a while you may have to get out the lawnmower. Or as one adman recently commented, advertising is like wetting your pants while wearing a blue serge suit: it gives you a nice warm feeling without anybody usually noticing (Rosene 15).

Certainly one of the most important reasons for advertising expenditures has to do with the tax code. Advertising is deductible as a business expense. If you have the choice of paying the government or running ads with the same money, which would you do? You don't have to be a genius to realize that if you take away the tax benefits of considering advertising a cost of doing business, commercial speech would turn to a whisper. The fact of the matter is that aside from comforting purchasers by assuring them they made the right choice, aside from comforting CEOs and employees that their work is important, and aside from certain unpredictable *short-term* increases in consumption, most advertising does not move product off the shelf. Two immutable facts: when times are tough the first expenses to be cut are invariably the advertising budgets, and the first thing a client does in such tough times is consider changing agencies. If advertising were effective, one would expect that rational industries would pour more money into advertising and quit playing musical chairs with agencies. Instead, what happens in a recession is that advertising expenses dry up and agencies get fired.

But from the macrocosmic view the story is different. Advertising helps make buying possible not because it sells specific goods but because it sells buying stuff as a way to consume meaning. Advertising serves to order both time and matter in such a way that to complete the self, to create the "lifestyle," you will have to make a purchase. Modern consumerism is therefore not a replacement of religion but a continuation, a secularizing, of a struggle for order. Salvation through consumption is not a contradiction but a necessity. So while capitalism requires people to be pious in the workplace, to believe *labore est orare*, to "lay not up for yourselves treasures on earth" as Jesus said, to be Calvinistic in the assembly line, it survives by encouraging us to be raving maniacs at the cash register, to be pagans at saturnalian events like Christmas, and to be woefully insecure about ourselves, especially about our body size, our odors, our face, and even about our gender. The other side of work, work, work is spend, spend, spend, and *here* advertising is efficacious.

✳ *WHAT WE ARE TO ADVERTISERS*

Mass production means mass marketing, and mass marketing means the creation of mass stereotypes. Like objects on shelves, we too cluster in groups. We find meaning together. As we mature, we move from shelf to shelf, from aisle to aisle, zip code to zip code, from lifestyle to lifestyle, between what the historian Daniel Boorstin calls "consumption communities." Finally, as full-grown consumers, we stabilize in our buying, and hence meaning-making, patterns. Advertisers soon lose interest in us not just because we stop buying but because we have stopped changing brands.

The object of advertising is not just to brand parity objects but also to brand consumers as they move through these various communities. To explain his job, Rosser Reeves, the master of hard-sell advertising like the old Anacin ads, used to hold up two quarters and claim his job was to make you believe they were different, and, more importantly, that one was better than the other. Hence, at the macro level the task of advertising is to convince different sets of consumers—target groups— that the quarter they observe is somehow different in meaning and value than the same quarter seen by their across-the-tracks neighbors.

In adspeak, this is called *positioning*. "I could have positioned Dove as a detergent bar for men with dirty hands," David Ogilvy famously said, "but I chose to position it as a toilet bar for women with dry skin." Easy to say, hard to do. But if Anheuser-Busch wants to maximize its sales, the soccer mom driving the shiny Chevy Suburban must feel she drinks a different Budweiser than the roustabout in the rusted-out Chevy pickup.[7]

The study of audiences goes by any number of names: psychographics, ethnographics, macrosegmentation, to name a few, but they are all based on the ineluctable principle that birds of a feather flock together. The object of much consumer research is not to try to twist their feathers so that they will flock to your product, but to position your product in such a place that they will have to fly by it and perhaps stop to roost. After roosting, they will eventually think that this is a part of their flyway and return to it again and again.

---

7. Cigarette companies were the first to find this out in the 1930s, much to their amazement. Blindfolded smokers couldn't tell what brand they were smoking. Instead of making cigarettes with different tastes, it was easier to make different advertising claims to different audiences. Cigarettes are hardly unique. Ask beer drinkers why they prefer a particular brand and invariably they tell you: "It's the taste," "This goes down well," "This is light and refreshing," "This is rich and smooth." They will say this about a beer that has been described as their brand, but is not. Anheuser-Busch, for instance, spent three dollars per barrel in 1980 to market a barrel of beer; now they spend nine dollars. Since the cost to reach a thousand television households has doubled at the same time the audience has segmented (thanks to cable), why not go after a particular market segment by tailoring ads emphasizing, in different degrees, the Clydesdales, Ed McMahon, Beechwood aging, the red and white can, dates certifying freshness, the spotted dog, the Eagle, as well as "the crisp, clean taste." While you cannot be all things to all people, the object of advertising is to be as many things to as many segments as possible. The ultimate object is to convince as many segments as possible that "This Bud's for you" is a sincere statement.

Since different products have different meanings to different audiences, segmentation studies are crucial. Although agencies have their own systems for naming these groups and their lifestyles, the current supplier of much raw data about them is a not-for-profit organization, the Stanford Research Institute (SRI).

The "psychographic" system of SRI is called acronomically VALS (now VALS2+), short for Values and Lifestyle System. Essentially this schematic is based on the common-sense view that consumers are motivated "to acquire products, services, and experiences that provide satisfaction and give shape, substance, and character to their identities" in bundles. The more "resources" (namely money, but also health, self-confidence, and energy) each group has, the more likely they will buy

THE VALS2 NETWORK

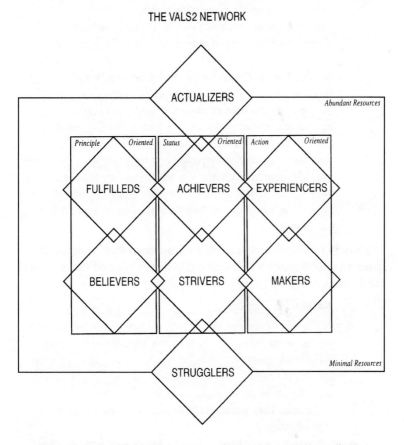

➤ The VALS2 paradigm. Lifestyle styled: a taxonomy of taste and disposable income. (Stanford Research Institute)

"products, services and experiences" of the group they associate with. But resources are not the only determinant. Customers are also motivated by such ineffables as principles, status, and action. When SRI describes these various audiences they peel apart like this (I have provided them an appropriate car to show their differences):

> Actualizers: These people at the top of the pyramid are the ideal of everyone but advertisers. They have "it" already, or will soon. They are sophisticated, take-charge people interested in independence and character. They don't need new things; in fact, they already have their things. If not, they already know what "the finer things" are and won't be told. They don't need a new car, but if they do they'll read *Consumer Reports*. They do not need a hood ornament on their car.

> Fulfilled: Here are mature, satisfied, comfortable souls who support the status quo in almost every way. Often they are literally or figuratively retired. They value functionality, durability, and practicality. They drive something called a "town car," which is made by all the big three automakers.

> Believers: As the word expresses, these people support traditional codes of family, church, and community, wearing good Republican cloth coats. As consumers they are predictable, favoring American products and recognizable brands. They regularly attend church and Wal-Mart, and they are transported there in their mid-range automobile like an Oldsmobile. Whether Oldsmobile likes it or not, they do indeed drive "your father's Oldsmobile."

Moving from principle-oriented consumers who look inside to status-driven consumers who look out to others, we find the Achievers and Strivers.

> Achievers: If consumerism has an ideal, here it is. Bingo! Wedded to job as a source of duty, reward, and prestige, these are the people who not only favor the establishment but *are* the establishment. They like the concept of prestige. Not only are they successful, they demonstrate their success by buying such objects as prestigious cars to show it. They like hood ornaments. They see no contradiction in driving a Land Rover in Manhattan.

> Strivers: A young Striver is fine; he will possibly mature into an achiever. But an old Striver can be nasty; he may well be

bitter. Since they are unsure of themselves, they are eager to
be branded as long as the brand is elevating. Money defines
success and they don't have enough of it. Being a yuppie
is fine as long as the prospect of upward mobility is possible.
Strivers like foreign cars even if it means only leasing a BMW.

Again moving to the right are those driven less by the outside world but
by their desire to participate, to be part of a wider world.

- ➤ Experiencers: Here is life on the edge—enthusiastic, impulsive,
  and even reckless. Their energy finds expression in sports,
  social events, and "doing something." Politically and personally
  uncommitted, experiencers are an advertiser's dream come true
  as they see consumption as fulfillment and are willing to spend
  a high percent of their disposable income to attain it. When
  you wonder about who could possibly care how fast a car will
  accelerate from zero to sixty M.P.H., they care.
- ➤ Makers: Here is the practical side of Experiencers; they like
  to build things and they experience the world by working on it.
  Conservative, suspicious, respectful, they like to do things in
  and to their homes, like adding a room, canning vegetables, or
  changing the oil in their pickup trucks.
- ➤ Strugglers: Like Actualizers, these people are outside the pale
  of materialism not by choice, but by low income. Strugglers
  are chronically poor. Their repertoire of things is limited not
  because they already have it all, but because they have so little.
  Although they clip coupons like Actualizers, theirs are from the
  newspaper. Their transportation is usually public, if any. They
  are the invisible millions.

As one might imagine, these are very fluid categories, and we may
move through as many as three of them in our lifetimes. For instance,
between ages 18–24 most people (61 percent) are Experiencers in desire or deed, while less than 1 percent are Fulfilled. Between ages 55
to 64, however, the Actualizers, Fulfilled, and Strugglers claim about
15 percent of the population each, while the Believers have settled out
at about a fifth. The Achievers, Strivers, and Makers fill about 10 percent apiece, and the remaining 2 percent are Experiencers. The numbers can be broken down at every stage allowing for marital status, education, household size, dependent children, home ownership, household income, and occupation. More interesting still is the ability to
accurately predict the appearance of certain goods in each grouping.

SRI sells data on precisely who buys single-lens reflex cameras, who owns a laptop computer, who drinks herbal tea, who phones before five o'clock, who reads the *Reader's Digest,* and who watches *Beavis and Butthead.*

When one realizes the fabulous expense of communicating meaning for a product, the simple-mindedness of a system like VALS2+ becomes less risible. When you are spending millions of dollars for a few points of market share for your otherwise indistinguishable product, the idea that you might be able to attract the owners of socket wrenches by shifting ad content around just a bit makes sense. Once you realize that in taste tests consumers cannot tell one brand of cigarettes from another—including their own—nor distinguish such products as soap, gasoline, cola, beer, or what-have-you, it is clear that the product must be overlooked and the audience isolated and sold.

✴ CELEBRITIES ARE THE PRIESTS IN THE EMPIRE OF THINGS

It is easy to see how commercial speech is able to imply a connection between a fungible product and an aspirational goal. Matters become slightly more complex, however, when this aura gets attached to a fellow human being.

The condition of being celebrated is doubtless one of our most central socializing devices as it separates leaders from the tribe. In all cultures certain people are capable of *celebratus,* or the condition of being honored, not just for what they have done but for what they can continue to do for us. This recognition is not always a function of the individual's specific acts but of the role played. In fact, the elevation of certain people—celebrities—is often dependent on their being able to perform certain rites for the rest of the tribe. In the church we still honor not so much the particular individual but the role of the priest in celebrating certain events like baptism, the Eucharist, marriage, or the rites of death. In the way we live now, the celebrity is that leader; he is our priest.

The celebrity/priest is the central character of the commercial world. He has one foot in our world and one foot in the magical world of adland. He must be recognized as "one of us" and "one of them." More important still, he has to be able to make us believe that he is sincere when he endorses a product that we know full well he is paid to use. This phenomenon is hardly new. Look at the walls of Renaissance churches and you will see an endless procession of martyrs and saints who are invariably undergoing the most exciting pictographic experiences in the service of what we are being invited to join. They are not supernumeraries on the stage, but foils for those of us in the audience. In their heroic deeds and sufferings they are endorsing a product, renting their glory, if you will, for the corporation. We see them rewarded with salvation, the same salvation proffered to us. If St. Sebastian is willing to endure a bodyful of arrows for an eternity of pleasure, why should we complain about our sorrows?

While the process of contrived reward is hardly new, neither is the conflating of fame and celebrity. But the linking of such glory to a manufactured object certainly is. In a universe of interchangeable products, the celebrity endorsement becomes a central part of the brand magic. "Be Like Mike," the Gatorade slogan promises. If you replenish your lost bodily fluids with their greenish slime you will not just be drinking Mr. Jordan's brand but will be participating in his majesty. This is what we have for the Eucharist.

The ability to quickly generate celebrity and then attach that value to a product is a hallmark of modern selling. The holy grail is to find a celebrity, rent his glory to endorse some product thereby increasing its value, and in so doing make the celebrity better known. Apocalypse occurs when the celebrity, the product, and the consuming audience are branded together as one. Consumable object, identification character, and consumer can't be separated. Not only can you drink Michael Jordan, you can even wear him as a shoe (Nike's Air Jordan) and as a cologne.

We accept the interpenetration of fact and fiction almost without hesitation. If life imitates art, then advertising imitates both. Magical thinking is not an occupational hazard, it is the *only* way to understand much in the supposedly material world. For instance, when Alan Alda and the cordial gang of misfits from *M*A*S*H* rented their celebrity to IBM in order to sell a product hardly available during the Korean War— the personal computer—they even pretended to be behaving just as they did in countless medical emergencies. Sometimes a star will so cover the product in the persona of the role he or she plays that the role takes over even though we are told who the endorser really is. It is not Candice Bergen but Murphy Brown who has the take-charge persona necessary to plug the business efficiencies of Sprint, even though the ad tells us differently. It is not Tim Allen who is touting the values of Builders Square, but the other Tim—the character on *Home Improvement*. When Jerry Seinfeld extols the American Express Card it is his sitcom self doing the plugging. Ditto Angela Lansbury doing her impression of the *Murder, She Wrote* sleuth discovering the hidden value in Bufferin. Sometimes this interpenetration can be downright confusing, as when Coach Quincy and his female co-star banter about Kraft products while calling each other by their names from the show *Coach*. The confusion is purposeful as it catches our attention.[8]

✳ *YOU ARE WHAT YOU BUY: THE EXAMPLE OF AMERICAN EXPRESS*

To observe the bizarre synergy between celebrity and materialism, we might look at a short-lived campaign called "People & Their Stuff" done by Ogilvy & Mather for the American Express Company. Credit cards are notoriously hard to advertise because the service they offer is almost totally interchangeable. After all, a dollar of debt is a dollar of debt. In advertising jargon the attempt to differentiate between fungibles is commonly called USP, or Unique Selling Proposition. Truth is not important, staking a claim is.[9]

---

8. It also catches the attention of the networks. ABC rejected ads by Jerry Seinfeld and Bart Simpson (for Butterfingers) saying they were too promotional for their respective non-ABC shows, and CBS has not let Sprint run its Candice Bergen ads during *Murphy Brown*. The real problem with celebrities is that the risky lifestyle that makes them shine in the public eye can so quickly produce a corporate black eye. Let Michael Jordan experience the debacle of Michael Jackson and the poles of charismatic attraction can be immediately reversed. So Bruce Willis pitched Seagram's Golden Wine Cooler until it was rumored in tabloids that he had a drinking problem. Ringo Starr had the same problem with Sun Country wine coolers. Once Mike Tyson and Robin Givens stopped cooing and started punching, Diet Pepsi headed for the showers. Rumors that Michael Jackson did not touch Pepsi, but young boys instead, collapsed an icon almost overnight. When Macaulay Culkin, star of *Home Alone,* said of Sprite, "I'm not crazy about the stuff. But money is money," admen reached for the bourbon. James Garner underwent heart surgery; the beef industry bled. When Cybill Shepherd, spokeswoman for L'Oreal, admitted she didn't dye her hair, many admen pulled theirs. Hertz fell over itself running away from O. J. Simpson.

9. Supposedly, Claude Hopkins discovered this concept of "ownership" selling carpet sweepers, canned meat, and beer. For instance, although all brewers steam-cleaned their bottles in the 1930s, Hopkins's claim that Schlitz steam-cleaned all their bottles established the notion that purity of product was unique to this brewer and no others.

Often the claim has nothing to do with the product. So, for instance, Pepsi "owns" the concept of a new generation while Coke owns friendship. Kodak owns the special moment of maturation, like the first haircut or first day at school. For a while Chevrolet attempted to own Americana as in "hot dogs, apple pie and Chevrolet," Miller Beer attempts to own early evening with Millertime, and "the night belongs to Michelob." Merrill Lynch owns not just the bull but the concept of confidence in the market; Ford owns quality in manufacturing; Marlboro owns the cowboy; Nike owns basketball; and Virginia Slims even pretends to own the women's movement.

American Express doesn't know what to own. After all, it provides the same service as MasterCard and Visa but it charges a considerable price for it. For a while it tried to own the importance of the cardholder with the "Do you know me" campaign in which a famous person is known not by face, but by the name on the credit card. So we see Stephen King or Martha Stewart having trouble charging a room until the concierge sees the name on the card and then knows he is in the presence of a celebrity. The assumption is that with this card you too will finally be known for the personage you are.

What Ogilvy & Mather did for Amex was to extend the ownership motif from association of the individual with the charge-card celebrity to association with all the celebrity's stuff as well. Using the card now joins you not just to the star but to all the star's things. In some ways this campaign is the triumph of commercialism, for now you too can get what celebrity gets—all that stuff—by magic.

In the first of the ads we see Mary Matalin and James Carville on their lawn surrounded by their favorite things. In the foreground are two spaniels and a fax machine; in the background, a Viking stove. In the middle, next to a wine rack, is a baby. The arrangement is not random; children seem just part of the inventory of a well-equipped life. There is some truth in advertising, for the couple really does have a Virginia farm (ninety-four acres, twenty-seven cows), and that barn in the background is theirs. However, the rest of their stuff can be on your front lawn too. Just use the card.

Matalin and Carville are presented as Grant Wood's *American Gothic* made modern—he with pitchfork, she slightly behind to his left. For the political cognoscenti there is a frisson of recognition. Opposites are not just in a state of attraction, but in positive unity. For these two have clearly put aside their political differences (she a Republican operative, he a Democratic insider) in order to use the card and consume.

Although they may find themselves on opposite sides of the partisan divide, the ad indicates that Carville and Matalin clearly share a conception of the good life. Love conquers politics, and things trump squabbles.

In consumption we resolve differences. By getting and spending we are held together. The family that pays together, stays together. In fact, in the upper left-hand box of the ad we see those things drawn in outline and glossed at the bottom. What are they? They are metonymies of the good life. Stuff to garden with, flowers to court with, riding mower to farm with, books (nonfiction) to spend time with, pots and pans to cook and entertain with, Maalox to recuperate with, and fax and paper shredder to practice their trade with.

Best of all, the ad certainly doesn't say this, but it is there nonetheless: the reason these two—who, as the copy text says, "don't always see eye to eye"—have gotten together is because they are in love. And as a result they have created that baby—the smiley character in the middle background. Is she, as the baby happens to be, not front-and-center but in the background because of the Carville/Matalin ability to afford all the stuff that doubtless also includes someone to take over child care?

84

 ➢   How political strategists, writers, and lovebirds go nesting. (American Express, 1997)

Not clear. But the legend in upper left tells us that the baby jogger (behind the kid) has gone "3.2 miles" while the easy chairs (distant background) have "more mileage logged than baby jogger." First things first.[10]

In the next ad in the Amex campaign, we come to a man whose comic routine is often centered around store-bought things. These things have names, and if you have ever watched the show you know exactly what the things are: a Pez dispenser, Dockers pants, Shredded Wheat cereal, Snapple soft drinks, Calvin Klein perfume, Junior Mints, Jujyfruits, Drakes Coffee Cake, Snickers, Tupperware ("with the patented burp"), Kenny Rogers Fried Chicken, Oh! Henry chocolate bars, the Cadillac Jerry gives his parents, his own black Saab convertible, stuff advertised in the J. Peterman catalog, to name just a few. To a degree unique in American culture, if you understand Jerry Seinfeld's humor, you know the meaning and names of Jerry's things. The same is true of Jerry's friends. We know Elaine buys her black-and-white spectator shoes at Botticelli, Kramer hits Titleist golf balls, George has a huge Gore-Tex coat, and, well . . . you get the point. When asked what he

---

10. To sound like a college professor, one might also say that, at a slightly deeper level, the American Express ad is a nice illustration of the failure of both liberals and conservatives to address questions of political meaning, letting *things* carry the day. In this ad, meaning is bracketed; things do the talking. Carville, famous for his 1992 campaign motto, "It's the economy, stupid," stands for the liberal preoccupation with issues of material well-being at the expense of any concern for matters of meaning. Matalin, on the other hand, is more likely to handle clients on the right who would speak about the collapse of families, the difficulty of teaching family values, the fear of crime, and the absence of spirituality. Out on the lawn amid her latest purchases from Williams-Sonoma and FAO Schwarz, she signifies the failure of the American right to understand the contradiction between its defense of "traditional values" and its promotion of the market economy that has done much to undermine those values. Meanwhile he, surrounded by his tools and toys from Jim's Appliance and Sports Depot, mutely acknowledges that the inequitable distribution of wealth cannot be controlled by government interference or the redistribution of that wealth. Let's hope the kid won't mess them up.

wants to do now that his hit show is over, Jerry doesn't miss a beat: start his own ad agency.

In old-style commercial television programs such as *All in the Family* or *The Mary Tyler Moore Show,* which were clearly anchored in real places like Queens and Minneapolis, it would have been unthinkable to ever show real products in such a way that the audience could recognize them as brands.[11] *Seinfeld* was new-style commercial television. On this show you saw the branded products because the show *depended* on a shared vocabulary of name brands to make its connection with its hip audience. After all, since we speak to each other in the language of commerce, it would violate the premise if a nonbranded product was used. In fact, the only example of a concocted product used so far was in the episode, "The Rye," in which Kramer moonlights as a hansom cab driver. Earlier Kramer has bought a huge supply of Beef-A-Roni from a shopping club and, since he now has too much, he feeds it to the horse. Realizing that the odoriferous results would not redound to their credit, Chef Boyardee asked that their name not be used and the producers complied.

Seinfeld repeatedly plays off against our knowledge of specific commercials and products. In one episode Jerry and his girlfriend finally break up because she likes the Cotton Dockers ads in which the camera pans the butts of guys standing around talking. Jerry does not like the ads. "But they're not talking about pants," he says. "That's just the

---

11. This changed in the late 1980s as the gentleman's agreement to keep recognizable products out of sight was dropped. Shows like *Cheers* or *Roseanne* started to use not Blitz beer but Stroh's and Budweiser right out in the open. Just as product placement started to be accepted in Hollywood as a way of off-loading the expense of production, so television started its own version. But the FCC has not allowed television producers to take money for showing specific brands; instead, there is a system called payment-in-kind, whereby the cast and crew of a production company get cases of the product in return for air time. When you saw a red Coke machine in the series *TV 101,* that Alf was eating only Hershey bars, that Oneida silverware was identifiable on the tables of *Dynasty* and *Dallas,* you knew that the production crews were going home with cartons of the stuff. *Seinfeld* and other popular shows have dispensed with payment in kind. They showcase the products for free.

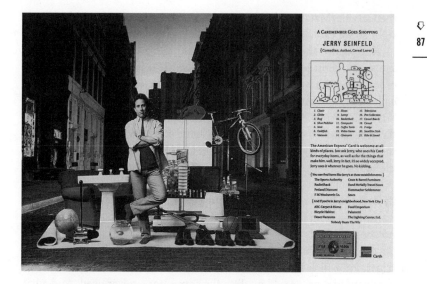

A CARDMEMBER GOES SHOPPING

JERRY SEINFELD
{ Comedian, Author, Cereal Lover }

1. Chair	8. Shoes	15. Television
2. Globe	9. Lamp	16. Pez Collection
3. Rug	10. Basketball	17. Cereal Bowls
4. Shoe Polisher	11. Computer	18. Cereal
5. Sink	12. Coffee Table	19. Fridge
6. Goldfish	13. Video Game	20. Satellite Dish
7. Vacuum	14. Cleansers	21. Bike & Stand

The American Express® Card is welcome at all kinds of places. Just ask Jerry, who uses his Card for everyday items, as well as for the things that make him, well, Jerry. In fact, it's so widely accepted, Jerry uses it wherever he goes. No kidding.

{ You can find items like Jerry's at these establishments: }
The Sports Authority   Crate & Barrel Furniture
RadioShack   Rand McNally Travel Store
Petland Discount   Hammacher Schlemmer
F.W. Woolworth Co.   Sears

{ And if you're in Jerry's neighborhood, New York City: }
ABC Carpet & Home   Food Emporium
Bicycle Habitat   Palanzeti
Disco Vacuums   The Lighting Center, Ltd.
                Nobody Beats The Wiz

Cards

➤   Some of Jerry's things in a show about nothing. (American Express, 1998)

point," she replies. Later, when the girlfriend meets George and Kramer, they both say to her, "Oh you're the one who likes those ads." She storms out. The joke here is not so much that Jerry has violated a confidence as it is that he has found her aesthetic judgment lacking. She has bad taste in—gasp!—commercials. Commercials are not just the way the characters know other humans, it is how they know reality.[12]

With this kind of rapid-fire decontextualization characterizing the show, it is to be expected that the American Express print ad makes no effort to disguise the brandnames or the place of purchase. We see the cereals: Corn Chex, Froot Loops, Total. If we look carefully we can see the brand of bicycle, bottled water, vacuum cleaner, and satellite dish (!). We recognize the motifs of cleanliness—the shoe polisher, the vacuum, the cleansers—as being part of Jerry's neatnik persona. We may not have seen this stuff in Jerry's television abode, but we know it could be there, like everything else, surrounding the refrigerator. Again, as with

---

12. In another episode George describes his dating strategy in terms of a commercial. First date, you show your stuff, second date, "they are humming your name like an ad."

the Carville/Matalin ad, we are provided the outline gloss at the upper right so we can check our recognition of Jerry's material world.

And again, those who can appreciate the joke will recognize why the smirk is on Jerry's face. He is this stuff. It is his persona, his way of knowing the world. And it is our way of knowing him. Take the Pez collection, for instance. It extends across the lower middle, to the left of Jerry's left knee. For those of us who grew up with these nifty fruit-flavored candies dispensed from a hand-held click dispenser, seeing them part of Jerry's life is a validation of our own nostalgic commercial life together.

Jerry Seinfeld's comedy "about nothing"—which is actually a heavily notational comedy about impulses, embarrassment, and everyday minutiae—is replicated in this ad. It is about nothing. The scene makes no sense. Why is Jerry out there in the middle of a Manhattan street? Yet everything about the tableau is tied to commercial things: Jerry's refrigerator, which Kramer so often raids, is stage center; the bike is forever hanging, never ridden; ditto the computer—never used. And what of the satellite dish (we know Jerry has cable), the goldfish (he hates pets), the globe (Jerry's intellectual curiosity is zero), and all those hiking shoes (he always wears no-name sneakers). They are not part of the show's mise-en-scène. In a way, *that* is the pitch. The American Express card can take Jerry, and by extension you, beyond the world of stuff you recognize into creating a different self, a different Jerry, a different you.[13]

This ad works because the product—the charge card—is so much the key to the storehouse of value. The text says as much: "The American Express card is welcome . . . it is widely accepted." You get the card, you get access, you get more things. But to understand the world of things or, better yet, the "empire of things," as Henry James prophetically called it, we need to turn to the core of the way we live now. For

---

13. The other members of Jerry's troupe have not been so lucky tying their celebrity to brands. Jason Alexander plays George for Rold Gold pretzels and the Intel chip (!), Michael Richards is Kramer all lathered up for a Gap magazine ad and for Mercedes (!!), and Julia Louis-Dreyfus shakes Elaine's fabulous silky tresses for Clairol Nice N' Easy. In each case, understanding the character provides the code to understand the often ironic endorsement.

without knowing how to fit things together, we could never have an inkling of creating a lifestyle, let alone an outfit, let alone a coherent self. That core is over there in the corner inside that big box, that radio running a picture track, that single most important part of commercialism, the greatest selling machine of all times—your television set.

3

But First, a Lot of Words from Our Sponsor

How We Hear What Things Have to Say

What I would like to know is how you Americans can successfully worship God and mammon at the same time.

—Lord Reith, founder of BBC, to CBS executives, 1952

WHENEVER a member of my paunchy fifty-something set pulls me aside and complains of the dumbing down of American culture, when he complains of how everything is commercialized, when he says that there is nothing in this culture but worthless junk for kids, whenever he invokes the lowest-common-denominator bugaboo, whenever he tells me that the golden age of books/radio/movies/television is long past, I tell him that if he really wants to turn the clock back he should go buy a lot of what economists call "Fast Moving Consumer Goods" (FMCGs). And every time he buys soap, toothpaste, beer, gasoline, bread, aspirin, and the like, he should make it a point to buy a different brand. He should implore his friends to do likewise. At the same time he should quit giving so much money to his kids. That, I'm sorry to say, is his only hope.

Here's why. As I have mentioned, the culture of the way we live now is carried on the back of advertising. I mean that literally. If you cannot find commercial support for what you have to say, it will not be transported. Much of what we share, and what we know, and even what we treasure is carried to us each second in a plasma of electrons, pixels, and ink, underwritten by multinational advertising agencies dedicated to attracting our attention for entirely nonaltruistic reasons. These agencies, gathered up inside worldwide conglomerates with weird sci-fi names like WPP, Interpublic, Omnicom, Saatchi & Saatchi, Dentsu, and Euro RSCG Tatham, are usually collections of established shops linked together to provide full service to their global clients.

Their service is not moving information or creating entertainment, but buying space and inserting advertising. That's how they are paid—usually as a percentage of what that space costs. Or, put another way, agencies buy newspaper space, radio and television time, and magazine pages wholesale, and then sell them retail to their clients. The real creativity in advertising is not in creating copy but in negotiating payments, usually figured in CPM or cost per thousand of readers/viewers/listeners. Logically, of course, the agency should be paid a percentage of the increase in sales caused by its advertisements, but no one has been able to put a needle on an advertising campaign to figure out how it works, let alone if it works at all.

Understanding this bizarre remuneration process is a key to modern popular culture. Agencies essentially rent our concentration to other companies—sponsors—for the dubious purpose of informing us of something that we've longed for all our lives even though we've never heard of it before. Modern selling is not about trading information as it was in the nineteenth century, as much as about creating an infotainment environment sufficiently alluring so that other messages—commercials—can get through.

Okay, you get the point. We all agree that commercial speech is so powerful that it drowns out all other sounds. But sounds are always conveyed in a medium. The media of modern culture are print, sound, pictures, or some combination of these. Invariably, conversations about materialism focus on the supposed corruption of these media, as demonstrated by the sophomoric quality of most movies, the banality of television, the mindlessness of most bestsellers, and the tarting up and dumbing down of the news in *USA Today* or *Time,* or on ABC or *Inside Edition.*

The media make convenient whipping boys particularly because they are now all conglomerated into huge worldwide organizations like Time Warner, News Corp., General Electric, Seagram, Viacom, Bertelsmann, Sony, and the like. But, alas, as much fun as it is to blame the media, they have little to do with the explanation for the explosion of commercialism.

❋ *THE CENTRALITY OF COST EXTERNALIZATION*

The explanation is, I think, more fundamental, more economic in nature. These media are delivered for a price. We have to pay for them, either by spending money or by spending time. Given a choice, we prefer to spend time. We spend our time paying attention to ads and in exchange we are given infotainment. This trade is central. Economists call this "cost externalization." If you want to see it at work, go to McDonald's. You order. You carry your food to the table. You clean up. You pay less. Want to see it elsewhere? Buy gas. Just as the "work" you do at the self-service gas station lowers the price of gas, so consuming ads is the work you do to lower the price of delivering the infotainment. In the contemporary world the trade is more complex. True, you are entertained at lower cost, but you are also enculturated in the process.

So far so good. The quid pro quo of modern infotainment culture is that if you want it you'll get it—no matter what it is—as long as there are enough of you who (1) are willing to spend some energy along the way hearing "a word from our sponsor," and (2) have sufficient disposable income possibly to buy some of the advertised goods. You pay twice: once for the ad and once for the product.[1]

❋ *THE CENTRALITY OF CHOICE*

So let's go back a step to examine these media because, strange as it may seem, they are at the center of the never-ending stream of packaged things in American culture.

As we have seen, advertising is invoked when the objects are interchangeable. Such objects, called parity items, constitute most of the commercial stuff that surrounds us, from toothpaste to beer to cars to airlines. What they have in common is that they are all machine made. There is really no discernible difference between Colgate and Crest, Miller and Budweiser, Ford and Chevrolet, Delta and United. In fact, the

---

1. In truth, you really pay three times. Since advertising is considered a business *expense*, it is taxed at a favored rate. From time to time, a state attempts to remedy this, as Florida tried to do a few years ago, but the howls of outrage, not from producers but from media, have stopped it dead. Since World War II, the national government has been wary of fiddling with the deductibility of commercial speech, but if they ever did it would profoundly change popular culture, perhaps for the better.

only difference is usually in the advertising. Advertising is how we talk about these fungible things, how we know their supposed differences, how we recognize them. So, obviously, we don't consume the individual products as much as we consume the advertising.

For some reason, we like it this way. Logically, we should all read *Consumer Reports* and then all buy the most sensible product. But we don't. Why do we waste our energy (and billions of dollars) entertaining fraudulent choice? I don't know. Perhaps just as we drink the advertising, not the beer, we prefer the illusion of choice to the reality of decision. How else to explain the appearance of so much superfluous choice?[2]

We are now closing in on why the rampant materialism in American culture has occurred with such startling suddenness in the last thirty years. We are also closing in on why the big complainers about commercialism are me and my paunchy pals. The people who want things the most and have the best prospects to get them are the young. They are also the ones who have not decided which brands of objects they wish to consume. In addition, they have a surplus of two commodities: time and money, especially the former. If you can make a sale to these twenty-somethings, if you can "brand" them with your product, if you can make them part of your "family," you may have them for life. But to do this you have to be able to speak to them, and to do that you have to go where you will be heard.

✳ *A MODERN HISTORY OF COMMERCIAL MEDIA ON A THUMBNAIL*

The history of modern mass media can be summarized in a few words: If it can't carry advertising to those aged fifteen to thirty, it won't survive. Period. New paragraph.

---

2. A decade ago, grocery stores carried about 9,000 items; they now stock about 24,000. Revlon makes 158 shades of lipstick. Crest toothpaste comes in 36 sizes and shapes and flavors. We are even eager to be offered choice where there is none to speak of. AT&T offers "the right choice"; Wendy's, "there is no better choice"; Pepsi, "the choice of a new generation"; Coke, "the real choice"; "Taster's Choice is the choice for taste." Even advertisers don't understand the phenomenon. Is there a relationship between the number of soft drinks and the average number of television channels—about 27? What's going to happen when the information pipe carries 500?

Books are the exception that *almost* proves the rule. Books used to carry ads. Initially, publishing and advertising were joined at the press. Book publishers, from William Caxton to modern university presses, have advertised forthcoming titles on their flyleaves and dustjackets. No doubt publishers would have been willing to bind other material into their products if only there had been a demand. While we may have been startled when Christopher Whittle marketed his Larger Agenda series ("big ideas, great writers, short books") by inserting advertising into what was essentially a long magazine article bound in hardcover, he was actually behaving like a traditional book publisher. When Whittle published William Greider's *The Trouble with Money*—ninety-four pages of text and eighteen pages of Federal Express ads—book reviewers turned away, aghast. But when Bradbury & Evans published Charles Dickens's *Little Dorrit* in 1857, no reviewer or reader blanched at seeing the bound-in ad section touting Persian parasols, smelling salts, portable India-rubber boots, and the usual array of patent medicines.

The reason books stopped carrying ads is simple. There was a cheaper medium—the magazine. The death knell of book advertising is still being rung, not by publishers but by the postal service. Put an ad in a book and it no longer travels at fourth-class book rate but at third-class commercial rate. A prediction: advertising will return to books; UPS, FedEx, and other commercial carriers make no such distinction about content, only about weight and size. Nor does Amazon.com. In addition, since Dr. Spock fought Pocket Books to have cigarette ads removed from his baby-care book in the late 1940s, the Authors' Guild has advised writers to have a no-advertising clause inserted in the boilerplate of their contracts with publishers. What would it take to reverse this? Not much, I suspect. Put a few ads in, drop the price 10 percent, and most people would accept it. Of course, the real reason books are currently ad-free is that the prime audience for advertisers, namely the young, is functionally illiterate.

Books aside, magazines and newspapers flourished because of advertising. In fact, all the innovations that made these media successful were forced on them by ad agencies. You name it: the appearance of ads throughout the pages, the "jump" or continuation of a story from page to page, the rise of sectionalization (news, cartoons, sports, financial, living, real estate), common page size, halftone images, process engraving, the use of black-and-white photography, then color, and, finally, discounted subscriptions were all resisted by publishers.

Look at the *New York Times* over the last decade and you can see this operating in slow motion. The gray lady of newspapers is putting on sneakers. The increase of infotainment throughout all sections, the inclusion of Tuesday's "Science Times" section to showcase computer ads, "Dining In Dining Out" on Wednesday for food and wine ads, "House & Home" on Thursday for furniture and real estate ads, the two-section entertainment sections on Friday for massive movie ads, the jazzy "Styles" section of Sunday for designers' ads, and above all, the use of color. Advertisers demand color; it leads to better product recall. Notice also the appearance on the front page of stories that used to be deemed tabloidlike and were therefore relegated to the back sections. The *Times* is even running a jazzy national TV and print campaign under the tagline "Expect the world," which is clearly meant to appeal to younger readers. All these changes are attempts to find the "proper" readership, not to find "All the News That's Fit to Print." If newspapers want to survive, they have to think of themselves not as delivering news or entertainment to readers but as delivering readers to advertisers.

One might even see newspapers and magazines in the current psychobabble as members of a victim class. They are remnants of a print culture in which selling was secondary to informing. To survive, they had to replace their interest in their reader-as-reader with the more modern view of the reader-as-commodity. Still, print media might have maintained their cultural standards had not radio and television elbowed them aside. Ironically, print had to conglomerate, to fit itself into huge oligopolies like Scripps-Howard, the Tribune Company, the New York Times Company, News Corp., Gannett, The Washington Post Company, Times-Mirror, and Meredith, in order to sell advertising space profitably. As advertising will flow to the medium that finds the target audience cheapest, the demographic specialization of print is a direct result of the rise of commercial culture.[3] Most of print culture today aspires to the condition of women's magazines, in which the ratio of advertising space to print space is about ten to one, and to the editorial condition of newspapers, which is as bland as vanilla.

---

3. This struggle to find targeted audiences has led to two interesting extremes. On the one hand are magazines that are pure advertising, like *Colors* from Benetton, *Le Magazine de Chanel*, or *Sony Style*, which erase the line between advertising and content so that you cannot tell what is text and what is hype. At the other extreme are magazines like the reincarnated *Ms.* or *Consumer Reports*, which remain ad-free for political or economic reasons.

✳ RADIO, HIS MASTER'S VOICE

The electronic media have turned the screws on print, have made it play a perpetual game of catch up, and have forced it into niches so that only a few national magazines or newspapers have survived. Broadcasting has forced print to *narrow*cast. Television is usually blamed, but the real culprit is radio. Radio started with such high hopes. It has achieved such low reality. Rush Limbaugh, Don Imus, and Howard Stern are not stars of this medium by accident. Understanding radio is a key to understanding the way we live now.

After World War I, Westinghouse had a surplus of tubes, amplifiers, transmitters, and crystal receivers that had been used during the war. So in November 1920, it started station KDKA in Pittsburgh on the *Field of Dreams* ("if you build it, they will come") principle. It worked. Once transmitters were built, Westinghouse receiving apparatus could be unloaded. You could make them at home. All you needed was a spool of wire, a crystal, an aerial, and earphones—all produced by Westinghouse. Patience and a cylindrical oatmeal box were supplied by the hobbyist. By July 1922, four hundred stations had sprung up.

Rather like users of the World Wide Web today, no one then seemed to care what was on as long as they were hearing something. However, in the 1920s great plans were being hatched for radio. Universities would take advantage of this new way to dispense their high culture by building transmitters. The government would see to this by allocating special licenses just for universities. This medium would never dumb down, it would uplift. It would never sell out to commercial interests.

The problem was that everyone was broadcasting on the same wavelength. When transmitters were placed too close together the signals became mixed and garbled. AT&T suggested a solution. They would link stations together using their already existing phone lines, and soon everyone would hear clearly. They envisioned tying some thirty-eight stations together in a system they called toll broadcasting.

The word "toll" was the tip-off. Someone was going to have to pay. The phone company suggested that time could be sold to private interests, and they called this subsidy ether advertising. The suggestion was not an immediate success. Secretary of Commerce Herbert Hoover, considered a presidential possibility, warned that it was "inconceivable that we should allow so great a possibility for service . . . to be drowned in advertising chatter," and that if presidential messages ever "became the meat in a sandwich of two patent medicine advertisements it would destroy broadcasting" (in Barnouw 15). Such Cassandras were uniformly ignored. This would never happen. The universities would see to it by their responsible use of education.

In 1922 AT&T started WEAF (for Wind, Earth, Air, Fire) in New York. They tried all kinds of innovative things, even broadcasting live from a football stadium. They tried letting companies buy time to talk about their products. Such talk was always done in good taste; no mention of where the products were available, no samples offered, no store locations, no comparisons, no price information, and never, ever, during the "family hour" (from 7 to 11 P.M.)—just a few words about what it was that they offered.

At 5 P.M. on August 28, the station manager even let a Mr. Blackwell step up to the microphone and say his piece about a housing development. He only spoke once. This is what he said, and it is every bit as important as Alexander Graham Bell's "Come here Mr. Watson, I need you," only a bit longer. It was to be the mayday distress call of high culture. It was the siren song of commercial culture.

It is fifty-eight years since Nathaniel Hawthorne, the greatest of American fictionists, passed away. To honor his memory the Queensboro Corporation has named its latest group of high-grade dwellings "Hawthorne Court." I wish to thank those within sound of my voice for the broadcasting opportunity afforded me to urge this vast radio audience to seek the recreation and the daily comfort of the home removed from the congested part of the city, right at the boundaries of God's great outdoors, and within a few miles by subway from the business section of Manhattan. This sort of residential environment strongly influenced Hawthorne, America's greatest writer of fiction. He analyzed with charming keenness the social spirit of those who had thus happily selected their homes, and he painted the people inhabiting those homes with good-natured relish. . . . Let me enjoin upon you as you value your health and your hopes and your home happiness, get away from the solid masses of brick, where the meager opening admitting a slant of sunlight is mockingly called a light shaft, and where children grow up starved for a run over a patch of grass and the sight of a tree. Apartments in congested parts of the city have proved failures. The word "neighbor" is an expression of peculiar irony—a daily joke. . . . Let me close by urging that you hurry to the apartment home near the green fields and the neighborly atmosphere right on the subway without the expense and trouble of a commuter, where health and community happiness beckon—the community life and the friendly environment that Hawthorne advocated. (Archer 397–98)

Three weeks later the Queensboro Corporation had sold all its property in Hawthorne Court (named for "America's greatest writer of fiction," who had clearly never been read by Mr. Blackwell) in Jackson Heights, Queens. The genie was out of the bottle.

"Giving the public what it wants" had its price. Like television yesterday and the Internet today, the messenger was soon being blamed for the message. Commercial radio broadcasting was debasing American culture with its incessant repetition of mindless humor, maudlin sentimentality, exaggerated action, and frivolous entertainment. Worse yet, it was forever talking about things: manufactured things, things to buy, things to have in your house, things you can't do without.

Proving yet again the power of Gresham's Law when applied to culture, radio programming by the 1930s was supposedly selling out to the lowest common denominator. Typical of highcult outrage was James Rorty, erstwhile advertising copywriter turned snitch for such leftward-leaning periodicals as *The New Republic:*

> American culture is like a skyscraper: The gargoyle's mouth is a loudspeaker (the radio), powered by the vested interest of a two-billion dollar industry, and back of that the vested interests of business as a whole, of industry, of finance. It is never silent, it drowns out all other voices, and it suffers no rebuke, for is it not the voice of America? That is this claim and to some extent it is a just claim. . . . Is it any wonder that the American population tends increasingly to speak, think, feel in terms of this jabberwocky? That the stimuli of art, science, religion are progressively expelled to the periphery of American life to become marginal values, cultivated by marginal people on marginal time? (32–33, 270)

But wait! What about those universities? Weren't they supposed to make sure the airwaves would be full of "the best that had been thought and said"? While there were more than 90 educational stations (out of a total 732) in 1927, by the mid-1930s there were only a handful. What happened? Surely, the universities would never participate in any sell-out to commercial interests.

Alas, the universities had done exactly that. They had sold their radio licenses to the burgeoning networks—called nets or, better yet, webs—emanating from Manhattan. In one of the few attempts to re-capture cultural control from commercial exploitation, the National Ed-ucation Association (NEA) lobbied Senators Robert Wagner of New York and Henry Hatfield of West Virginia to reshuffle the stations and re-store a quarter of them to university hands. These stations would for-ever be advertising-free, making "sweetness and light" available to all. The lobbying power of the NEA met the clout of Madison Avenue. No contest. The Wagner-Hatfield bill died aborning, defeated by an almost two-to-one margin.

One of the reasons the Wagner-Hatfield bill floundered so quickly was the emergence of a new cultural phenomenon, the countrywide hit show. Never before had an entertainment been developed that an entire nation—by 1937 more than three quarters of American homes had at least one radio—could experience at the same time. *Amos 'n' Andy* at NBC had shown what a hit show could do. NBC thought a hit was the way to sell their RCA receivers and they were partially right—more than 100,000 sets were sold just to hear the minstrel antics of two white men pretending to be black. But CBS knew better. Hits could make mil-lions of dollars in advertising revenue. Although not yet called a block-buster (that would come with the high-explosive bombs of World War II), the effect of a hit was already acknowledged as concussive. One "hit" could support hundreds of programming failures. And it could sell millons of dollars' worth of soap and toothpaste.

✳ THE "WORK" IN NETWORK

In truth, CBS or not, television never had a chance to be anything other than the consummate selling machine. It took twenty-five years for radio to evolve out of wireless; it took only five years for television to unfold from radar. And while it took a decade and the economic de-pression to allow advertiser control of the radio spectrum, it took only a few years and economic expansion to do the same with television. Advertisers had rested during the war. They had no product to sell. No surplus = no advertising.

Even though radio not only survived but prospered during the war, the new kid on the block was too tough to beat. From the first nar-row broadcast, television was going commercial. The prophetic Philo T. Farnsworth presented a dollar sign for sixty seconds in the first public demonstration of his television system in 1927. Once Hazel Bishop became a million-dollar company in the early 1950s, based on television advertising, the direction of the medium was set. It would follow radio.

Certain systemic changes in both broadcast media did occur: most importantly, the networks recaptured programming from the agencies in the 1950s. Although this shift away from agency control took scandals to accomplish (most notably the quiz-show scandals rigged by advertising agencies, not networks), it would have happened anyway. Simple economics made it cheaper to sell time by the ounce than by the pound. The nets could make more by selling minutes than by selling half or full hours. Magazines maximized ad revenues by selling space by the partial page; why not television? The motto of this new medium became, "Programs are the scheduled interruptions of marketing bulletins." How could it be otherwise?

We need not be reminded of what is currently happening to television to realize the direction of the future. MTV, the infomercial, the home shopping channels, and even Web-TV are not flukes but the predictable continuation of this medium. Thanks to the remote-control wand, the coaxial (soon to be fiber-optic) cable, and the dish antenna, commercials will migrate from their pods and enter programming. Like product placement in the movies, commercials will be written into the television text. Remember, the first rule of the commercial world is: given the choice between paying money or paying attention, we prefer paying attention.

What all this means is that if you think things are bad now, just wait. Just as the carnival barker doesn't care what is inside the tent, only how long the line is in front, the pooh-bahs of the television industry only care who's looking, not what are they looking at. The bestseller lists, the box office, the Nielsens, the various circulation figures for newspapers and magazines, the number of double-clicks as you surf the Web are the meters. They decide what gets through.

Little wonder that so much of our popular culture is derivative of itself, that prequels and sequels and spin-offs are the order of the day, that celebrity is central, and that real innovation is so rare. What if you lose audience share, or get the wrong audience interested? This culture, what is sexily called postmodern culture, is recombinant culture. This is how it has to be if advertisers are to be able to direct their spiels to the appropriate targets for their products. It's simply too expensive to be any other way.

✳ *TELEVISION: THE COMPLETE SELLING PACKAGE*

> In day-to-day commerce, television is not so much interested in the business of communications but in the business of delivering audiences to advertisers. People are the merchandise, not the shows. The shows are merely the bait. (Brown 15–16)

Call television whatever you want—"idiot box," "American dada," "Charles Dickens on LSD," "the greatest parody of European culture since *The Dunciad*," "wallpaper," "child molester," "plug-in drug," "thief of time," "pain killer," "chewing gum for the eyes," "the bland leading the bland" "summer stock in an iron lung," "Hollywood films for the blind," "dream killer," "dream machine," "vast wasteland," "white noise for the brain," "a toaster with pictures," "a Frankenstein monster boasting a bullet-proof vest of irony," this electronic medium is the greatest selling medium ever concocted, bar none.

Television is *the* primary force in the material world. Whereas generations ago, growing up was defined by a progression of books read, then for my parents by movies seen, for those of us born since World War II, it has been marked by a progression of television jingles memorized. Print took about two centuries to gain currency as communal memory; photography was in general use after 1900; the telephone took half a century to become part of everyday life; radio was absorbed in thirty-five years; and the cinema in twenty. Television happened overnight.

At some mysterious point in the 1950s, television ceased to be just an odd-looking gizmo—a radio running a picture track—and entered the bloodstream. It became part of our nervous system. It is who we are. It is what we do. In our culture most people watch it for most of their free time. After sleeping and working, watching images on a video tube is what we do with ourselves. It is our favorite way to pass time. More than 95 percent of American households have at least one television set, and it is on more than six hours a day. We spend the equivalent of one day a week watching it. Well more than 90 million households have this thing as part of their lives, and asked if they would give up the thing or a family member, most respond that the thing stays. More American households have televisions than have indoor plumbing. The New York legislature passed a bill stating that television is a "utensil necessary for a family." On any given evening as many as 60 million people are observing this utensil.

The experience of watching television has become the social and intellectual glue that holds us together, our "core curriculum," our church. Television has co-opted many of the ceremonies of American life. Religion, politics, and sports have gone into the box. "Did you see?" has replaced "Do you know?," "Did you read?," or "Have you heard?" Television displays most of what we know and much of what we believe.

This all sounds rather ominous to those who vibrate while reading *Brave New World,* but I'm not so sure. What's on television is what most consumers—*not* viewers!—most of the time want to watch. The ad agencies that support programming have no agenda other than to assure the sponsor that the network is providing the audience as promised. Audience share is the commodity that ABC, CBS, NBC, ESPN, and Fox sell—not the shows. Or, seen another way, production companies sell video sequences to the networks that broadcast them in order to rent the attention of the audience to advertisers.[4]

The current experience of watching television is like listening to the radio while driving a car. In the early days, one had to turn the station selector knob, then in the 1960s press a preset button. Now you hit "scan" or "search" and wait for "your" culture to come forward. "Hurry up and choose," the machine says, but many of us just let it continually search. The radio generation is a "one thing at a time" generation, a "you can't do two things at once" generation. The TV generation, by con-

---

4. No one in the business pretends otherwise. Robert Niles, vice president of marketing for NBC, puts the matter like this: "We're in the business of selling audiences to advertisers. They [the sponsors] come to us asking for women 18 to 49 and adults 25 to 54 and we try to deliver" (Harmetz 21). Mr. Niles's predecessor, Sonny Fox, now an independent producer, made the point more politely at a lecture series sponsored by the Annenberg School at USC: "The salient fact is that commercial television is primarily a marketing medium and secondarily an entertainment medium" (Andrews 64). And Roger King, in charge of syndication for King Brothers (*Wheel of Fortune, Jeopardy*) contends, "The people are the boss. We listen to the audience, see what they want, and try to accommodate them. I know it sounds simplistic, but that's exactly what it is" (Dunkel 80). Or here is Arnold Becker, CBS's vice president for research: "I'm not interested in culture. I'm not interested in pro-social values. I have only one interest. That's whether people watch the program. That's my definition of good, that's my definition of bad" (Andrews 64).

trast, does multitasking: homework, talking on the phone, watching a number of TV programs, and listening to the radio all at once.

Contrasted with reading, television almost requires us to do something else while we are choosing what to watch. You can eat—the TV dinner and the TV tray showed almost from the first what the medium was for. You can recline; you can walk around. An entire generation has raised their children with the machine on. You are still in perfect contact with the medium, still changing channels. Most of us use peripheral vision to consume most television. Television reads us to sleep and reads us awake. Did I see that on television, or did I dream it? "Do I sleep or view?" asks the modern Keats.

The producers of television flow know this. That is why so much is made of being the sleepy viewer's comforting friend. "Welcome to . . . ," "Good evening, folks." "We'll be right back." "See you next week." "Stay tuned." "Don't touch that dial." "You wouldn't turn your back on a friend, would you?" the machine almost whines, aware that nothing will overcome the channel-changing impulse. "Stay with me a bit longer. By the way, did you hear the story of . . . ?" "Yep," we say, punching the key, "already heard it."

Formula and fungibility are the hallmarks of television fare. As the television semiologists say, shows are "homologues" of each other, and "semilogues" of those in the genre; entertainments share diachronic and synchronic similarities; they refer both to individual texts and to all precursors and successors. What the academics mean is that repetition and redundancy are what viewers want. We want choice among equals. Media reformers have found this out to their dismay. The availability of three channels or thirty channels does not change the lack of product differentiation. All networks ultimately behave as one, as do all shows inside a genre. This is also true of commercials.

✳ PROGRAMMING CLUTTER

The purpose of television is to keep you watching television, at least long enough to see the advertisements. The illusion of choice is the tribute the medium pays to the attention span. Programs are the scheduled interruptions of marketing bulletins, and marketing bulletins are successful only to the degree that people see them. "We break through the clutter," says the promotion campaign of a major network, wisely neglecting to mention not only where the clutter comes from, but also that clutter is what we now watch television to see.

Part of the attraction of the Super Bowl, television's most watched sporting event, is the promise of a glut of clutter. There is almost as much written about the Super Bowl ads as about the Super Bore itself. In a four-hour show, the ball is moved for all of seven minutes. The genius of MTV is that it is so cluttered that one does not need to change channels. The flow is endlessly shifted for us by a programmer with an itchy remote-control finger. In the jungle of television one need not study individual entries to understand the species. Each episode condenses the whole show as well as the entire genre, as well as the entire medium. In television phylum, ontogeny recapitulates phylogeny. So too does each commercial seek to sell its own product while acting out principles formulated over generations of other commercials. Like a language made up entirely of idioms, we never need to pay attention to the phonemes. Television is an eternal void that must be refilled each day from beginning to end. Watch it once, you've watched it a hundred times. And that is precisely its attraction.

Every programmer's worst fear is that we might turn the set off. Especially fearsome are the edges of shows where, after 22 or 55 minutes of sequences, we are moved through the boundary rituals of changing shows. Viewers tend to go off on their own as pods of commercials are broadcast. That is why in the last few years the shows have been blended together over the half-hour breaks. The commercials are randomly staggered. These commercials are still built on a ten-second scale (ten, 30, 60, 120 seconds) inherited from radio days when they were split around station identification. Each show is under stress to keep the audience from drifting not only to other shows, but especially away from the set. Television shows are chosen in part for how well they "deliver" an audience across these half-hour breaks—called flowthroughs.

Since this hiatus is the riskiest time for programmers, here we often find the newsbreak, a conflation of a "break" in programming with the "breaking" of an urgent story. We hear the news music and see the newscaster at the news desk telling us to stay there for the news—complete story at eleven. So too, the opening credits of each show are punchy with the promise of pleasure to come, and are contrived to hold us through the next commercial pod and past the impulse to choose again. This is the same principle that the financial networks follow when they run the ticker "crawl" along the bottom of the screen during commercials.

Moreover, when a show is being "spun off," as *Frasier* was from *Cheers* or *Melrose Place* from *Beverly Hills 90210*, the station break will be postponed until the audience has been ushered across danger by having the two shows temporarily joined. And when programmers are convinced that a show is never going to build audience quickly enough, it will be "bonged" or shown twice during the same week at different times, as has happened to *3rd Rock from the Sun*. Since no one knows what is playing when, NBC touts its endless summer reruns with the admission, "It's new to you." The assumption is that the audience will never know when they saw it, and won't care. Often wishful thinking is all that is left to programmers.

✳ *HOW THINGS FIT TOGETHER: LIFESTYLE CHANNELS*

The impact of television on materialism is not via specific commercials. Along with commercial speech comes commercial context, and here television is supreme. We see on television how things fit together. Television illustrates a thousand times each hour how branded objects are dovetailed together to form a coherent pattern of selfhood, a lifestyle. If you are successful and happy you drive a new car, you wear designer clothes, you have a house full of branded appliances, you have an entertainment center, you travel a lot, you have a cell phone or whatever new gadget is making the rounds. We see, as we first saw in the movies, what a coherent pattern of consumable objects does in creating the stereotype of success and happiness.

Again, this did not originate with television but was lifted across the electronic divide from radio. But radio was a pallid comparison. For instance, when you listen to the old soap operas of the 1930s, you can see how repeated references to consumables was a key to generating character. Of course, this was aided and abetted by advertisers who were then allowed out of their commercial pods to appear on the air inside the story. This intrusion into programming accelerated during the 1930s as advertisers really took control of separate texts and made them essentially infomercials.

The real advances in lifestyle creation took place during the Great Depression. Ironically, as general want and deprivation increased, so too did rapid advances in mass consumption, and even more rapid changes in a general understanding of what it took to consume/create a coherent self.

It was in the 1930s that phrases such as the "American Way of Life" and the "American Dream" became associated with material as well as social and political well-being. For the first time such diverse groups as middle-class whites, blacks, and working-class ethnics could share a kind of material literacy. Just look at the ads of the 1930s and you will see buddings of the ZIP code demographics we recognize today, from Blue Blood Estates to the group that caused such a ruckus, Public Assistance.

✳ THE DAYTIME RADIO SOAP OPERA AND THE SALE OF SOAP

We might not have known much about these shifting social dynamics as they were tied to new consumption practices, but we all knew about how common objects like cigarettes, patent medicines, beer, canned meats, thread, and the like were being packaged into distinct brands and marketed to different audience segments. Take soap, for instance. Like shirt collars and tie-up shoes, soap was becoming one of the ways to craft a lifestyle in the 1930s. On the farm you used soap made from lye and animal fats; in town you used soap made from vegetable oils. On the farm you used soap maybe once a week; in town, once a day. On the farm, soap lasted only months and then started to stink; in town, store-bought soap, say like Palmolive (the name says it all), would last forever. When you ran out, you just bought more of the exact same soap. You used the same kind of soap as your Ma did on the farm, but in the city you used the same kind of soap as European royalty or Hollywood stars.

Radio made this knowledge possible. While we did not all read the same newspapers, we listened to the same radio programs. Of all the radio formats that originated in the 1930s, the soap opera was the best suited to play a central role in encouraging mass consumption. First, serial programming turned individual housewives across the nation into a mass audience that faithfully tuned in to each daily episode. Second, soap operas provided role models of "real-life" families who overcame the adversity of *want,* and successfully attained the American dream of middle-class well-being and happiness through *purchase.* And finally, serial programming permitted the development of characters with whom the audience could identify and who could serve as trusted friends and experts on how to use manufactured things.

This late-morning–early afternoon genre was a creation of the advertising agencies that controlled their content. Initially, agencies such as J. Walter Thompson, N. W. Ayer & Son, Young & Rubicam, Lord & Thomas, and especially Blackett-Sample-Hummert began to interweave casual references to the sponsor's product into program dialogue. The agencies enlarged their radio departments to begin production of radio programs specifically tailored to their clients' needs. In exchange for the now standard 15 percent commission on gross costs, the agencies hired writers, announcers, actors, and directors. They also supervised scripts, wrote commercials, booked air time, devised premium offers, and oversaw broadcasts. The sponsor's booth was above the broadcast studios at Radio City for a reason. From here the agency made sure the sponsor got its money's worth. That worth was considerable: a potential audience of 23 million housewives in the population of 37 million women between the ages of 16 and 64 who were making most of the consumer decisions for the entire family.

The agency never forgot it was creating the show not for the network but for the sponsor. Whether it be Zion Curtains, Brown Beauty Baked Beans, La France bluing, SnoSheen Cake Flour, or Satina laundry starch, the soap opera was the primary classroom of consumption. So on Irna Phillips's groundbreaking *Today's Children,* Mother Moran, a trustworthy teacher if ever there was one, would try the product during the show and then pronounce it successful beyond belief. The announcer would politely interrupt to tell her the product was now available at your neighborhood store. After a pause for the housewife to dutifully write down the necessary information, the action would recommence.[5]

As part of New Deal optimism, the Federal Communication Commission insisted that commercial speech be separated from the text.

---

5. Phillips positioned Mother Moran as the modern housewife not "stuck in her ways." So, while frosting a cake, she would explain to Lucy, her granddaughter, "I got the new kind of flapper that you can be icing the cake right on the platter." Or, later in the episode while admiring her finished product, she wistfully comments: "And to think that this cake is not one of my own recipes but a recipe I took right off the flour box" (in Lavin 80). A few seconds later we segue to the Pillsbury commercial that, at that time, was printing recipes on the package to encourage increased usage of its flour.

The formal commercial "load" was established whereby some seven minutes per hour were set aside for the pitch. It never really worked. Not only was the load continually being negotiated and subverted, but radio stars like Arthur Godfrey insisted on talking about Salada tea while interviewing his guests, and Jack Benny made fun of the restriction by starting his show with the sly plug, "Jello Again."

But no matter. While radio could introduce a product and make a claim that it was new and improved, it could not literally show how the product fit into a constellation of other goods. It could not show how a product fit into a brand family or extended an already existing brand.

Only television can do that, and that is why product placement of various sophistication has been so important on television. While we may think the display of branded product during a show is recent (and the showing of the "trade dress," or packaging of an object certainly is), the more subtle forms of placement have been there from the first broadcast.

✳ THE PRIME-TIME TELEVISION SOAP OPERA AND THE SALE OF AUTOMOBILES

What radio did for soap, television did for cars. Long before the quid pro quo of exchanging free products for exposure, Detroit was busily supplying its newest models to the networks. All they asked in return was that they control who was shown driving what. As long as the guys in the white hats were driving new Fords, it was worth it to supply cars free of charge—especially if the bad guys were in Chryslers. Woe to the television producer who put a bank robber, embezzler, drug dealer, sleaze merchant, or especially a child molester, behind the wheel of a late-model, recognizable car from Detroit.

The power of this kind of brand association was obvious in the movies. What red-blooded boy does not remember the green Mustang Steve McQueen drove in *Bullitt* or the Pontiac Trans Am that launched roguish Burt Reynolds through all the *Bandit* pictures? What American male does not know of James Bond's Aston Martin, and how shocked we were when he sold out, first to a Continental Mark VII LSC, and now to a BMW Mazda Miata knock-off. The problem with the movies, however, is that they are always a day late in spreading the word about what is down at the showroom.

Television is the medium of right now, this year, here at hand, on sale now. Ironically, television was even more current in the glory days of pre-cable when reruns were only a summertime event. Then Detroit hit pay dirt. Car brands were literally created on television. If they gave an award for perfect placements, the all-time winner would be Chevrolet for the Corvette that Martin Milner and George Maharis seemed to live in on *Route 66*. But also high up on that list would be the talking Trans Am on *Knight Rider*, which was seen every week for four years. Or what of the muscle cars that rocketed the Dukes of Hazzard around Tennessee, or the one that laid so much rubber in New York, driven by Starsky and Hutch?

Such star billing may help sell performance cars to testosterone-poisoned males, but the real money is to be made selling station wagons to Mom and sedans to Dad. Here, no one outdid Ford, which made sure its steering wheels were in the bejeweled and Rolexed hands of the rich and powerful. Those were all Fords you saw on *Dallas, Dynasty, Knots Landing,* and *Falcon Crest*. Even though the major action was adultery, business skulduggery, spousal abuse, and murder, who cared? These protagonists had the right zip codes, lived in big houses, wore stylish clothing, and spent the day at the country club. You want lifestyle? They got it.[6]

The car companies have led the way to what must ultimately happen in television. Network television programming is rapidly going back to the habits of early radio. The commercials are slithering out of their restricted pods and reentering the entertainment. The Great Wall that the FCC attempted to erect between church (programming) and state (commercials) has already crumbled. As we will see, since the late 1980s, all broadcast media have been moving to the pure form of the infomercial.

✳ "COME AWN DOWN," THE PRICE IS INDEED RIGHT

Television does more than wrap commercial speech around entertainment, and it does more than show how branded objects fit together in

---

6. Pity the poor foreign car companies. Since they don't change their styles yearly, they are not as eager to provide cars gratis. Porsche had to settle for the leftovers. The German car company was only too glad to provide a 911 and a 924 for the famous episode of *Dallas* in which J.R. Ewing was shot.

the material world. It also provides us with the most far-reaching, albeit gossamer, web of knowledge. If being in a culture means that those in it are instantly able to connect separate pieces without explanation, then indeed, as oxymoronic as it sounds, television culture is what we are in. If E. D. Hirsch and William Bennett want cultural literacy and national standards, just flip on the set.

Consider game shows, for instance. All cultures have nonathletic games. They are fun to play because in them the connections that we share are made. When you make such a connection, you feel a frisson, a thrill or pleasure. If you want to see (and feel) these thrills turn on your set from noon to early prime time.[7] Game shows all depend on an eager audience's willingness to bond emotionally with the contestants and play along. The referee/host, who encourages this sympathy, is central. That's one reason the quiz-show scandals of the 1950s so devastated the genre. By giving Charles Van Doren the answers, Jack Berry cheated every viewer who had ever shouted out an answer at home. The ump, not the contestants, makes the game believable.

Some of the most popular game shows are those that reward your knowledge of commercial culture. Currently there are a slew of such shows, with names like *The Price Is Right, Let's Make a Deal, The New Shop 'Til You Drop, Shopping Spree,* and *Supermarket Sweep.* They all test your ability to know the price of branded objects.[8] The roots for such entertainment go deep, all the way back to early television and late radio. In 1946 the Dumont network had the first TV shopping show called *Cash and Carry,* which copied radio price-guessing shows like *Pot O' Gold* and *Take It or Leave It.* Clearly, when we first started pricing machine-made objects, we also started to share a new culture, a culture in which (as

---

7. While game programming today isn't the 1960s (when game shows were all over the TV landscape—including four in prime time), they are around in the off-peak hours. Television game shows fit into families. For instance, there have been many members of *The Dating Game* and *The New-lywed Game* genre—now resurrected as MTV's *Singled Out* and *The Big Date.* There are tests of knowledge like Merv Griffin's goldmines, *Wheel of Fortune* and *Jeopardy!. Family Feud* tests family knowledge, the *Newlywed Game* tests individual knowledge, and so forth. But the payoff is the same: you see someone make a connection and vicariously you play along.

8. I should also mention in passing *Debt,* in which contestants, who clearly have not known the prices of objects, compete for the right to have their loan and credit card balances wiped out.

Oscar Wilde said of accountants) knowing value was replaced by know-ing price.

Two of our current pricing shows are worthy of note: the first be-cause it has proven to be not only long-lasting but also the progenitor of many clones, and the second because, as a clone, it shows how univer-sal commercial knowledge is in our culture. And it should be. After all, commercialism is not second nature to us, it is primary.

The Price Is Right and its new, improved model, *The New Price Is Right* is the *locus generis* of many game shows. *The Price Is Right* is the most watched network game show. It has been on for a generation (start-ing on ABC in 1965 with a hiatus from 1966–1971), and features a mas-terful master of ceremonies with the wonderfully appropriate name Bob Barker.[9]

You don't have to know the format of the game to watch *The Price Is Right*. But you have to watch it a number of times to really figure it out. Here's how it generally goes: In the first round, the "Bidding Round," four contestants must guess the price of some object without over-bidding. The closest bid wins. In the second round, called the "Pricing Round," the winner meets winners of other first rounds and has to play some kind of number game: guess the digits of some object's price, figure out how to pay for some object with a certain amount of money,

---

9. One can only marvel at Mr. Barker. He is suave and debonair in a smarmy car-salesman way with nifty suits and richly oiled coif. He treats contes-tants with measured scorn when they flub, and treats his female assistants with measured chauvinism, calling them "my girls," or "my gorgeous Daphne," or "the lovely Holly." He gives a never-ending commentary on their physical proportions, outraging the PC viewers who love to hate him. When speaking to us or to the studio audience Mr. Barker acts like a Kmart doll with a string-pull on his back. He speaks in riffs, all lingo. He out-Bert-Parks Bert Parks and he out-Dick Clarks Dick Clark. Mr. Barker is a peren-nial winner of Emmys. He is also a hit with some GenXers who love his role as evolutionary throwback. In fact, in a movie a few years ago called *Happy Gilmore,* Bob tangles with Happy Gilmore, a hockey player who has taken up golf. The humor, what there is of it, is based on subverting your parents' game—golf—with the outrageous behavior of hockey. Happy hits the ball like a puck. He insults club members, just like in hockey. But in the big Pro-Am tourney he ends up insulting Mr. Barker—bad mistake. Happy gets worse treatment than do the dimmer contestants of *The Price.*

write a check for any amount, and, if the price of the branded object plus the check amounts to some number, say $6,000, then win; guess each of four digits in the price of a car and give up one dollar for every number away from correct digit, and win if you have as much as one dollar left. The point is you need a little math and a lot of knowledge about prices. But the real point is that doing the math allows us to concentrate on the branded object. In the next round, "Showcase Showdown," the remaining winners spin a huge wheel and then collect money depending on the luck of the spin. Finally, the pièce de résistance is the "Showcase" itself. The two finalists have to guess the value of not one but a bundle of objects—a 19.2-foot Sea Ray Sorrento powerboat and Sturdycraft trailer, a trip to the Climax Hotel in Bakersfield, a hair transplant from House of Elizabeth—and this time the numbers are huge.

If you have ever watched the show, you do not need to be reminded of the two aspects that critics glom onto. First, all the contestants act as if they are hyped up on speed. They are experiencing what looks like terminal ecstasy over winning a skidoo or a four-piece linoleum dining room suite. They can't stand still, they can't think straight, and they can't figure out the simplest math. Their frantic mania only encourages the studio audience to yell out answers. And second, more distressing to Galbraitheans, is that the real stars of the show are the never-ending shiny branded objects described by the off-screen announcer as if they were the kneebones of Christ.

> A new car! A Buick Skylark! A 4-door sedan—distinctive looking, lots
> of room, comfortable, and generous in appointments—equipped with
> all standard features and California emission system *plus* floor mats.

And without the floor mats?

The cause of all this pandemonium is not the *promise* of something for nothing; it is the *fact* of something for nothing. The knowledge these people have is the knowledge of a ten-year-old running loose in Kmart. Sourpuss critics never cease to point out that the Nielsen ratings clearly show that the primary audience (the show is on just before noon) are young mothers and middle-aged to elderly women. The commercials bear this out: they are for haircare and feminine hygiene products, home cleansers, laundry and dish detergents, kitchen appliances, pregnancy tests, and magical potions to wash away gray hair color and remove wrinkles.

But how much knowledge of FMCGS (Fast Moving Consumer Goods) do these women have? Alas, not much. Morris Holbrook, W. T. Dillard Professor of Marketing at Columbia University Business School, has examined the show carefully and concluded that the knowledge of the consumer world evinced by this group is close to nil. He concludes his book, *Daytime Television Shows and the Celebration of Merchandise: "The Price is Right"*:

> In sum, when tested empirically, the level of performance achieved by even the best player on *The Price is Right* corresponds to an informative proportional reduction in error of only about one-quarter. Hence three-quarters of the true price information remains as error variance. When all is said and done, these contestants demonstrate a knowledge, say, that a car costs more than a couch or that a trip to Hong Kong costs more than a weekend in Las Vegas (if you start from Hollywood). But they do not demonstrate much more than that. (101)

There is a kinder, gentler version of *The Price Is Right* appearing just a few hours after Bob Barker has called it a day and headed for the links. The game is *Supermarket Sweep* and it also rewards a kind of knowledge thought useless by many. This game has also been around for television eons, starting on ABC in 1965. It takes place not in a studio but in the supermarket.

It's a three-act game. Here's how it goes. In act one, players compete for time by correctly guessing such things as the prices of various objects found in your supermarket. Then, in act two, being timed, groups of two are sent hurling through the aisles to pick up the most valuable cartload. We see them frantically toss salamis, canned hams, hunks of beef, turkeys, and ground coffee from one side of the aisle with one hand, while tossing Nestea, contact lens cleaner, cold medicines, and vitamins with the other. In addition, they compete for bonuses by returning with special items that are getting special airtime plugs. The winning couple makes it to the bonus round—act three—in which the contestants must go fetch special branded objects by following clues. The winning couple therefore not only knows what is the priciest stuff in the store but also knows the location of specific brands and can drive the shopping cart like Mario Andretti.

The only way such a show can be successful is if the folks at home also know the store. And of course they do for, as we will see in the next chapter, supermarkets are laid out with a recognizable, countrywide format. The show ends with our cherubic master of ceremonies gleefully announcing, "Next time you are in the checkout line and you hear (beeping sound of scanner) think! *Supermarket Sweep*."

As opposed to *The Price Is Right*, the referee and the off-screen announcer of *Supermarket Sweep* are supportive and affirming old friends. The contestants are a cut above those on *The Price Is Right*, being mother-daughter teams, school friends, or just childhood chums. But the knowledge base is the same: what things cost. While Professor Holbrook prefers the airy bon ami of *Supermarket Sweep* to the hard-edge *Price*, he concludes: "Every image, every detail, every nuance in the shopping-oriented game show moves toward the worship of possessions and toward the sanctification of materialism," and, "Disturbingly, both [shows] seem to justify a way of life in which material consumption is the target of existence" (41, 111).[10] These shows do more than demonstrate that material consumption is the target for existence; they show that in shopping we share a real sense of community, a sense of shared experience and knowledge, a common culture.

Admittedly, *The Price Is Right* is a self-conscious and often ironic display of materialism gone ballistic, of vulgarity raised to valor, of a cele-

---

10. Just for the sake of argument, let's go downtown to Wall Street where the fruits of the professor's teaching endeavors are currently hard at work on the trading desks of multinational brokerage houses. These young people are, oddly enough, in somewhat the same demographic profile as the television game show audience except for gender and degrees. Some of them, the young men with hands on the telephones and fingers on the keyboards, are also trying to guess prices—not the prices of projection TVs or a six-ounce can of Spam, but the prices of parts of hogs, bits of copper, and railroad cars full of barley. To be sure, they are trying to guess not the retail price but the future price; and so it is a more complex guess. But, after all, they have that Columbia M.B.A. and a few hundred Intel chips to help them. What they do, however, is very close to the game show. First, they are not guessing in order to do good. Their goal is to get something for as close to nothing as possible. And second, when they guess correctly, what do they often do? Well, if Hollywood and Tom Wolfe are any guides, they jump up, whoop, and give the "Master of the Universe" high-five to each other. So in many ways, not only do they mimic the pricing game, they even behave a lot like the studio audience and contestants.

bration of shine and hype. The whole show, in fact the whole of commercial television, is struggling for the condition of a "blurmurcial," in
which commercial speech so intrudes on entertainment that they cannot be separated.

✳ THE INFOMERCIAL: TELEVISION'S FUTURE

The infomercial was born in 1981 when Marc Fowler, a Reagan campaign stalwart, was appointed to head the FCC. Mr. Fowler's most important statement was his definition of television as "just another appliance—a toaster with pictures," but his most important rulings had
to do with what happened if two stations on cable were showing the
same program at the same time? What if some superstation like WTBS
in Atlanta and your local independent station were both showing *Gilli-
gan's Island* for the umpteenth time. The FCC essentially said that the local station could then show anything it wanted. Anything! It could show
only ads if it wanted. The twelve-minute-per-hour commercial (it had
risen steadily from seven) load was lifted.

For those in the "find a niche and fill it" school of capitalism,
Mr. Fowler had provided just such a protected spot. If you were to program your local station precisely to be in conflict with another station,
you could be guaranteed safe passage around the FCC restrictions on advertising load. Of course, at this time there was no contraband programming available—at least not yet. No one had envisioned what a full
half-hour ad even looked like.

As is often the case, children's programming led the way. Selling
toys caused the Great Wall between advertising and programming to
crumble. In the 1970s, the afternoon airwaves were overrun with toy-
based shows like *He-Man, GI Joe, Thundarr the Barbarian, Blackstar,* and
Mr. T, in which plasticine vigilantes literally pounded good sense and
manners into evil villains. The progenitor of the modern bash-'em-up
storm troopers was Prince Adam, aka He-Man, who, together with the
Masters of the Universe, was continually at war protecting his natal
Castle Grayskull from the evil Skeletor.

The show's real job, however, was to sell toys. In a merchandising
coup, Filmation Associates, a subsidiary of Westinghouse, animated
a fantasy around this five-and-one-half-inch warrior and tried to sell
it to the networks. *He-Man and the Masters of the Universe* was a crude,

poorly crafted cartoon, but it was full of screen bursting violence. The networks, still cautious about the relationship between advertising and entertainment, were timid.

However, hundreds of independent stations on the cable were desperate for "filler" shows before the profitable prime time began at 8:00 P.M. The number of independents had tripled between 1972 and 1980, and most of them were unable to afford the prices of afternoon syndicated reruns that the majors ran primarily to cover these mid-afternoon doldrums. The independent stations bought *He-Man* and in so doing essentially allowed the toy companies to create their own temporary networks. These independents, through the prototype of what is now called barter-syndication, were paid by exchanging air time for programming. The station receives the programming gratis and then sells part or all of the commercial time and pockets the proceeds.[11]

Soon there were other ways to narrowcast to a target audience. About the same time that "kidvid" was moving across the afternoon programming horizon, Warner Amex Satellite Entertainment Company (now owned by a consortium of conglomerates—the usual suspects) was starting a nonstop, twenty-four-hour commercial channel beamed via satellite across the United States. The channel was called Music Television or just MTV. And instead of picking the time slot to program, it used the entire channel all day long.

Musicians had made performance films of their acts since the Vitaphone recorded musical acts in the 1920s, so why not continue the process to sell tapes and CDs? The impact of these "videos" was immediate, transforming not only the recording industry but show business as well. Quick cutting, slow dissolves, computer-generated images, animation, wild angles, multiple-image montages, hallucinatory special effects, Chromakey, magnified close-ups, masked screens—every-

---

11. By the time *Thundercats* came to the market in the mid-1980s, Lorimar Telepictures cut a deal whereby they paid a percentage return to the station that was based on how well the toys were selling in the broadcast area. In order to maximize its return, the television station saturated its audience with specific toy-driven cartoons. The more toys sold, the larger the station's cut. They carved a direct path from airwaves to shopping aisles. Others would follow. These shows were to television what the soap opera was to radio. They showed that you could use *broad*casting to *narrow*cast if you could find the right time slot.

thing that is implied in that portmanteau term "state of the art" was involved.

For a while even the advertisers, who had introduced the music video, were the adapters of their own frantic styles. Coke, Levi's, and Ford spots were almost interchangeable with what could be seen on MTV, except that these clips were in thirty-second segments. In fact, the advertisement and the music video occasionally interpenetrated. Michael Jackson promoted Pepsi in his videos and made Pepsi commercials that were knock-offs of these videos.

If romantic art struggles for the condition of opera, and if Newtonian science aspires to pure mathematics, then television—all modern, free-market, commercial television—seeks the state of pure advertisement. Ideally, the entertainment and the advertisement would melt into a seamless "advertainment." Put that in the past tense. It's already happened. The infomercial and the home shopping networks have removed the last membrane separating entertainment content from advertising commercial.

Both these genres depend on a number of propitious developments. First was the removal of legal restrictions on advertising load. Second was the excess supply of both time (as opposed to print media where pages can be added to increase space, in electronic media you *must* add programming to fill up the time) and transmission capacity (the current coaxial cable can easily carry fifty channels). Third, the viewer needs a way to crudely interact with this programming if a sale is to be made. The 800 and 888 numbers were the beginning of interactive media, for they allowed consumers to place orders and enabled the sponsor to collect customer data within hours, not days. "Call now! Operators are standing by." [12] And finally, the method of payment is the credit card. Quick, efficient, and ripe with yet more information (this time for the bank), the sixteen-digit number completes the circuit.

The infomercials look so much like real programs that it is often only in the last few minutes that you realize the film noir that you have been watching, and that is making you feel afraid to go out on the street, is

---

12. The ad agency is also standing by. They can test a spiel over the weekend in an isolated market and know by Tuesday whether they can roll it out nationwide by the next weekend. That would be suicide in print, where the time frame is in months, not days. But because most of the televised products can only be bought by phone, the sponsor has one of the very few chances to know exactly how well the ad draws.

really trying to sell you mace. Or the instructional exercise show is trying to sell you a home gymnasium in easy payments. Or those pleasant celebrities chatting in the living room are really huxtering vitamin supplements. For a while, the most often shown infomercial was the Soloflex ad in which godlike youngsters worked themselves into an almost sexual lather while the voice-over suggested reverently that such bodies could also be possible for us couch potatoes at home. We potatoes, if we watch television long enough, can now also learn how to inhibit baldness, become rich in real estate, cut rocks with ginsu knives, cook in woks, become thin with body cream, quit smoking without using willpower, wax our cars so that they can resist a flame thrower, and learn to dance so that we'll never be dateless again.[13]

Usually there is nothing particularly objectionable about these infomercials other than that they are being passed off as documentaries or spontaneous talk shows. If you are willing to sell time to Oral Roberts or to He-Man and the Masters of the Universe, whom can you deny? Anyone with a fistful of dollars can get on the public airwaves. Not only do stations get rid of excess time called remnants, they are also not liable as transmitters of deceptive ads. Best yet, in the commercial tradition that transformed newspapers, they get paid up front. No wonder that the Lifetime channel airs about forty-three hours of infomercials each week (more than six a day) for almost 25 percent of its schedule;

---

13. The snake oil salesmen of carnival days are alive and well, with characters like Jay (the Juiceman) Kordich, Richard Simmons, and Tony Robbins in the first rank, and over-the-hill celebrities in the second. The burned-out star is often the "channel stopper," slowing down the nervous remote control finger. So we see Cher, E. G. Marshall, John Davidson, Robert Vaughn, Joseph Campanella, Monty Hall, John Ritter, and Michael Reagan enthusing us on to shell out $39.95 for hair cream, $297 for real estate hints, $69.95 for no more smoking, or $59.95 for a food substitute. To show that there really *are* standards, the FTC disallowed an infomercial hosted by Lyle Waggoner from extolling the virtues of Y-Bron Homeopathic Formulation as a sexual stimulant and impotency cure, and scolded Art Linkletter for a reprehensible scam selling Craftmatic chairs that never were delivered. But it allowed Michael Landon to continue hawking a plan to get your kids better grades ("Where's There's a Will There's an A"), although he was long since dead and buried. A contract is a contract. And it allows The Psychic Friends Network, an infomercial hosted by Dionne Warwick, to dispense advice from "trained tarot readers and seers" over a 900 number at $3.99 per minute.

the Nashville Network airs some forty-two hours a week, the Family Channel twenty-eight hours, usa Network nineteen hours, and so forth.

Now that infomercials have stopped growing like algae at the edges of the programming pond, they are about to edge into prime time. To make the transition, they are being called long-form marketing and direct-response television and are sponsored by companies like Volvo, Kodak, Cuisinart, Sears, MCI, Saturn, and Corning. This genre is no longer a "withhold and thrust" kind of carnival selling but a way for companies to make an extended point, much the way the famous "hands" ads for Kraft introduced new products like Cheez Whiz to the market. You can demonstrate complexity. You can show your audience how to use your product. Clearly, the ads now have a life of their own for they have moved from sopping up excess time on cable channels to becoming channels of their own.[14]

In the last few years infomercials have been jumping from their upper-tier channels to become standard programming. By far the most interesting mutation of such advertainment was "The Ringers," an infomercial created by Jordan McGrath, Case & Taylor for Bell Atlantic. In this half-hour show we see a sitcom family with plumber dad, working mom, teenage kids, and various in-laws dealing with life's problems in the Al Bundy/Bart Simpson manner. As the show progresses, the dad occasionally turns to us in the audience and demonstrates how call waiting, call forwarding, and return calling all work to help his mildly outrageous family. It's corny. "America's funniest PHONE-IEST family" we are told in the typically dimwitted theme song, "If you want to meet the Ringers, just pick up the phone/Cause no one in this family can leave the phone alone." But it is effective, especially cost-effective. To broadcast "The Ringers" in the Baltimore area for eight hours after midnight cost $8,000. The press coverage of the ad alone was worth that much.

Although *Seinfeld* accepts no money for its display of commercial goods, you can see it is right at the edge. What would prevent Castle

---

14. In fact, there is now a cable channel not just for infomercials (ATV or advertising television) but for short-form commercials as well. Twenty-four hours of commercials! The reason such channels are all over your cable is that these infomercial networks pay vast sums to your cable supplier to be included in the basic service. It hardly seems fair that you should have to pay to have them take up programming space, but of course, the cable companies say they really help defray the expenses of educational programming—cost externalization at work.

Rock entertainment, which produces the show, from subvening the extraordinary salaries of the troupe (almost a million dollars an episode) by trading air time for product display? Nothing. In fact, we may go back to the "good old days" in which the name of the sponsor was in the name of the show. Remember *Philco Television Playhouse*, *Kraft Television Theater*, *Firestone Hour*, or *U.S. Steel Hour?* Prepare yourself for the *American Express Seinfeld Show*.

The influence of the infomercial should not be minimized. It only looks like the Rodney Dangerfield of television. The infomercial has spawned print relatives, the "advertorial" (the exploded advertising section that acts as a roadblock to reading, yet looks like surrounding text) and the "outsert" (the advertising section that is literally "bagged" with the magazine, often prepared in the same editorial manner as the mother text). Moreover, the infomercial is the ontological basis of the home shopping networks.

To completely remove the entertainment meat from the programming sandwich is no easy job. ABC tried to run *Nitecap* in the same twilight zone as infomercials. Although it flopped, the show was instructive of the direction of television. At a glamorous soirée in a luxury penthouse apartment in Manhattan, Robin Leach and Rae Dawn Chong chat up various telegenic guests. Halfway through the conversation, the subject subtly changes to pitch our guest's product. So a pleasant talk about sports segues into a motorized tie rack, or vapid comments about weather drift to a vibrating beeper. ABC convinced a few stations to carry *Nitecap* by promising them a percentage of the gross. No sale, at least not in this form.

✳ *HOME SHOPPING ON YOUR TELEVISION AND THE INTERNET ON YOUR COMPUTER*

One of the keys to direct selling on television is *not* to kid the customer into thinking you are *not* selling direct on television. Most selling on television is like door-to-door selling. The foot must be placed carefully and the commercial interruption is that foot. The home shopping networks and the Internet, however, are like selling inside the store. The customer's foot is already at your counter. You have to close the sale. Advertising is not so important. Getting the money is. So, in a sense, the electronic home shopping phenomenon is much more like catalog selling or direct mail. The quid pro quo of exchanging entertainment for pitch is lessened as pure information (object, color, size, price) increases.

As has usually been the case, technology is driving this shift. On television this circuit is already crudely interactive since you have to use your phone to complete the loop. With Web-TV you use your receiver as transmitter. You move a cursor on the screen to indicate choice and then click. What goes inside these information pipes is a problem analogous to deciding what you print with a high-speed printing press. The answer is . . . everything, including the store.

Home shopping started in 1982 when Roy Speer, stuck with a surplus of electric can openers he received when one of his Tampa radio station's advertisers went bankrupt, realized he could make more selling the gadgets to listeners then selling air time to advertisers. He was right. And when he changed media from radio to television, the market exploded. His Home Shopping Network (HSN) now has twenty-three thousand incoming telephone lines that field up to twenty thousand calls a minute. Using an automated system, most purchases are made by keying in various numbers with the touch-tone phone, but there are two thousand operators for those who need the personal touch. Better yet, all sales information is immediately available to the station and displayable on a computer screen: how much inventory left, which pitches are working best, at what price do they bite.

Supposedly when Barry Diller (who used to make movies for Paramount and television shows for Fox) saw his friend Diane Von Furstenberg sell $1.2 million worth of clothing in ninety minutes, he too was hooked. He anted up $25 million for a stake in QVC (Quality Value Convenience), a competitor of HSN. The days of ersatz gold chains, zirconium diamonds, radio earmuffs, spray-on vitamins, music box-cum-toilet paper dispensers, and autographed Bibles were over. Now here come Donna Karan, Calvin Klein, Saks Fifth Avenue, Macy's, and Nordstrom with suitcases full of stuff, as well as the usual valets—Time Warner, Viacom, Phillips, Blockbuster, Turner, Tele-Communications Inc., and the "Baby Bells"—eager to lend a hand. What this portends is not clear. Will it be good-bye mall, hello video wall? Who knows? One thing is certain, however. If home shopping behaves like other innovations in selling or delivering the goods, the ramifications for commercial culture will be considerable.

You can almost see exactly this process happening in microseconds on the World Wide Web. The main difference is that the Web did not develop to unload surplus goods, but to speed military and academic intelligence. As search engines made access to any site possible in seconds, commercial interests started to encroach. At first they were fiercely battled; you were flamed and shamed if you used the medium to sell stuff, but now selling is second nature—about to become first.

As I write this, the major problem with advertising on the Web is that the sponsor really has no way to evaluate his investment. Those banner ads, that currently help underwrite the medium and allow you to waste huge quantities of time traveling to far-off places of human interest, are of unknown value. That is why the double-click or click-through protocols are gaining importance. When you point and click on a banner you are triggering two connections. First, you are making an Internet connection to the banner's Web site, and second, you are making yourself known to the company's computer.

One would think that at last the holy grail has been found because now the sponsor knows exactly who has observed the bait, who has read the message, and who has bit the hook. More important still, this information now allows push technology, in which the banners you will see are dependent on the banners you have clicked on. As the Web and television come together into some form of Web-TV, it will be possible to so target the audience that Ford could put an Escort into the image that I see, while it puts a Lincoln towncar in the one you see.

Alas, home shopping and Web shopping have not proven as successful as hyped. The Home Shopping Network pulled its own infomercial channel, called HSN Entertainment, a few years ago. IBM has already shuttered its World Avenue station, Wal-Mart has had second thoughts about going online, and Sears too has taken a breather from establishing itself on the Net. What is clear is what has always been known about shopping: it may result in buying stuff. But that is not why we do it. True, shopping services on the Web that electronically take you to the cheapest price are successful for a few people, but until the human element is present, until the "touch and feel" is present, most of us will get in the car and drive down to the bazaar. Like televangelism before it, home shopping and Internet selling may find that most people most of the time like to take their salvation together. So let's leave the high-tech world and have some fun. Let's do some real shopping!

Boxed In

The Power of Packaging

Packages understand people much better than people understand packages.
—Thomas Hine, *The Total Package*

I love to go to the supermarket. It is called *super*market because it really is an ancient market blown up to mega size. Stalls have become aisles and aisles are entire markets of produce. "Grocery" store is also an appropriate term because this is a store in which things are bought and displayed *en gros*. Other names also tell much about the modern experience: Safeway, Publix, Stop & Shop, Grand Union, Food Fair, even Piggly Wiggly and Food Lion.

✳ WHAT'S SUPER ABOUT THE SUPERMARKET IS THAT YOU DO ALL THE WORK

We have come a long way from the "pile it high and sell it cheap" days of the first supermarket retailers in the 1930s. King Kullen on Long Island and New Jersey's Big Bear, set in dingy warehouses and deserted garages, were dreary places with food scattered on plain wooden tables and pineboard shelves. The gleaming modern supermarket is a comparative Arcadia with its magical cornucopia of never-ending stuff coming at you from all sides.

What I like about grocery shopping is that it can be done at any speed. It's just like watching television, except that your feet are the remote control clicker. You can shop as a close reader, or you can shop as a gestalt reader; you can go on automatic pilot, or hands on. Every aisle is different and similar. Each aisle tells a different story. Like a modern Keats you can stop and consider every aspect of the commercial life, ponder history and taste, pause to figure out the cost per ounce, comparison shop, touch and feel everything. What colors, what sizes, what shapes!

I also like the free coffee and the nice ladies passing out free samples. I often buy their products because they are so friendly. They are the only people who go out of their way to talk to you, aside from the checkout people who ask the feared "paper or plastic?" In fact, silence is the secret of successful shopping. Foreigners often hate it.

Once you learn the terrain of your nesting grocery store you can go into other supermarkets across the country and feel right at home. Most supermarkets are in the standard 40,000-square-foot, 24,000-item maze format. This geography must reflect the ordinary shopper's attention span for objects stacked in space. Usually, you enter this maze down an aisle with refrigerated goods, then proceed like a pen on a heart monitor up and down aisles, moving to your your left, swinging to and fro past a multitude of Fast Moving Consumer Goods with frozen foods meeting you on your turn, until you are in the farthest reaches of the store. There—at the most distant point from any cash register—you are usually in fresh fruits and vegetables. Sometimes this pattern is reversed but produce, meat, and dairy products almost always are located on the store's circumference. This placement makes time-efficient shopping difficult.

Cans, bags, wrappers, tubes, and boxes are in the center of the store. This stuff sits on shelves, and the shelves are in aisles, and aisles end in stacked displays. Your grocer tends these high-visibility turnarounds with special care as they are often part of the elaborate kickback system called slotting allowances. He is paid extra by suppliers for access to these aisle abutments. Suppliers have to fight for these spaces as well as for their other display areas, which is why you often see their delivery men stocking the shelves, not the store employees. If you were essentially paying rent on this space, you'd be checking your turf too.

The maze pattern seems so logical but the concept of aisles is recent, an innovation of the wonderfully named Piggly Wiggly Supermarkets. During the Depression, Piggly Wiggly executives realized that labor costs could be saved by forcing the shopper to do the work of the errand boy. Add to this the shopping cart and it was all over for clerks. The wire cart, introduced in 1937, was the innovation of Sylvan Goldman in Oklahoma, who realized that the problem of aisles was really a problem of transport. To complete the cycle, the National Cash Register Co. provided a machine in the 1940s to speed you on your way down the checkout line. It computed change *and* produced an itemized customer receipt. Not only was checkout time nearly cut in half but, more important, consumer confidence in the self-service supermarket was strengthened.[1]

Two more innovations were necessary for the "cheapies" (as supermarkets were first called) to elbow aside the long-established local grocer. The hermetically sealed tin can and the freon-cooled refrigerator meant you no longer had to buy out of the barrel, and you no longer had to shop twice a week. Advances in cooling and canning meant you could control the amount of food in your house, thereby turning the supermarket into your personal larder. For this reason, as markets have grown into supermarkets, pantries have disappeared and kitchens have grown much smaller.

✸ THE CENTRAL PRINCIPLE OF COMMODITY CULTURE: EXTERNALIZE COSTS

The supermarket is a tribute to cost externalization. You are not aware of it, but you do a tremendous amount of work in the self-service market. You are hunter and gatherer doing the work of many, from maid to clerk to chauffeur. The only thing you don't do is stock the shelves. The most fundamental difference between a traditional open-air market

---

1. If you want to see the modern mutation, go to Sam's Club or to any of the membership warehouses or price clubs. Here the aisles stretch vertically up to the ceiling and the commercial loading cart replaces the wire boxed cart. The choice is small, only about 1,500 items, but it is all branded merchandise. Neat trick: small retailers pay for cooperative advertising to build brands and the Wal-Mart Corporation comes to harvest their investment. In addition, Wal-Mart then cuts special deals with manufacturers to get even lower wholesale prices. Everything about these buying clubs tells you that you are no longer in the supermarket, you are in the warehouse. They are very much like the first supermarkets, King Kullen and Big Bear.

and the places through which you push your cart is that in a modern retail setting nearly all the selling is done without people. The product is totally dissociated from the personality of any particular person selling it. The salesperson is there all right, but is outside the store, appearing only in the advertising and inside the store on the package.

The supermarket purges sociability. Although no one talks to you, the visual "static" is deafening. Almost two thirds of the buying decisions are made once the food shopper has set foot in the aisle. Nothing is made easy. Capitalizing on these last-minute decisions is why grocers don't alphabetize soup sections, why all the raisin bran cereals are not bunched together, and why high-profit toothbrushes are both nestled with toothpastes and stacked almost at random elsewhere. With more than fifteen hundred new items introduced to supermarkets each month, the need to inform and confuse the querulous shopper is intense.

So a company called Ad-Tiles puts its ads on the floors in Pathmark stores and charges the advertiser what amounts to fifty cents per thousand impressions. Flashing coupon dispensers are omnipresent, except near the upright freezers and open fresh dairy case because shoppers do not like to open doors—too cold. The current hot places in the store are in the shopping cart and at the checkout line.

The humble shopping cart is about to become electronic. VideOcart is here, almost. This shopping cart has a six-by-nine-inch screen affixed to what used to be the kiddie rumbleseat and it is activated by infrared sensors on the ceiling to flash ads, messages, and recipes as you pass various products. The same technology that scans the Universal Product Code on your can of beans now scans the shopper. You are the can.

The greatest problem at the checkout line used to be how to navigate Junior past the sugar bombs packaged as snacks, but may soon be how to get past the television monitor. The resident geniuses of place-based media—Ted Turner and Chris Whittle—are still experimenting with "checkout channels," at which eye-level monitors broadcast a continuous loop of tabloid news and commercials. If you have four thousand to five thousand supermarkets on one channel, the demographics are better than *Seinfeld*. Even the publisher of the *National Enquirer* was pleased since he was losing hundreds of thousands of dollars as readers scanned his tabloid in the six or so minutes a usual trip to the register takes, instead of purchasing it.

Although it was a great idea, checkout television hasn't worked as planned. A few crucial problems: the store personnel keep turning off the sound (a problem also faced by Chris Whittle with Channel One in schools) and, even more horrendous, the checkout line is where you go *after* you have made those hundreds of in-store decisions. Turner lost about $30 million finding this out. NBC may yet have the successful system. Their Shoppers' Video monitors are scattered throughout the store and are soundless.

✳ THE SUPERMARKET AS JUNGLE

It's a Darwinian world, the grocery store. Most of the activity happens in the jungle of aisles. Things are forever trying to jump off the shelves into my cart and I push them back. "Take me!" they scream. Nope, not today, I briskly reply, try me next week.

Packages allow manufacturers to talk. If advertising is the first word, then the package is the last one. The point of packaging design is to close the deal. Only about half the items on the shelves in the typical American supermarket are promoted by media advertising. The others have to catch the customer's attention, and simply by standing there, persuade him or her to try them. It's not easy to do, as the 90 percent failure rate of new products attests.

At the supermarket each box, can, and jar, every standup pouch, tube, and squeeze bottle has been very carefully considered. Human test subjects have been strapped into pieces of heavy apparatus that measure their eye movement, blood pressure, and body temperature. Which package can make the connection? Will the packages be understood in a nanosecond? Psychologists even get people to talk about packages in order to get a sense of their innermost feelings. Imagine you and this can of Franco-American spaghetti are chatting about your favorite television show, the white-coated researcher asks. What would you say? And does the can agree?

Package designers have worked and reworked the patterns of seduction on their computers and have tested mock-ups on the store shelves long before you ever see the packages in their "trade dress."[2] The shelves themselves are constantly being adjusted to make sure the high-

---

2. In the commercial world, wrapping is known by the legal term "trade dress." It is one of the few legal terms that is elegant and appropriate. Trade dress has a noble heritage, being the branding of the rose and crown on objects approved of by James I in 1623. Since most products today are not as unique as in James's day, how they are covered is what makes them special.

profit packages are there at eye level, while those with a low markup, like milk, are put in less prominent places. Refinements are measured in shades and millimeters. Market researchers have even studied photographs of families' kitchen cupboards and medicine chests to get a sense of how packages behave when they are put in their final resting place. After all, the package is going home with you and should not be an embarrassment.

Once on their store shelves, products, like library books and children, are supposed to stay still. They don't, of course. They are forever wandering around finding slightly different habitats. Certain high-profit items like razor blades, batteries, and camera film get repeated throughout the store, other items get stocked at the turnarounds to make sure you don't miss them, some foods like sugar cereals for Junior are placed at knee level while others are a far reach, like slow-moving cooking wares. Stores even periodically rearrange products just to make sure shoppers don't become too habituated to certain pathways.

The supermarket is full of evolutionary subtleties. For instance, waffles once were four products—flour, butter, eggs, and milk. It wasn't hard to make the batter, but it was a nuisance to clean the waffle iron. Now, on supermarket shelves sit more than thirty variations of already pressed perfect waffles. From Eggo Nutri-Grain waffles to bite-sized Aunt Jemima bran waffles to Belgian Chef restaurant-style to Hungry Jack full-plate waffles, the waffle has become a new shape of food. Once such a shape has been established in the shopper's mind, producers will attempt to extend it from the simple home-base product outward. So you might have Pillsbury waffle mix, then Pillsbury Lite Waffle mix, then Pillsbury syrup, and so on, as the host product attempts to inch onto more and more shelf space.

Want to see the battle really raging? Check out the caffeinated, caramelized, carbonated sugar water. There is Coke, Diet Coke, Cherry Coke, Tab, plus the caffeine-free versions, each one struggling not just to catch your eye, but to deny space to Pepsi, Diet Pepsi, Crystal Pepsi, and all their caffeine-free versions. It is clear that some of the cola extensions are on financial life support. What are they doing there? Clearly, more to keep the competition *off* the shelves than to really find a customer base.

While we are moving through the FMCGs, things are happening at blink speed. In the average half-hour trip to a large supermarket, thirty thousand products vie for your eye. Those that get noticed have only a sixth of a second to make their sales pitch. Since you have a finite number of eye blinks (an estimated five thousand a day), the package needs to literally get "into your face"—and quick.

Today's marketers know they have to pull the trigger at the speed of light. Since the contents of most of the supermarket stuff are fungible, much of the responsibility of selling has to fall to the trade dress. The dress must both cover the product and assert its difference. Little wonder that one packaged food out of four costs you more for the container than for what's inside.[3]

The package is the Venus's flytrap for humans. Sometimes this mechanism is open (those transparent windows on pasta packets); at other times the wrapping is a cunning disguise. No matter what the package form, everything depends on color. We are in the jungle: the least shift in tint tells us "look sharp—danger ahead!" Yellow is always out there telling us medicine is nearby—it's the color of pus and irritation. Blue is trustworthy, but hardly appetizing, so it is around many home supplies. Red is all over the place, used for cookies, crackers, and frozen foods, especially on "comfort foods." Green, which was thought to be taboo on packaged goods because it signified vegetable life, not hermetically sealed protection, has come to mean "good for you" not in the wholesome sense but in the guilt-free sense. It is slathered over Healthy Choice and Snack Well's foods, which make claims that eating

3. If you really want to see this process, go to the liquor store. Premium vodkas offer the most obvious example. Not since Uneeda biscuit in 1901 has an advertising campaign been so focused on a package as that of Absolut vodka. The bottle has a very distinctive profile and Absolut was a pioneer in the use of transparent labels to allow shoppers to see the product within. The advertising seeks only to establish that silhouette as a prestige item. It never mentions the contents at all, ever. In fact, the whole vodka aisle is a bottle beauty contest. Finlandia's highly-sculptured bottle looks just like Ittala crystal. Newer brands follow Absolut's lead in establishing a distinctive profile. Frïs (complete with umlauts) resembles the Citicorp building; a brand called Icy is clearly knocking off Absolut's label-as-bottle format; Belvedere, Chopin, and Grey Goose all achieve 3-D effects with etched images on the inside back surfaces of the bottle that shimmer through the front label, and Skyy is in a sky-blue bottle looking just like something you might have found on granny's bedside table. No wonder with such elaborate packaging that a book about Absolut's packaging and advertising—*Absolut Book*, natch—was published and became a bestseller in 1996.

this goo is somehow better than your previous choice. When the package graphics announce "10% less fat than our usual cookies," chances are this claim will be against a green background.

✳ *YOUR GROCER WAS NOT ALWAYS SO FRIENDLY*

The war, as they say in marketing, has always been in the store. Whereas we now are pitted against large food corporations like General Foods, Stouffers, Carnation, Campbell's, Pepsico, Pillsbury, Ralston Purina, Kellogg's, ADM, and Progressive, we used to lock horns with the "no credit—don't ask for it" storekeeper. Now the grocer has his big friendly face prominently displayed near the office and his thumb far from the scales. Our wariness is ancient, but now almost forgotten.[4]

The package resolved this ancient feud. Not only did it allow you to carry your booty home, it did something more important—it assured you that you were not being stiffed. The illustration shows the H. J. Heinz Company playing on the shopper's anxiety of the 1920s. Although they claim the grocer is chum to both processor and shopper, the imagery here says something different. The packaged goods company has rendered the grocer's careful wrapping and weighing scale unnecessary.

Only the ignorant would like to go back to the good old days of the neighborhood store. Most shoppers would say we've come a long way from the days when you'd go to the grocer to get your own container filled from the flour barrel and not know whether you were getting the right amount or price, or even whether it would be full of grubs and weevils. An ounce is an ounce and the package says so. Even in the post–Civil War days when factories started to pack goods in paper so that you could buy a "paper" of coffee, soap, or dried yeast, an unscrupulous grocer might unwrap, separate his cut, then rewrap the paper so that the unwary customer would never know. Packaging really began when the papers could be written on and then sealed.

---

4. Many of the assertions in the Magna Carta have to do with fair dealing by the grocer. What equals one measure of wine, beer, or corn? To resolve the complexities of having different grocers mandate different measurements, the first acts of constituted government was to stipulate uniform sizes, weights, and measures.

But to a cynic we have simply transferred deceit from inside the paper, as it were, to the outside of the box.[5] More important than any claim of nutrition, more important than any standardization and quality assurance, however, is the expression of identity that the package establishes with the consumer. This relationship replaces, or at least supplements, any relationship that the buyer might have had with the storekeeper or even the farmer. Through the promotion of trade characters, such as the dour Quaker, the Jolly Green Giant, the playful Campbell's soup kids, the irrepressible Pillsbury Dough

➤ The grocer is our friend, but the can keeps him honest. (H.J. Heinz, 1922)

Boy, the joyful Tony the Tiger, or the long-suffering Aunt Jemima, packaging took part in separating us from the grocer. In a sense, the mercurial grocer has moved from behind the counter to the outside of the package. He has been packaged—literally.

---

5. Nowhere is this more ridiculous than on the supposedly honest nutritional sidebars established in 1992 by the FDA. My favorite subterfuge was the association of junk food with the word "nutrition," thereby easing guilt in purchasing the products. For a while cracker packages showed the crackers and soup together as a "serving suggestion." The nutritional chart looked terrific but all the crackers contributed was flour and sodium. The rest of the nutrition came from the soup that was pictured on the package, but not contained inside. The FDA has tried to stop this deceit, but labels on breakfast cereals (with or without milk) are still hard to understand.

✷ *TWO OF MY FAVORITE THINGS AND THEIR PERSONALITIES: WONDER BREAD AND COKE*

Over my keyboard, atop the modern altar of the computer monitor, sit two forbidden icons of my youth. They are a cellophane-wrapped loaf of Wonder bread and an aluminum can of Coca-Cola. My parents despised these products. To my father, Wonder bread was air and water and to my mother the Coke was sugar water that would "rot your teeth."

To me they represented the off-limits of my youth, the bread and wine of the new commercial culture. The analogy is not haphazard, for everything I loved was from the forbidden mass culture. It was mass produced, mass marketed, and consumed en masse. If I wanted to celebrate the unholy Eucharist of modern life, I would have to partake of it outside the home, for we "simply" (and that was the word used) would not countenance them inside the family circle.

My parents were waging a feckless battle separating the sacred from the profane. They, along with Dwight Macdonald, the Van Dorens (alas, not Charles), Robert Hutchens, Mortimer Adler, and all the rest, were fighting a rear guard campaign against the new packaged culture. In the showdown between junk and jewels, between trash and treasures,

➢ A few of my favorite things: Coke and Wonder bread.

the vulgar would not just survive but prevail. It prevailed partly because it came in such interesting packages.

Machine-made bread is a hallmark of commercial cultures, and American-made processed bread is unique. It has few defenders. Even Henry Miller found it obscene:

> What do I find wrong with America? Everything. I begin at the begin-
> ning, with the staff of life: bread. . . . If [Americans] knew what good
> bread was, they would not have such wonderful machines on which
> they lavish all their time, energy and affection. . . . Here is the se-
> quence: poor bread, bad teeth, indigestion, constipation, halitosis,
> sexual starvation, disease and accidents, the operating table, artificial
> limbs, spectacles, baldness, kidney and bladder trouble, neurosis, psy-
> chosis, schizophrenia, war and famine. Start with the American loaf of
> bread so beautifully wrapped in cellophane and you end on the scrap
> heap at 45. (in Harrington 12)

One can only imagine what he would have said about Coke, let alone about my other favorites: Spam, Twinkies, and Jell-O.

There is probably no better introduction to the power of commercial culture than to describe the delivery systems of Coke and Wonder
bread. And probably no better way to explore the vagaries of packaging
than to realize that one of these products now barely exists in a corner
of the bread aisle, while the other has gone on to conquer the world.

❋ WONDER(FUL) BREAD

Wonder bread, the one-time king of all packaged bread, was introduced
in sliced form in the 1930s. The bread first gained national attention at
the famous 1939 World's Fair. The Wonder Bakery was a popular exhibition inside the "World of Tomorrow" section, which envisioned the
technological utopia of 1960. What better symbol of perfection than
repeatable bread slices? How grand the 1960s would be! Each slice of
Wonder was machine perfect, a marvel of progress—smooth, identical,
without imperfection—indeed, America's bread.

Wonder was malleable enough to be rolled up on the palm into a
little ball while stable enough to support the viscous mixture of
peanut butter and marshmallow fluff, or Velveeta and deviled ham. It
deserved its transcendent name; this was no sacrilege. This was the
bread for the new world, a bread characterized by mass-produced purity

and freshness, the staff of life, vacuum-sealed and wrapped in red and blue polka dots.

When the war came the government required that white bread be fortified. Wonder was on the front line, a favorite of our doughboys. What little nutrition it had, had already been milled out, so chemicals were pumped back in. Wonder made a marketing niche out of this legal necessity. By the mid-1940s, it switched advertising claims from freshness to nutrition. In the war years was born the assertion "Helps build strong bodies" that would later be followed by either twelve or eight ways or, finally, as the lawyers descended like locusts, no number at all.[6]

Clearly the people who made this bread—at this time it was baked by a consortium called Continental Bakery that had acquired the Wonder name when it gobbled up the original Indianapolis bakery in the 1920s—knew what was happening in my house. Mothers were suspicious of a food that tasted nothing like it should. Wonder was yummy bread. You didn't have to "Give it to Mikey, he'll eat anything." We all ate it. So Continental hired the Ted Bates Advertising Agency to combat the anxious moms.

The Bates agency was run by a new kind of advertising executive who actually had a theory to explain selling. The executive was Rosser Reeves and his theory was called USP, or Unique Selling Proposition. The selling proposition did not have to be true, but it had to be unique. For instance, when Reeves wanted to sell Colgate toothpaste he claimed, "It cleans your breath while it cleans your teeth." This was malarky, but it gave the impression that clean-smelling was a characteristic only of Col-

---

6. At the same time Wonder was making its claims, the electric home toaster was born. Mothers could magically transform this gooey mattress of malleable white dough into a perfectly crunchy slice of brown toast. It is hard to imagine how magical toast was to those of us who grew up just after the war. The world's first automatic toasting device (eventually majestically called the Toastmaster) could warm and brown sliced bread into a kind of rigid, crusty cake that could then be buttered and jellied. The transformation to toast itself was the miracle. The white bread went in the maw of the Toastmaster, it was lowered automatically, we waited, then the bell sounded, the toast sprang up. Was there ever a more powerful image of American technology than this? Each day we observed the transformation of unformed and weak sponge bread into the firm, hard, oven-tough wafer of what? American manhood, perhaps? We watched, like the Magi, the scent of a golden future wafting before us.

gate. In the same manner, he claimed that "Anacin is like a doctor's pre-scription," and that "M&Ms melt in your mouth, not in your hand."

When it came to Wonder bread Reeves coined the infamous "Helps build strong bodies twelve ways." It was a dazzling bit of jujitsu, for he made a deficiency into an advantage. The twelve ways were never ex-plained. This stuff was just flour, yeast, and water, to be sure, but it was those additives that helped add strength to those bodies. All the other sliced white breads had almost exactly the same additives. In a world be-fore chemicals got a bad reputation, Reeves made it seem that Wonder was adding special stuff like cod-liver oil and vitamins that would oth-erwise never be consumed by kids. For a decade Continental Bakery got away with this claim. Wonder prospered.

But, alas, in 1971 a Federal Trade Commission complaint alleged that Wonder's ads claiming children grow to "90 percent of adult height" during the "Wonder years" ages one through twelve was simply false. The company did nothing but change the claim from twelve ways to eight. Finally, the FTC determined that the Wonder ads falsely implied that Wonder was an extraordinary food for producing dramatic growth in children, which, of course, was exactly what it wasn't. Continental, by now a minor subsidiary of the giant conglomerate ITT, gave up the dis-puted ads without a whimper, but, as they say in advertising, an outpost had already been established in the customer's mind. USP at work.

Great advertising could introduce the product with claims of value and uniqueness, but it was the package that clinched the deal. Although we may now see Wonder as a sham, it was looked at in the 1930s as an honest bread. For it came wrapped in a new material, a material that showed the manufacturer had nothing to hide. The wrapping was al-most as clear as glass and far more pliable than waxed paper. It was a new kind of wrap pioneered by Du Pont and it was perfect for this bread. It was cellophane.[7]

---

7. When that smug Los Angeles businessman took baby-faced Dustin Hoff-man aside in *The Graduate* and whispers, "I just want to say one word to you—just one word—'Plastic,'" he knew what he was talking about. Cello-phane is simply plastic at its most plastic. It had been invented in 1911 by a Swiss chemist in an unsuccessful effort to find a coating that would keep tablecloths from becoming stained, and it was first manufactured in France in 1913. Du Pont licensed that patent in 1923 and began producing it the following year. Although it was conceived and born far from the United States, if any product was associated with America, this was it. In 1927 Du Pont made a crucial improvement. It made its translucent shield

At first manufacturers shied away from cellophane because it was too revealing. So Du Pont's promotions showed retail displays featuring paper bags filled with macaroni, nuts, beans, spices, vegetables, and other commodities that you could see through a cellophane window. But you could also use cellophane *as* the bag. You could even print on it. Bread was the perfect commodity to bag in cellophane because you could keep it airtight and visible. Air-and-water bread, by its nature indistinguishable from all oth

"What a lovely transparent wrapper!"

Cellophane

➤ Transparent Cellophane lets you peek inside. (Du Pont, 1928)

ers, could now be bagged *and* branded. And so it was. In large red letters the single word "Wonder" was surrounded by yellow, red, and blue balloons. What kid sitting in the newly designed grocery store shopping cart would let such a sight go by without a whoop of desire?

In his delightful book, *The Total Package: The Evolution and Secret*

---

moisture-proof, allowing it to be used as a protective covering for food. This clear, flimsy product remained close to invisible, however, until a few years later when Du Pont began a pioneering marketing campaign to make what had been a little-known component into a household word. Cellophane was one of the first packaging products to be advertised as a reason to buy what it covered. As opposed to waxed paper, which was not airtight, this wrapping would keep food fresh. Better yet, you could buy the stuff to cover your own food at home. The company's success in creating a celebrity substance was affirmed when, in his 1934 song "You're the Top," Cole Porter climaxed a list of superlatives with the accolade, "You're cellophane."

Meanings of Boxes, Bottles, Cans and Tubes, Thomas Hine, design critic of the *Philadelphia Inquirer,* draws a straight line between the monstrance—the heavily adorned container for the wafer used in the Roman Catholic liturgy—and the Wonder bread bag. The job of both is to call attention to the invisible essence within—the body of Christ within the bread in the case of the monstrance, and the nutritional additives in the case of Wonder. Mr. Hine, who did not know the provenance of the multicolored balloons, proposed one of his own.[8] He considered the colored circles to be like the precious stones on the monstrance, designed to catch the eye from a considerable distance and command recognition. He may not have caught the letter of the wrapper, but he certainly caught the spirit.

If you look at the Wonder package today you can see how the guardians of truth-in-packaging have had their way with all those balloons. On both sides of the package we are greeted by a cartoonish bow-tied "identification character" who assures us that this product "helps build strong bodies," but then adds the words, "Now nutrition experts recommend six to eleven servings daily from the bread, cereal, rice and pasta group. Wonder bread is a versatile and convenient way to add a grain-based food to every meal." Below this petty caviling is a Food Guide Pyramid (along with all the "Nutrition Facts" mandated by the Food and Drug Administration) squarely sited over the bread/cereal/rice/pasta group. Rosser Reeves would be turning over in his grave. Wonder bread not only has been robbed of its uniqueness, it has been associated with the foods of the damned: cereal, rice, pasta. Why not add spinach and broccoli?

Wonder bread was the beginning of junk food, the progenitor of Twinkies, Hostess Cup Cakes, and Ho-Hos, the beginning of food already digested. As great as its package was, and as outrageous as its claims were, Wonder was destined to be deflated. First, private label and generic breads could produce the same product cheaper. Air and water is air and water. And second, variety breads and fancy breads made

---

8. The wrapper graphics were happenstance, inspired by a balloon race at the Indianapolis Speedway that was right across the street from the bakery. These balloons caused enough consternation, however, for a Wonder executive to explain in 1938 that they were not to imply that Wonder was full of air.

powerful health claims every bit as outrageous as Wonder's.[9] But they made them stick.

White bread itself has become a relic, and not in the religious sense. The bread police have won. In 1967 Americans ate 8.8 billion pounds of white bread. In 1982 we ate 6.2 billion pounds—a 30 percent drop in fifteen years. The rates are now stabilizing. In between, in 1975, Wonder ranked number one on the Center for Science in the Public Interest's "Terrible Ten" list of foods—above sugar, Pringles, and even the dreaded Coca-Cola (Harrington 12). Wonder was a symbol, all right, but unlike 1939, when it reflected the feats of technology, Wonder has come to stand for all the excesses technology could commit. Wonder has had the air squeezed out of it and now sits at the edge of the bread aisle gasping.[10]

✳ COCA-COLA

I see a strange connection between your slogan "The pause that refreshes," and Christ's own words, "Come unto me, all ye that travail, and I will refresh you."   —A minister, to his local Coca-Cola bottler

If the balloon-festooned Wonder bread wrapper is the monstrance for our times, then the twelve-ounce fire-engine-red can of Coca-Cola is the chalice. Of all the liturgical objects, the chalice is the most important and one of the most important containers in all Western culture. This

---

9. How the mighty have fallen. According to the company's own studies, Wonder is now consumed almost exclusively by blue-collar and lower income white-collar households with several children. About 40 percent of all heavy white bread users earn less than $15,000 a year and the biggest eaters are men and teenagers. About half of Wonder's sales are to people older than fifty. Such an irony that the very bread that was once a badge of affluence has now become just the opposite.

10. So the Wonder years are over. Still popular culture protects its own. A few years ago there was a television show called *The Wonder Years* that was based in the 1960s. The show's name was a lifting of the commercial—remember, the "Wonder Years" themselves were "the crucial growth period between ages 1 and 12."

container is not just magical in itself but holds the central magic of the entire religion. Transubstantiation happens beneath its brim.[11]

One can be quite certain that Asa Chandler and his followers in Atlanta, Georgia had no such metaphysics in mind when they developed, packaged, marketed, and advertised their caramel-colored sugar water to what would become a worldwide audience of gulpers. It is not happenstance, however, that of the two myths associated with this beverage—that it was at one time tinctured with cocaine (it was), and that it is created by a secret formula that still resides in a bank vault at the Trust Company of Georgia (it is)—are dim analogs to the magical properties of a far more ancient transubstantiation.

Now I realize that only a tenured professor could make the outrageous claim that the Coke can is in any way analogous to the sacred chalice. I ask only that you find a recent can and hold it in your hand. More time and energy and imagination and dedication has been lavished on this container than on any other vessel except the medieval chalice. Not only is the Coca-Cola name considered one of the most recognized in the world—valued by studies conducted by *Financial World* at almost $50 billion—but the iconography of this can is universally recognized. More people around the globe now know what this can "means" than can interpret the sign of the cross. (But then again, the Marlboro package, Mickey Mouse, the Golden Arches, and even Tony the Tiger are equally famous.)

---

11. Recall that at the Last Supper, Christ established the new covenant with his blood: "This is my blood . . . which is shed for many" (Matthew 26:28; Mark 14:24). Luke (22:20) locks the metaphor of wine as blood to the chalice so that the receptacle becomes an equivalent of the sacrificial blood: "This cup is . . . my blood which is shed for you." No other object in all Christendom is like this vessel. No one now looks to the Holy Roman Church to innovate packaging, but a recent contribution of the American Catholics has been the disposable communion package. True to the concerns of an AIDS generation, this delivery system consists of a plastic-wrapped wafer and a tear-off container of grape juice, rather like the creamers served with coffee. The patented, hermetically sealed, disposable, grape juice-filled "Celebration Cup" costs about ten cents each and is already a staple in about one thousand Catholic churches. Appropriately layered over the commercial culture, it has already has been dubbed "Fast Food Communion."

Much ink is spilled each time Coke changes containers, so let's just observe the most recent makeover done to the can in 1997. After the debacle of New Coke, and after the brouhahas made by Pepsi with its almost monthly redesign, Coke rededicated itself to packaging. More than ads, more than product placement, more than all the public relations, the can must have the final word. Have a look at what it says.

On the front of the can against the trademarked Coca-Cola red is an extraordinary sight: a rendition of the old greenish glass contoured container. Much has been made of the female form of this hourglass bottle, how pleasant it was to hold and heft, how ergonomic. The original glass bottle, first made in 1915, was later dubbed the Mae West for a reason. But here, pictured on the outside of the aluminum can, it is slightly canted over to one side as if ready to be poured. Its fluid level, however, plays an optical trick by making us think that it is upright while the can is tilted. I know of no other package in which the center image is an erstwhile package foregrounded.

Since Coke has been notoriously tightlipped about what is going on here, one might surmise that the old package reinforces the fact that this is Coke *Classic,* not New Coke or any of the other brand extensions like Cherry Coke, Caffeine-free Coke, Diet Coke, Caffeine-free Diet Coke, and Diet Cherry Coke. This is the real McCoy, the old wine, as it were, just in a new bottle.[12]

As I write this, Coke is planning to introduce a contoured aluminum can in the shape of the old glass bottle. Coke has already succeeded in 1993 with the plastic twenty-ounce contoured bottle based on the Mae West design. But the contoured can is far more difficult. Will the cans be able to keep their shape when stacked one on top of another? Will consumers pay more for the can? The big problem is not just cost to the consumer, however. Bottlers now continuously fill cans, changing only the fluid as the cans fly down the assembly line. Whether it is Sprite or Diet Coke, the can is always the same. But this new contoured can means that everything will have to stop, machines be reset, and then

---

12. But there is another possibility: that Coke has been under siege not just from Pepsi but from all the "New Age" beverages that sell the container not the drink, as well as from competitors like Richard Branson, whose Virgin Cola appears in a glass bottle shaped like a woman (called the Pammy after Pamela Anderson Lee). In the beverage business this is called drinking the can, and Coke needs to protect its role as packaging leader.

run only as long as the hourglass cans run. If you ever wondered about the importance of the container, realize that Coke is already making these cans in Germany and will be test-marketing them in this country. Industry insiders suspect Coke will never earn back its development costs. Take heart; it was the flip-top box that accounted for much of Marlboro's success.

Coke will run this risk, for this is the flagship can, this is the chalice from Atlanta, this is the one that "says it all." Have another look at the can. The familiar logo spirals up the can, whereas on earlier cans it was horizontal. Likewise, on all the other brand extensions of Coke, like Diet Coke and Cherry Coke, the curve graphic is featured underneath their individual product IDs. The logo seems to read as the label on the new can, while it also takes the place of the label on the older bottle.

Meanwhile, the red "Always Coca-Cola" disk has been inflated to push its edges beyond the container's boundaries, giving the illusion that the can is larger than it really is. Inside the company, this logo is known as "the red disk," "the bull's eye," or the "trademark disk," and it is intended to serve as the worldwide symbol.

This "Always Coca-Cola" advertising campaign, introduced in 1993, calls attention to its archrival Pepsi, which is anything but *always* Pepsi. In fact, Pepsi, true to its wavering claim to be the choice of a new generation ("Generation NeXt"), and for those who think young, is *always* changing its chalice. Perennially also-ran Pepsi seems to use its can to acknowledge that if you can't get attention by remaining the same, you had better never stop changing.

What is also interesting from an art-historical point of view are those new typefaces on the Coke can. Crude typewriter-style words—"delicious," "refreshing," "unique"—float on the surface in several colors. This new Typeka lettering, which has been manipulated electronically to make almost every letter a different weight and level than the one before, is arresting. It looks as if some of the words have been typed by an old Underwood machine that has been knocked around so much that every letter now carries a different load of ink. In fact, the type looks as if this had been written at the same time that the Mae West bottle was in use.

And what are the antecedents of these words "refreshing" or "unique"? Is it the sugar water or the container? Observe the word "Refreshing" down at the bottom of the can. The FBI crime lab would doubtless claim that the letters were typed by three different machines as each letter seems a different size and font. And on the spine appears the now mandatory boilerplate nutritional ingredients, the Universal Product Code, and the touching little box that assures us that this is Coke Classic ORIGINAL FORMULA. Again, here is a company that has not forgotten the trauma of New Coke that so infuriated loyal drinkers of the original, that it was poured out into the streets like so much bad wine.

To understand this Coke container you need to understand that in American culture you either drink Coke or Pepsi. No one knows why this is; why Dr. Pepper or RC Cola could not make it a triad, why other noncola drinks are not included even though 7-UP tried to be one of the "uncolas," why no such distinctions divide the drinkers of beer (although Anheuser-Busch has tried to make its package central to its one-time claim to be "King of Beer"), and why no such distinction exists between drinkers of various brands of bottled water, whiskey, or gin.[13]

I think—and again this is what you'd expect from someone who makes his living obscuring the simple—that Coke and Pepsi must separate along some deep fault line of human personality. Think about it: don't you know people who refuse to drink one or the other cola? Yet in taste tests few people can reliably separate the taste. Who cares who can pass the "Pepsi Challenge," the campaign of a few years ago where more drinkers supposedly preferred Pepsi? No matter. Back in the 1930s blindfolded cigarette smokers were found to be fiercely loyal to a brand, although they could not distinguish its taste. What separates cola drinkers is that their allegiance transcends reason. A Lucky Strike smoker will puff on a Camel, a Miller man will drink a Bud, but a Coke drinker will not sip a Pepsi.

This is not a consistent dichotomy. It doesn't crop up elsewhere. It is not like Republican/Democrat, paper/plastic, good to eat/bad to eat. I don't want to give it too much semiotic spin, but it is interesting that Coke eternally fine-tunes its packaging, while Pepsi eternally re-creates theirs. Pepsi is at the forefront of product design. Its ads—usually from BBDO—are usually unusual. Pepsi is always taking chances, going off

---

13. Pepsico has found this out much to its discontent as the market share of its flagship brand has been eroded. Pepsico's marketing plan of the 1970s was to use its fast-food restaurants like Taco Bell, KFC, and Pizza Hut as outlets dedicated to pouring only Pepsi. What they found was that, while they had a captive audience, a much larger one lurked at the doorway not wanting to come in because they had to drink Pepsi. Pepsi learned the hard way and spun off the food divisions.

to the hinterlands with great special effects. Pepsi has energy; it is pro-lific; it is on the road of excess. Coke is staid; it is reflexive; it follows the center line. While its ads come from numerous agencies, includ-ing CAA, the one-time premier Hollywood talent agency, they are rarely edgy. Pepsi celebrates everything, even failure. Coke agonizes over everything, even success. Is Pepsi platonic while Coke is aristotelian? I don't know, but I do think that in the world of goods, in the commer-cial land of what seems multitudinous choice, it is noteworthy that here worldwide culture funnels down to a single either/or. Clearly, here is a place where you drink the marketing along with the soda.

✳ THE METAPHYSICS OF WRAP

One cannot think about the world we now live in without thinking about packages. Certainly at one level the concept of packaging is pro-found: once there is meaning, there is a surrounding husk, a surface and a depth, worlds within worlds, things inside things, and so on. Where do we draw the line between contained and container? Quan-tum mechanics tells us that energy like light comes in bundles; religion essentially provides a package of beliefs and images; politics, a world-view; our bodies are the packaging crate of our genes. The nut is just the seed's package. The onion a packaged package, endless.

Eggs, pods, rinds, clam shells, even cellular structure itself may tell us that the unmediated world is a world that simply does not exist. The deep truth may not be imageless; there may simply be no deep truth, only veil behind veil, endless packages. Interiority and exteriority, clo-sure and exposure, reveal and conceal—there is almost always some film between ourselves and what we consume, be it made of airy noth-ing, or tin, paper, cellophane, and cloth. What we need to acknowledge, and perhaps even appreciate, is that very often it is the sheathing that we desire; the wrapping is more important than what's inside.

People are forever complaining about packaging. The really perplex-ing aspect of packaging is not why it is omnipresent but why we so re-sist our complicity. Could it be that our disdain for packaging is really our uneasiness with needs unmet, desires unfulfilled? The container is the Trojan horse of commercialism, the used car salesman, the smarmy and insincere pander, the veneer.

When we don't like a political candidate we say he's packaged—run-ning a packaged campaign, giving a packaged speech. When we think of a packaged tour we think that it is for people who, unlike ourselves, need to be told where to go and what to experience. They are tourists, we are travelers. Hollywood agents make package deals to wrap entertainment schlock; that's what makes them Hollywood agents. Disney World, Eurodisney, Disneyland: *yuck,* packaged junk, *dreck.*

Okay we say, some products need packaging such as lipstick, a book of matches, shaving cream, and a few other items like perfume, where separating the product from the package is virtually impossible. But elsewhere we act as if commercial culture has simply gone too far in enveloping *everything.* They are doing this to us, we say. We never asked for it, we say, as we pass by the colorless generics to grab the colorful box.

✳ PROBLEM PACKAGES

We sneer in disgust at overpackaging. Remember the uproar some years ago over the CD "long box"? True, it took a second-story thief to pry open, and it did seem exorbitantly large, but that was just the point. This package was made to be hard to move, as in to *re*move, from the store. The later jewel-box packaging also resulted from record companies recalling the late 1960s and early 1970s when album covers had special foldouts and die-cut covers that clearly added to sales. Many hits of the hippies owed their success to great psychedelic cover design. Tape cassettes didn't lend themselves to special packaging and that had affected sales for certain acts with hard-to-see "visuals." So the big package around the compact disc was an attempt to reassert the album cover.

Some products can't be sold without superfluous packages. Nike shoes, for instance. Why packages we put over our feet should be more attractive coming in individual cardboard boxes has puzzled the shoe industry for years. But this much is true: you cannot sell shoes without a box. Two generations ago, you could. All the shoes of one size were shipped to the retailer—twelve to a carton—from which he pulled out the individual pairs.

Let someone like John Malloy tell us that our dress is self-packaging and that you can become successful by changing the packaging by "dressing for success," and we recoil. When Thomas J. Watson, founder of IBM, called his white-shirt-only dress code self-packaging and in-

144
—
↻

sisted on displaying that packaging to his corporate customers, nay-sayers tut-tutted and rolled their eyes. What was the relationship between clean white shirts and electric typewriters? Watson knew, and that knowledge made himself and his stockholders rich.

Many of us revile a culture that has packaged daily life into vast franchised systems of conformity and predictability. "Isn't this plastic conformity awful," we say as we drive into McDonald's for the styro-foamed, clamshell-packaged Egg McMuffin after spending the night at the cellophane-wrapped Holiday Inn.

Perhaps our hostility to packaging is linked to our embarrassment that *res non ipsa loqitur,* things don't say enough, that we need training wheels for reality, that we "cannot see life steadily, and see it whole." And the fact that once packaging has been removed, it becomes trash exacerbates the problem. After unwrapping, we dedicate some of our most vehement scorn to such trash. When it is on the road we call it lit-ter. The rest of it—almost four hundred pounds per person per year—is suffocating us, or so we are told, and so we like to believe. We are run-ning out of landfills, says Chicken Little, furiously wrapping and un-wrapping Christmas presents, expecting others to do the same.

Our Puritan anxieties, which gave rise to the consumer revolution (work, work, work, spend, spend, spend), also fuel our willingness to point fingers. Our guilt at creating waste is undeniable, but pales be-side our desire to claim others should feel not only just as guilty but profoundly ashamed. In truth, "trash" is a word very much like "weed" or "predator"; it denotes a category, but connotes disdain. Alas, a very small percent of real trash is from packaging. Ironically, most trash re-sults from using the medium favored by the largest complainers about packaging, namely, newsprint.

✳ AN ONTOLOGY OF MODERN PACKAGING

At the risk of putting Pangloss to shame, let me assert what I hope is obvious. Packaging has not just succeeded but triumphed because both producer and consumer have been rewarded. The producer has been able to talk with the end user without having to go through the salesman. Just as advertising allows him to speak over the head of the retailer, the package allows him to speak around the clerk. The con-sumer accepts the package because it assures him that what is inside is what he wants—no grubs, no thumb on the scale, no chocolate chip cookies containing less than one thousand chips per package. Plus he can carry the package easily and display his good taste to others. Department stores know this, which is why Tiffany's, Barney's, Saks, and other downtown stores go to great lengths to provide shoppers with elegant paper shopping bags complete with store logo prominently displayed. Shoppers eagerly comply. As with the τ-shirt, shoppers want to be publicly associated with the product.[14]

Clearly, we often prefer the commercial husk to the honest seed because we prefer the commercial language of advertising to the plain-speak of reality. The package is not just the identity of the product; it is the identity of the consumer. *You,* you're the one. You've made the right choice. You are special. So along with the advertising, we eat the container. Along with the slogan, we drink the beer. If the package acts as the confidence man for the product, then it does the same for ourselves. The package faces us and with it we face others. The package is the magical voodoo doll.[15]

---

14. Should you want a bizarre testament to the mutual benefits of packaging, witness the singular failure of the cooperative food store and the so-called generic product. One of the many lessons we can learn from the rise of commercialism is that most of us seem to prefer the depersonalized transaction with the elaborate package to the humanized interchange of real feeling and honest goods. Give a consumer a choice of buying unpackaged food in bulk and saving money, or buying overwrapped smaller portions in containers and paying more, and we all know which will prevail. Put generic products into neutered containers and they might just as well be in a barrel. Who knows? Let a depression set in and we may prefer the language of money to the language of graphics, the coin to the trade dress. But until then let the box, bag, and tube do the talking.

15. Industrial designers like Walter Dorwin Teague, Norman Bel Geddes, Henry Dreyfuss, Donald Deskey, and most of all, Raymond Loewy were discovering this central truth of modernity in the 1930s. Just as clothes make the man, covering makes objects. In a series of classic experiments in the 1930s, Louis Cheskin demonstrated that package design actually altered the way test subjects experienced the taste of the beer or crackers they sampled. With a nod to Freud, Creskin called the phenomenon "sensation transference," and this voodoo provided the packaging industry with a sense of legitimacy, if not necessity.

✳ *THE HISTORY OF PACKAGING ON A THUMBNAIL*

The first successful commercial packages were those in the mid-nineteenth century that held over-the-counter nostrums—the ones we now so love to mock. Carter's Little Liver Pills is about the only survivor of a vast family of potions designed to live up to their outrageous labels. Thanks to the Civil War battlefields, the empirical proof was presented that pain could be alleviated by soporifics. Why not use these potions at home?

All that was needed was the technology to brew these elixirs (most of them were alcohol-based), bottle, and distribute them. The claim of pain prevention had already been made. The rise of a countrywide magazine media reinforced these assertions with advertising and, accompanied by halftone illustrations, showed exactly what the package looked like.

Since the contents were similar, the only way to achieve product differentiation was with packaging. By the turn of the century both the packages and the labels had been transformed. Patent medicine—two parts claim, one part medicine—was every bit as important as soap in transforming the way we live now. It is still alive and well down at your local drug store and on your television set; just look at most over-the-counter drugs.

What chromolithography did to labels, new machinery did to containers. Bottles of various sizes had been around for a century and these new colorful labels were easy to apply. Folding boxes were introduced in the 1850s, becoming cost-effective with the invention of automated box-making machines in 1879. Canning technology had been used to provision Napoleon's army as well as the Royal Navy, and canned meat and vegetables (sometimes tainted with lethal doses of lead) accompanied explorers searching for the Northwest Passage in the 1820s through the 1840s. Since you couldn't see inside, such cans demanded labels to make the package complete.

Gail Borden started selling canned condensed milk to the New York market in the 1850s and, during the Civil War, was faced with such a heavy demand that he had to license plants in other parts of the country. His Elsie the contented cow was a label of genius that not only made the contents known but also asserted the satisfaction and safety of the donor. The invention of the easy-to-use can opener in 1865 secured the place of cans once and for all.

Next was the metal tube. Invented in the 1840s for holding artists' paints, it was first filled with toothpaste in 1892. In a nifty irony, the tubes that once held colors now were brightly colored to hold a vast array of colorless emollients and medicines. In the 1880s and 1890s, along with innovative packaging, promotional stunts, and a memorable trade character, Henry P. Crowell transformed the cylindrical form to paper, filled it with what was essentially finely milled animal feed, and called it a breakfast cereal. We still know the memorable, stern Quaker on the canister.

The turn of the century saw further technological advances, but perhaps the most far-reaching development was the way in which coordinated packaging, branding, and advertising wrested power from wholesalers and retailers, and placed it in the hands of manufacturers. The advertising agency was crucial. It allowed Nabisco, for instance, to talk directly to the end user. Now the customer would walk into the country store and ask not for crackers, but for Nabisco crackers. The turning point was this Nabisco Uneeda biscuit ad from 1901, masterfully conveying not the product but the advantages of factory packaging. Have a look at this ad from the N.W. Ayer & Son agency. The waterproof kid who makes the visual metaphor for dryness was the son of the copywriter.

148

➤ Arguing by analogy: Nabisco's In-Er-Seal packaging is like the kid's slicker. (National Biscuit Co., 1890s)

While the main theme in postwar packaging has been the growing dominance of plastics, another consequential event was the discovery of synthetic detergents. Procter & Gamble introduced Tide in 1947, and its success spawned a large number of new packaged goods, ranging from shampoos and other hair care products to virtually every conceivable type of household cleaner.

And never underestimate the transforming power of television. On one hand the "tube" (itself a package of electronics, first in the shape of furniture and now in the shape of a movie screen) made packaging adapt to the fact that, after sleeping and feeding, we spend most of our time watching it. Packaging followed. In the 1950s TV dinners were launched, which led to the assault of frozen foods, all in colorful packages. You didn't cook the food, you boiled the package, or later, you microwaved it—package and all.

Still more important, if you can't show the package on television, you can't sell it. Package graphics depended not just on how the package sat on the shelf, but how it sat cupped in a hand shoving it out into the eye of the television camera. Marlboro took a woman's cigarette and redesigned the box in 1955. You had better remember it. The flip-top box was opened and shut before our eyes every night, at least until tobacco advertising was removed.

Television had another effect on packaging: it forced simplicity. If you can't recognize the object in a few blinks, you can't advertise it in thirty seconds. The simplicity of design in American products, commented on by every tourist who observes us, is really the result not of a shared sense of simplicity, but of the necessity of products having to fit into an average eighteen-inch diagonal screen. The massive relabeling effort in 1992 to comport with new federal regulations about nutritional facts reinforced the visual simplicity of American products. Designers had to work around the dense text of the nutritional information box, while making the rest of the package telegenic.

✳ RELIGION, ART, AND THE PACKAGE

Ironically, it is precisely the allure of packaging that made it the past handmaiden of religion and the present bride of art. How can you observe medieval Christianity and not be aware of its resemblance to a series of Russian dolls each fitting nicely inside each other? The soaring cathedral box supported by flying buttresses was built over and around a never-ending series of boxes extending deep into the catacombs. The central, smallest container of course was the reliquary, in which bits of bone, small pieces of fabric, chunks of wood were boxed and guarded. When a new church was being constructed, often a shard of an already certified relic was transported into the new box. More likely, however, the precious rarity had to be bought on the open market.

We are aghast at the medieval commerce in what are so clearly bogus relics housed in such magnificent containers. But when you realize that the talismanic power of objects still exists down at your local A & P, you appreciate what supply and demand curves do with market magic. When you have few objects, the level of concentration perforce increases. And when you have thousands, each individual object has to fight for attention. You can't whisper; you have to shout.

Thomas Hine cogently writes in *The Total Package* that the supermarket is the only modern space that resembles the church. "With its thousands of images and messages, it is as visually dense, if not as beautiful, as a Gothic cathedral" (4). This adulation is as breathless as it is true. What Hine does not say is that this was unavoidable. The men who pioneered packaged goods came directly from the Christian ranks; in e. e. cummings's line, they stepped from the "world of born" to the "world of made." The rise of Consumer Culture did not just come from the Christian tradition, it was a central, albeit highly conflicted, aspect of the Christian tradition.[16]

I don't mean to suggest that Chartres is a box of Tide or that the crucifix is a logo, but I do mean to suggest that similarities are not happenstance. The early church architects knew that in the package was the

---

16. Christianity is hardly alone in using containers as metaphors of magical belief. Many religions organize their worship around different sorts of containers of sanctity—open this, use me, be saved. How else to explain the small vessels many Chinese still use for making sacrifices of food to their spirit ancestors, the mummies and pyramids of Egypt, or the Jewish ark that holds the Torah. What separates the modern Western world is that, way before the Industrial Revolution, we acknowledged both the power and the threat of worshiping objects. We don't call these religious objects *idols*, but we certainly worship near them. Often in our current secular world we now call them *works of art*. Listen to highcult critics discuss Rothko's chapel, the sublimity of Abstract Expressionism, or the transcendental vision of Mondrian and you will think you are back in church.

promise. They knew what soaring forms do to the awestruck observer. Magnificent wrapping suggests the energetic glory within. Sometimes the wrapping becomes the glory as with the elaborate banner loincloth that flutters about Christ's midriff in countless crucifixion paintings— an inspired resolution of a complex problem. Ironically, the early church fathers abhorred the ornate painting and elaborate decoration that started to appear on the walls of certain churches. But once they realized that parishioners flooded to exactly those spaces where such wrapping appeared, the medieval concern with spare and empty space ended, and the renaissance of ornamentation began. Florence is hardly Disneyland, but the enthusiastic desire to wrap surfaces with exciting images is the same. Certainly Pope Julius II knew when he hired Michelangelo for the Sistine Chapel that he was hiring not a decorator but a conjurer. He said as much.

✳ *THE ART OF THE PACKAGE, THE PACKAGE AS ART*

To find the real appreciation for modern packaging, however, we need to turn from religion to art. In many ways art and religion are similar. They promise meaning for life by positing a system of belief and a canon of accepted works. Unlike religion, however, the art world has not just acknowledged the role of packaging, it has celebrated it. Modern art has demonstrated what religion implied: in matters ethereal, it is almost impossible to tell the dancer from the dance, the contents from the box. This celebration of modern ambiguity, known as pop art, represents the tribute art has paid to packaging.

The genius of pop art was, of course, that it never pretended otherwise. It loved the commercial package. Let the moody Guses of Abstract Expressionism like Franz Kline, Barnett Newman, and Clyfford Still mull things over down at Rothko's chapel; the pop artists of the 1960s were on their way to the grocery store. Then off to the bank. No lugubrious rigors, no tortured disquisitions on the meaning of paint, no metaphysics of marginality for them. Just get me to the package, pop said, no need to unwrap it.

Pop art was simply that—*popular* art: art that made no pretense about distinctions, art that collapsed hierarchies, art that celebrated what we shared not what separated us, and, most annoyingly for those who cherish the romantic myth of the alienated artist, art dedicated to making money. "To me," said Andy Warhol, "business is the highest form of art." He wasn't kidding. To conduct this business the artist detailed what we know and what we are attracted to. We all know exactly what that is; it is our carnival commercial culture of highly decorated surfaces.

If, to highcult pundits, packaging was the toxic gas of commercialism, to pop artists it was the divine afflatus. They reveled in it. Packaging was, after all, not just "the surface art of capitalism," not just "capitalism's way of saying 'I love you' to itself," it was the indigenous art of America. Product design and packaging was what we had. No critics were necessary; no priestly class of intercessionaries need apply; the subjects and the treatment of pop were as known to us as the stages of the cross were known to Florentines. Ballentine beer cans, Brillo boxes, Campbell's soup cans, Spaghetti-Os, VWs, Mott's apple juice, Kellogg's corn flakes, Del Monte peach halves, Lipton soup mixes, Lucky Strikes, Coca-Cola bottles, huge flaccid hamburgers and erect lipsticks, you name it. If it had life on the shelf, it was captured and moved into the museum. Pop was a labor of consumptive love.

Pop art appropriated the *mentalité* of wrapping things up. Better yet, it appropriated the methods of packaged production. Just as it was in the Renaissance, the process could be industrialized. The mechanized silk screen made this possible. Imitation was no longer a term of opprobrium. Appropriation became the modus operandi. Fine art could be dissolved into mass media, mass-produced for mass consumption.

Recall that before Andy Warhol became a foppish circus barker of the 1960s, he had spent the 1950s churning out magazine graphics, newspaper advertisements, menu illustrations, fabric motifs, record-album covers, book jackets, Christmas card designs, photographs of department store window treatments, and enough illustrations of women's shoes to indulge a foot fetishist's fantasy for a lifetime. Just as the Florentine painter and friar Lippo Lippi spent hours reflecting in church surrounded by what he loved, after Warhol became famous he spent most of his time shopping.

In many ways Warhol's artistic life was the epitome of commercial culture. It started with his debut exhibition in 1962 in the Los Angeles Ferus gallery where he lined up thirty-two paintings of Campbell's soup cans. This number was determined not by aesthetic necessity, but by the number of available soups. Warhol's wry repetition called attention to the iconic status of this humble container and the mindless repetition of packaging. Soup, a symbol of maternal love—the ultimate comfort food—was rendered immaculate and inhuman by its sterilized can.

This can of soup, Warhol all but stated, was the true Madonna of our secular times.[17]

Truman Capote once called Warhol "a sphinx with no secret," and the artist himself claimed that everything to know about him was on "the surface of my paintings and films and me." True enough. Warhol adored the surface, the wrapping, the container, the package. When you look at the stuff he consumed, from soup bowls to nut jars, you see it had one thing in common. It was stuff holding stuff. He had no pretensions, no secrets; he just loved packaging. The very act of mechanical creation turbocharged the process. He called his studio the Factory, and his means of production were the same as his habits of consumption: machined en masse.

But once you say that pop loved packages, what's left? Not much. Pop was a dead end. Like dada, which also idealized the container (recall Man Ray's *Pechage* or Duchamp's *Boîte en Valise*), it was bad *art*. It was meant to be. Pop was devoid of complex aspiration by design. It was a mirror always, never a lamp. By the end of the 1960s pop had essentially lost its way. Fast Moving Consumer Goods, canned food, cosmetics, plastics, glitz, oversize packaging, emblems, audio-visual aids, blinking lights left the studio and returned to the store. Again, as in the Renaissance, designers went to where the money was, and in commercial culture the money is on the outside of a package of reduced-fat chocolate-chip cookies, not inside the gallery.

Depending on your point of view, pop art was either the surrender to, or the victory of, worldly goods. Packaging *über alles*. The pop artists saw the commercial commodity in almost human terms. What they overlooked, or probably didn't care for, was the fact that advertising, packaging, marketing, branding, fashion—in short, buying and selling—was tied to deep-seated desires on both sides of the transaction.

---

17. Warhol accumulated an estate of almost ten thousand objects—from rare antiques to flea-market junk. Just to inventory all the items took several weeks, and the objects had to be grouped into three thousand lots with bid estimates based on the market value of comparable pieces lest the sale drag on for weeks. Rather like the recent sales of the estate of Jacqueline Kennedy Onassis, Princess Di's wardrobe, or the Duke and Duchess of Windsor's household effects, Andy's things in death had achieved the cartoon state of associational magnificence, "sensation transference" from celebrity to commoner. The objects themselves had become packages of value and the market reflected that.

Producer and consumer want to talk about, and even *with,* the things they manufacture and buy. What is now called brand personality (which, after all, pop enjoyed discussing) is not a concoction of com-mercialism, but the result of a deep desire to personify object reality and give it pizzazz.

✳ *TWO EXAMPLES OUTSIDE THE CANON: CORNELL AND CHRISTO*

One sees this interchange not just in the high pop of the 1960s, but in the earlier and later versions as well. Let us look at just two artists: one precursor, whose very private world consisted of telling tales in boxes—Joseph Cornell; and one more contemporary artist whose world is en-tirely public and whose creations consist of covering what has already been created—the provocatively named Christo.

Looking at the shadow boxes of Joseph Cornell, most made between 1940 and 1960, one sees nothing of the wry ironic humor of pop. In-stead one sees a kind of misty romanticism, a childlike innocence putting small things inside small spaces, a nostalgic placement and jux-taposition that quietly moves without disturbing. Cornell was quiet for a reason. Many of his boxes seem made as a kind of sentimental offer-ing of experience for his disabled brother, Robert. Joseph would pick up all manner of small objects on his job hawking textile samples around lower Manhattan. He brought them home to his dreary clapboard house on Utopia Parkway in Flushing, Queens and cached the booty in the cellar. Shells, butterfly wings, sand, buttons, stuffed birds, marbles, pictures of ballerinas and movie stars (his Marilyn Monroe predated Andy Warhol's), bits of costumes, pennies, feathers. Victorian toys, stuffed animals, letterheads from French hotels, clay pipes—you name it, he filed it away. Countless ordinary objects, toys, and other childhood treasures and mementos were saved, carefully stored in labeled shoe boxes and later retrieved for his work.

Putting things in boxes is ancient. There is safety in boxes. We recognize that little things likely to be lost are less vulnerable in boxes. Cornell transformed lowly old ephemera into evocative and appealing forms *because* they were confined in small spaces. They are trivial objects; that's just the point. But like Keats observing the forms on a Grecian urn, Cornell seems to be saying to us as to his brother: make of them what you will. There is ambiguity and mystery rather than clar-ity of meaning in these 3-D collages. In them we find a little world made cunningly of familiar things magically transformed into the realm of poetry, fantasy, and myth.

In a way Christo is Cornell's opposite partner. While Cornell wished to make the mundane mythic, Christo wants to make the mythic mundane. Christo's art (and many would dispute the term) is to cover, wrap, put away, package. He takes the present object that you think you know and makes it only a silhouette, a shadow. In a kind of playful unwinding of Bishop Berkeley's famous "essi est percepti," Christo makes you wonder if reality can be perceived at all. Maybe a tree falling in a deserted forest doesn't have to make a sound.[18]

Christo, who is now in his mid-sixties, was born Christo Javacheff in Bulgaria. As a child, he started by draping things, then in the 1950s he developed a penchant for swaddling things like cans, bottles, and oil barrels in fabric and rope. From these he went on to covering a car with cellophane and putting tinfoil on a statue. Christo was making his point about packaged culture. As children know and adults may have forgotten, cover/uncover, hide/find, conceal/reveal is a source of almost primordial excitement.

A decade later, Christo stepped up the current. In *The Wrapped Pont Neuf* in Paris, for example, the entire bridge was wrapped. See, he said, how arbitrary the Left Bank/Right Bank dichotomy had now become. The immortality and placement of art was being challenged. In *Ocean Front*, he covered some 150,000 square feet of watery cove in Newport, Rhode Island with white polypropylene, and in *Surrounded Islands*, he did the same, encircling islands in Biscayne Bay, Florida, with shocking pink fabric. For *Valley Curtain* he stretched some 200,000 square feet of orange nylon across the Grand Hogback valley in Rifle, Colorado.

Christo's pièce de résistance was draping the Berlin Reichstag. He had wrapped buildings before—always art institutions like the Kunsthalle in Bern, Switzerland (1968), or Chicago's Museum of Contemporary Art (1969). The old German parliament was a different object with a much different history. This was not a container of art, but a repository of nationalism. Built in 1894, gutted by a mysterious fire in 1933

---

18. Christo's oeuvre has a decided Emperor's New Clothes quality to it. How many times can you ring this bell? Then there is the (possibly apocryphal) story of the Christo wrapped chair sculpture delivered to an auction house where, to the horror of its owner, a porter unwrapped it. The objet d'art had to be sent back to the artist, to be wrapped again.

that Hitler used as an excuse to declare emergency rule, the building was captured by the Russians in 1945, restored in the 1960s, and left unused during the cold war years. Again Christo argued that his draping effaced history, for the Reichstag no longer sat on the West Berlin side of the Berlin Wall, but with Christo's art it sat nowhere.[19]

When interviewed, Christo usually encourages comparisons with Claude Monet's variations on the theme of Rouen Cathedral, or Rodin's covering his figure of Balzac with a cape. What they are doing, Christo claims, is shrouding the structure, hiding details and ornaments, and hence highlighting the internal truth. Christo maintains that throughout the history of art, the use of cover has been a fascination for artists. What Christo does not say is that it is precisely this activity that characterizes the commercial world of packaged goods, a world he claims to despise but is so clearly part of.

✳ POP IN RETROSPECT

To a remarkable degree, your estimation of pop art, even a pop that includes Cornell and Christo, will depend on how old you are and how deep you are immersed in the world of packaging. "Pop is about liking things," Andy Warhol once commented, but he might have added "especially certain things." The objects that mainstream pop liked best were those staples of the grocery store. In fact, one could write a treatise on pop at the supermarket. While Cornell would have made art from the detritus he found outside the store and Christo would have wanted to cover it in fabric, the store, filled with packages, is a central icon. Let's go shopping, pop said, and we did.

Canned, bottled, tubed, pressed, sealed, and processed goods are as much a part of the iconography of Warhol, Wesselmann, Rosenquist,

---

19. Christo loves to point out that the *Wrapped Reichstag, Berlin, 1971–1995* took twenty-four years to complete, much of that time spent convincing the German government the project should be done. Ninety professional climbers and 120 other workers took six days to cloak the building, with its four towers and two courtyards, in a thick chainmail of aluminum. Over this, polypropylene fabric was secured by ten miles of blue rope. Statues and stone vases were also covered under specially made cages to alter the silhouette's outline. Surely this was the ultimate package.

Rauschenberg, Johns, Oldenburg, and Lichtenstein as holy Madonnas and crucified Christs were for the Florentines. Claes Oldenburg knew exactly what he was doing when he assembled *The Store* in 1961. His store was filled with plaster reliefs and three-dimensional objects of ordinary commercial stuff. It seemed to be spilling out of the windows. Oldenburg's refusal to separate the commodities in the store from those put in an art gallery was more than a mischievous elevation of

➤   Is it an ad or is it pop art? (Scoresby Scotch Whisky, 1990)

such subjects, it was an admission that they can't be separated. Art and commerce are one in commercial culture, just as art and religion were one in the Renaissance.

I don't mean to stretch this hoary comparison too far, but if art does indeed reconfigure the world around it, then pop—short-lived as it was—had a far more lasting impact than most other modern movements. In a prescient way Lichtenstein's 1962 painting that he called *Masterpiece* effectively forecast the future. In stereotypical comic images of a beautiful blonde and her handsome companion, the balloon dialogue tells the story: "Why, Brad Darling, This Painting is a MASTER-PIECE! My, Soon You'll Have All of NEW YORK Clamoring for Your Work." The important clamor for pop was not only that it created a new breed of gallery owner and collector (it did) and annoyed most highcult critics (it did) but also that it changed the way we looked at the world around us. What it took from commercialism it more than returned by reshaping it. In the modern cant, it privileged packaging and made it safe to discuss without embarrassment. It made the commercial object, the package, just one remove away from the masterpiece.

Commercialism is now busily repaying the homage. Before you go to the store you see pop campaigns like the print ads for Smartfood popcorn showing thought balloons filled with smart-alecky ideas hovering above the heads of consumers; the slogan: "You can't get it off your mind." Or what of the long-running ad campaign for Scoresby scotch telling tales in huge benday dots of Cheryl and Todd? By the time you get to the store you are hardly surprised. Pop art is popping up on product packages. The brightly colored cartoon and comic strip images are in every aisle. Just look at soft drink cans, for instance: Pepsi-Cola, Cherry Coke, Diet Cherry Coke, and Hawaiian Fruit Punch are splashed with pop pictures of surfers, sunglasses, and lips outlined in cherry-red lipstick. Better yet, look at the supercaffeinated, pick-me-up drinks like Mountain Dew, Mellow Yellow, Jolt, or Surge and you will think you are in an explosion in a pop factory. Perhaps it is linguistic justice that soda pop and pop art should finally come together in one tribute to the enduring allure and cultural primacy of the package.

5

The Branding of Experience

Or Why the Label Has Moved from Inside the Collar to Outside on the Shirt

If this business were to be split up, I would be glad to take the brands, trademarks, and goodwill. You could have all the bricks and mortar—and I would fare better than you.

—John Stuart, Chairman, Quaker Oats Ltd., 1974.

AS the nineteenth century was coming to a close, Anthony Trollope wrote a fictional interpretation of his contemporary culture called *The Way We Live Now*. Trollope intended to explain how the everyday life of his time was held together. Like other popular novelists, he created upper-crust characters by moving them through a milieu of dinner parties, political squabbles, club activities, church functions, and trips between various country and city houses.

As it always does, art reflected life. And the art genre that described this kind of life was the "novel of manners." This term is one of the few appropriate litcrit terms because the reader really does learn about the hoity-toities from observing their social interactions.

The reading public then had as finely developed a sense of decorum as we now have toward what we see on TV. Knowing the appropriate fork at the Drones club was as important for them as our knowing how to behave on Super Bowl Sunday or during the Oscar telecast.

Along with a knowledge of class manners and family pedigree, the Victorian novelist established his dramatis personae by moving them through specific terrain, be it a fictional world like Barchester or a very real one like the City district of London. His readers understood the importance of place because geography also denoted social status. Place mirrored personality.

In *The Way We Live Now,* Augustus Melmotte, a Jew, comes from Paris to London with his daughter and his Bohemian wife. When the action of the novel is over and he has committed suicide because he cannot fit in, wife and daughter head off to America—to San Francisco, to be exact. Trollope is always exact in letting you know that geography determines character. These women could never breathe easily in London. So too we know that Ruby Ruggles and her bumpkin brother belong at Sheep's Acre Farm and that Roger Carbury should preside over Carbury Hall. Sir Felix Carbury, fallen from grace, must go to Germany—there is no room for his kind, no club that will accept him. Mrs. Hurtle comes from San Francisco and in the end must return there.

Any Trollope lover worth his salt can tell you much about the protagonists simply by such comings and goings. These paths are the code by which our grandparents recognized, in Dominick Dunne's felicitous title, those who are "people like us": our kind/not our kind.

The Victorian reading public needed such shorthand because *things* had no brand personalities—manners, places, sinecures—and bloodlines did. Salaries meant little, accomplishments even less. Characters were separated by city club, pew, country house, and family trees. The central acts of *The Way We Live Now* are the attempts by Augustus Melmotte to buy a titled husband for his daughter and get a named estate for himself. He can't do it, of course—how silly to try even if he is "the City's most powerful financier."

Trollope was hardly alone in charting this territory. All the great Victorian popular novelists—Dickens, Eliot, James, Thackeray, Meredith, Hardy, Gissing—outlined character in much the same way. They had to. What else was there? They focused on social status and minute description of manners because there was little else. It is not that the Victorians were snobs, although they certainly seem that way to us. They simply had no other social algebra into which they could compute the value of Mr. X and Miss Y.

What the modern chroniclers like Bret Easton Ellis, Tom Wolfe, Jay McInerney or Joyce Carol Oates do with the name of a restaurant, a brand of shoe, a T-shirt, or even a Mont Blanc pen, their Victorian predecessor did with a gentleman's club, a political affiliation, or the placement of the family burial plot. In the Victorian novel, characters are like sharks; they must move around from named place to place or die. In the modern novel, characters are no different. They must spend a little time going from store to store shopping for defining objects.

A popular novelist today can/must create character using manufactured things—not just any commercial things, but those with a peculiarly modern kind of modern thing: the branded object. Having them is what we have for manners.

✳ BRANDED GOODS AS CULTURAL MARKERS: A ROSE BY ANY NAME WOULD NOT SMELL AS SWEET

Consider just two of our modern popular novelists, Ian Fleming and Stephen King, in comparison with the great Victorian novelists. I don't mean to make them Trollopeans of our times (from John O'Hara to John Updike, we have not lacked for chroniclers of manners), but I do want to place them in the constellation of popular writers who have generated compelling characters almost exclusively by showing their associations with store-bought things. The named country estate for Trollope is the branded gin for Ian Fleming.

Just as our great-grandparents knew the social habits and family history of Augustus Melmotte, Eustacia Vye, Becky Sharp, or Uriah Heep, who among us does not know that James Bond drove an Aston Martin; that he was a bulk consumer of designer names like Guerlain, Lanvin, Yardley, Rolex, and Cartier; that he agonized over his martini (shaken not stirred); and that pages of descriptive prose would surround his choice of champagne (Mouton Rothschild 1953, if you please). When 007 in *Live and Let Die* goes with his wish list to the FBI he gets what he wants:

> a Swank tie-clip in the shape of a whip, an alligator-skin billfold from Mark Cross, a plain Zippo lighter, a plastic Travel-Pac containing razor, hairbrush and toothbrush, a pair of horn-rimmed glasses with plain lenses, various other oddments and, finally, a lightweight Hartmann Skymate suitcase to contain all these things. (72).

Linguists call this substitution of brandnames for generics "taxonomic particularizing." We call it "telling it like it is." In the modern consumerist world, this invocation of brandnames is not only a way to create the illusion of reality—it is reality. We may not know what the objects are, but we know the names.

Stephen King, who refers to himself as "the literary equivalent of a Big Mac and fries," writes stories awash in brandnames that all Americans know. There are few Rolls-Royces and Rolexes here and certainly no Mouton Rothschild 1953, but there are reams of brandnames. Here are a few from just one novella, *Art Pupil:* Schwinn, Nike, *Time,* A.1. Steak Sauce, Motorola, Kools, Keds, Kodak, Scotch tape, Ring-Dings, Coke, Hyatt, Diamond Blue-Tip matches, Krazy Glue, Porsche, Shell No-Pest Strip, Big Macs, *Penthouse,* Revlon, *Reader's Digest,* Wildroot Cream Oil, Budweiser, Lawn-Boy, IBM, Hush Puppies, Smokenders, and Winchester.

These popular writers are not alone in tying their fiction to the world we know. As Tom Wolfe has mentioned, the phenomenon of "Kmart realism" is upon us because the only recognized world is what we see in the aisles of Kmart. If our rites of passage are through a thicket of "advertised on TV" brandnames, why should we expect something different from our fictional counterparts?

Novels are hardly alone. Take a look at Wendy Wasserstein's 1990s hit *The Sisters Rosensweig.* Not only do the sisters know each other through their branded objects, but the play itself turns on one of the sister's possessing a genuine Chanel suit. This is a Broadway play, not a mid-cult novel, so the names are ratcheted up a notch or two. We make sense of the fictional characters because we already know the brand personalities of their defining objects.

So in *The Sisters Rosensweig* we are told who owns what. Louis Vuitton handbags, Asprey candlesticks, Manolo Blahnik mules, Ungaro suits, Birkenstock sandals, Wedgwood and majolica pottery, Retin-A, Susie Cooper china, Portobello Road antiques, Ralph Lauren shirts, Fruit of the Loom underwear, *Newsweek,* Diet Coke, Tanino Crisci, Harrods, *The Financial Times,* a Turnbull & Asser shirt, and even a Filene's bag are signifiers of personality and social status. One of the sisters—as you might imagine the most American of the lot—vows that if she gets the cable television job she's after, "I'm marching myself right into Saks and treating myself to Bruno Maglis, Ferragamos and Manulo Blanchikis." To get the joke not only do you have to realize that this last item is a mispronunciation of "Manolo Blahnik," but you also have to know what that is. (It's a snazzy shoe favored by fashion editors, socialites, and Hollywood stars.) You don't have to get the joke, but you do have to get the point: clothes don't make the woman, brands do.

✳ WHY NO ONE COMPLAINS WHEN BRANDED PRODUCTS APPEAR IN MOVIES

In the spirit of the times, on opening night, Chanel sent Ms. Wasserstein flowers and after the opening Ferragamo sent free shoes. They didn't have to. Ms. Wasserstein needed them as much as they needed her. The companies sent their products not to bribe but to acknowledge. What they were acknowledging is the intimate connection in popular culture between creating entertainment and sharing brand awareness.

The ability to generate instantaneous verisimilitude is why product placement has so quickly become part of almost every Hollywood movie. The more expensive and successful a movie, the more likely the appearance of branded products. If we ever saw a generic beer or an insignia-free automobile in a blockbuster movie we would say to ourselves, "Ah, this is just a poorly produced movie—they couldn't even get any payola." It is certainly a sign of our times that if a high-cult literary author were ever to take a kickback from a company for plugging a product, we would be outraged. But if Hollywood studios *don't* do it, we consider them tacky.

That is because novels are now a generation or two behind the movies. They haven't caught up. Whereas readers would probably join a class action to sue an offending author, no one ever thinks of suing a studio. Product placement will come to novels, but it will never really be successful. Readers are, by and large, unmotivated consumers, long past prime branding time—not too poor, but too old.

Moviegoers aren't. One of the most interesting lawsuits brewing in Hollywood has been over the matter of product placement run amok. Reebok, the shoe company, took Tristar Pictures, a subsidiary of Sony, to court for reneging on a promise to present certain brands of its athletic shoes in a positive light. The bone of contention is the movie *Jerry Maguire*, in which a mercurial professional football player, Ron Tidwell, played by Cuba Gooding Jr., rails against the sponsorship of commercial interests that have passed him by. Finally, after he has had a great season, he signs a whopping sponsorship deal with, you guessed it, Reebok. He hits the big time and makes a commercial. All ends happily. Or at least that was the plan.

Reebok certainly thought so. To make sure this happened, they had provided Tristar with more than $1.5 million in merchandise, advertising, promotional support, and other benefits. They even provided the very commercial they thought would be inserted at the triumphal ending. The happy audience would leave the theater remembering this commercial in which Reebok declares, "Rod Tidwell. We ignored him for years. We were wrong. We're sorry." Reebok planned to use this very commercial on television. What a coup! What synergy!

But in audience previews, the movie producers found that railing against Reebok tested better than the sellout, and so they left Reebok unredeemed. No deal with Tidwell. No commercial. No backscratching. So not only did Reebok not get positive play, it got hammered. Lawyers for the shoe company bolted across the line of scrimmage, filing suit just days after *Jerry Maguire* opened to critical acclaim and box-office success.

Although the parties reached an out-of-court settlement in which the commercial was restored to cable and videocassette versions, the Reebok suit underscores the growing importance and persistent practice of product placement. Everyone is served: the studio defrays cost, the manufacturer gets his message across to a captive audience, and the audience (supposedly) appreciates seeing the world it recognizes and can quickly associate with.

✳ THE BRANDNAME AS HERO

The migration of commercial names into the popular arts has been both sudden and far-reaching. In a study only an academic could appreciate, *A "Brand" New Language: Commercial Influences in Literature and Culture*, Monroe Friedman actually does a count of the brandnames of known commodities as they have become ligatures holding our shared fictional reality together.

Since he is a psychologist, a research consultant to numerous federal commissions, and a statistician, Professor Friedman did all kinds of sorting of his data to make sure they fairly represented the culture that was consuming/creating them. So for instance, when he was dealing with best-selling books since the late 1940s, he coded the 2,931,400 words by copyright date, time and place restrictions (eliminating historical novels and novels with foreign locales), as well as novels set in institutional environments outside the mainstream, such as mental hospitals, army bases, and the like.

In a graph is what he found about the frequency of brandname mention in popular American plays, novels, and songs, as well as British plays. You don't need to be an account executive to see that the explosive increase in use of brandnames occurs at the same time television advertising is becoming the dominant source of communal knowledge.

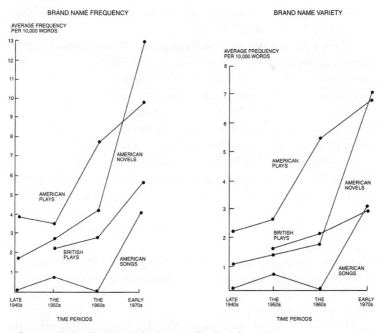

• Frequency and variety of Brand Names in Popular American Plays, Novels, Songs, and British Plays. SOURCE: From Monroe Friedman, A "Brand" New Language: Commercial Influences in Literature and Culture, pp. 78-79.

➤ Frequency and variety of brandnames in popular American plays, novels, songs, and British plays. (Monroe Friedman, A "Brand" New Language: Commercial Influences in Literature and Culture, 78–79)

✳ *THE BRANDING OF THE WAY WE LIVE NOW*

The reason these corporate names are all over the place is that branding is the keystone of commercial culture. Burning your mark on whatever is flying off the assembly line is at the heart of modern marketing. Branding was inevitable. It had to be. Once the machine could be applied to production, anyone who had the machine also had the ability to flood the market with his own version of your product. Without some way to differentiate your cigarette, shoe, or shirt, the very economies of mass production that could increase your profits could bankrupt you. The only thing worse than dearth is glut.

When we think of branding, we invariably think of the scene in the Western movie where the young cowpokes rope and brand steers under the watchful eye of John Wayne. Smoke sizzles off the red-hot iron. The calf bellows. Let Mr. Wayne find his branded dogies in somebody else's herd and you'll hear more bellowing.

At first, branding was not so violent in real life and had more to do with informing middlemen of shipping instructions than with marking personal property. A brand was essentially a sign applied with blacking brush or hot iron to a bale or cask, showing where contents came from as well as who had done the shipping. Once retailers passed on this information to consumers, it was only a matter of time before they too were asking for cotton or coffee from a certain container.

The next step was crucial. The end product soon carried the brand, even though such information was unnecessary to the middleman. In fact, if anything, the retailer was hurt by branding because it meant that he had lost control of the sale. If you walked into the candy store and asked for cookies, the confectioner would send you to the cookies he wanted to move, the ones with the highest markup. But if you asked for Oreos, you know, the ones with the orb and cross branded on *every* cookie, you had the power and the profit went to the manufacturer.[1]

---

1. If you want to see this branding process currently unfolding, look at the numerous ads and promos for pharmaceutical products flooding through print and electronic media. While the drug companies used to target the pharmacy or the doctor for prescription drugs, now they are heading for the end user. If they are successful, the patient approaches the doctor and says, "I need Rogaine. I need Proscar. I need Claritin. I need Prozac. I need

No one initially knew how powerful this process could become and that is why a few really powerful brands got loose and, ironically, shifted the process into reverse. Instead of becoming progressively proprietary a few brands became progressively generic. They became so popular that the brand became the name of the commodity. Think only of the linguistic transformations wrought on Band-Aid, Kleenex, Hoover, Walkman, Thermos, Jeep, Vaseline as well as on lower-cased, erstwhile trademarked, but now unprotected zipper, cellophane, aspirin, formica, and yo-yo, and you will see how dynamic the branding process can become. Little wonder Xerox® makes such an almighty fuss lest it become confused with generic copying.

❋ WHERE BRANDING CAME FROM

This transformation from generic to branded started about the same time Trollope was writing *The Way We Live Now.* By the late nineteenth century, brandnames were appearing on wrapping for, say, coffee, soap, tea, or yeast. The customer would purchase the product "by the paper," which referred to the rough weight of what could be held in an envelope.[2] With clothing, brand marks moved from the package to appear on tags, such as on Levi's jeans, or inside the collar as with Arrow shirts. In a curious example of what goes around comes around, the brand is now back on the surface—literally stamped on the product—like René Lacoste's alligator, Ralph Lauren's Polo pony, Gucci's G, or even Tommy Hilfiger's entire name.

There is a good marketing reason for this display of brand. You can't advertise without it. Make all the machine-made biscuits, shoes, ciga-

---

Viagra." And when the pharmacist then suggests that perhaps another version will do, the properly prepared customer looks just the way Duke Wayne looks at the cattle rustlers.

2. Look at the way cocaine and heroin are hawked today on the street and you will see how tea was sold in the nineteenth century, just as Thomas Lipton came on the scene. When drug pushers name their versions of dope Homicide, Stingray, Manhattan Special, Mad Dog, or Dead Presidents, they are behaving just like early captains of industry.

The New Salesman Rebuked.

"Excuse him, Madam. He has not yet learned that our best class of customers all mean **PETER'S** when they ask for Eating Chocolates. They know from long experience that it deserves its great reputation for Purity, Wholesomeness, and Digestibility."

Lamont, Corliss & Co., Sole Agents, New York.

➤ How brandnames are established: it's not candy, it's a Baby Ruth. (Peter's Eating Chocolates, 1920s) rettes, automobiles, or computer chips you want; you can't sell effectively until you can call it a Ritz, a Nike, a Marlboro, a Chevrolet, or an Intel 586. If everybody's biscuits are in the same barrel, and if they look pretty much the same, it probably doesn't reward you to tell people to buy biscuits. Chances are they won't buy *your* biscuit. The money you spend lauding biscuits will never be returned.

As Thomas J. Barratt said halfway through the nineteenth century, "Any fool can make soap. It takes a clever man to sell it." Barratt was a clever man. He made a fortune by calling his soap Pears' Soap and making sure everyone knew about it by defacing miles of Anglo-American wall and newsprint space with "Have you had your Pears' today?" He stamped the Pears' name on every bar of the pear-shaped soap.

Not only did Barratt know that repeated assertion was as good as established fact, he also knew that establishing brand value is based on association. Like so much else in the commercial world, magical thinking is the trigger that makes meaning. So if you want to associate your brand with good health, you simply show a happy doctor prescribing the brand to his trusting clients. Since we don't all know the same doctors, you could choose a mythical doctor and it would work just as well. Barratt was the first to use nurses in starched white uniforms to testify to his soap's therapeutic values.[3]

✳ HOW BRANDING WORKS

If you are selling a product like soap, where every competitor is using the same ingredients, you associate your product with the lasting values of some eternal verity like beauty, health, youth or, in Barratt's case, works of high culture—works of art. If you look at the lower right-hand corner of the Pears' ad, you will see that is exactly what Barratt has

---

3. When commercials were made some twenty-five years ago in which Chris Robinson and Peter Bergman, actors who portrayed doctors on soap operas, sold cold medicine by admitting, "I am not a doctor, but I play one on TV," the audience didn't care. Better yet was Robert Young. A film star who played various roles to an earlier generation, to us he was Marcus Welby, M.D. When he prescribed decaf coffee for upset nerves, many people thought it was medical advice.

done to sell soap. He has stamped his product name onto a work of art—literally![4]

And in so doing Barratt changed forever the nature of brand creation. He blurred the once bright line between art and advertising, between high culture and the vulgar. What the Victorians had rent asunder, namely, art and commerce, was now rejoined. In a strange sense, selling by brand returned to principles established by the mendicant orders of the Holy Roman Catholic Church. The renaissance of art as a selling tool began anew. Only now the sponsors had changed.

Barratt's great claim to fame in the advertising world was his dedication to saturation campaigns. Like modern-day cola ads, the Pears' brand appeared everywhere. It was said of the Catholic Church of the sixteenth century that a peasant would never be able to escape the iconography of the Church. The shape of the cross was purposefully built into his house—in the door frame, in the bedstead, and even into the place setting of eating utensils. Barratt, the modern pope of the new redemption through consumption, is said to have painted "Good Morning! Have You Used Your Pears' Soap?" on so many surfaces that genteel people were bashful about greeting each other with the Good Morning salutation lest they be contaminated with vulgar commercialism. In a variation of cleanliness being next to godliness, Barratt was even able to wrangle a testimonial from Henry Ward Beecher—the eminent American minister—one of the first celebrity endorsements in the modern world.

Lest you think Barratt was a lone wolf among Victorian sheep, James Gamble in Ohio was doing very much the same thing with Ivory Soap. Once he discovered (by not turning off the mixing machines in time) that if soap is superaerated it will float, he built the brand by

---

4. This sacrilege or miscegenation of cultures, depending on your favorite Victorian trope, had a curious history. Sir John E. Millais had painted his grandson watching a soap bubble he had just blown through a clay pipe. The painting was warmly received as *A Child's World* at the Royal Academy. Here was Victorian childhood personified. Sir William Ingram bought the painting to use as a full-page illustration in the 1887 Christmas number of *The Illustrated London News*. Like other magazines of the time, the *ILN* was then engaged in the circulation-building tactic of covering its pages with "images suitable for framing." Once he had used the image, however, Ingram sold the painting and all its rights to Barratt. Predictably, *A Child's World* soon became *A Child's World with Pears' Soap*.

➤   Art sells soap: Pears' commandeers John Millais's *Bubbles*. (Pears' Soap, 1880s)

claiming that purity was what causes flotation. The claim that "It floats!"—based on "99 44-100 per cent. pure"—stuck. If Barratt owned art, Gamble owned purity. We all know which association sells more soap.

✳ MODERN BRANDING À LA SEINFELD

Clearly the psychopathology of branding is buried deep in the human yearning for material to mean something, to matter. As we have seen, the soul of materialism is suspiciously close to the soul of heavenly redemption. Clearly, in many instances we want the sizzle not the steak, we want the signifier not the signified, we want the myth not the material.

Once again, if you want to understand modern commercial culture you can do no better than to watch *Seinfeld*. Although J. Peterman is a spacy and loopy character who employs Elaine to write catalog copy for his mail-order business, he is based on a

THE "IVORY" is a Laundry Soap, with all the fine qualities of a choice Toilet Soap, and is 99 44-100 per cent. pure.

Ladies will find this Soap especially adapted for washing laces, infants' clothing, silk hose, cleaning gloves and all articles of fine texture and delicate color, and for the varied uses about the house that daily arise, requiring the use of soap that is above the ordinary in quality.

For the Bath, Toilet, or Nursery it is preferred to most of the Soaps sold for toilet use, being purer and much more pleasant and effective and possessing all the desirable properties of the finest unadulterated White Castile Soap. The Ivory Soap will " float."

The cakes are so shaped that they may be used entire for general purposes or divided with a stout thread (as illustrated) into two perfectly formed cakes, of convenient size for toilet use.

The price, compared to the quality and the size of the cakes, makes it the cheapest Soap for everybody for every want. TRY IT.

SOLD EVERYWHERE.

➤ Ivory Soap: so pure it floats—a claim now more than a hundred years old. (Procter & Gamble, 1882)

real marketing genius. What the real J(ohn) Peterman knows is that you
don't wear clothes, you wear a story. In his catalog, called the "Owner's
Manual," he gives you a story for every object. Every sweater and sock
in the off-size catalog comes complete with a detailed drawing and a
witty—at times too witty—paragraph description. This description is
not of the object as much as of its ethos as seen by the quirky Peterman
persona. Here, for example, is a pair of black silk pajamas that you
could buy at any mall anchor store:

> Somewhere in December, somewhere between Gramercy Park and
> Basin Street a beautiful woman is opening a present. The man knows
> her, but not very well. He would like to. She would like him to. She is
> used to a certain lack of imagination from new admirers. She sighs. (36)

One can see why such loopiness would appeal to Jerry and the show's
resident genius, Larry David. Peterman is just so over the top. But what
he is doing is exactly what L.L. Bean, J. Crew, Talbots, and Eddie Bauer
attempt to do. He is trying to create a brand personality for each object
on the fly. As with the other catalog companies, Peterman has a "home"
product, the ankle-length cowboy duster that invests the other products
with a romantic air the same way L.L. Bean's rubberized winter boot
sets the rugged tone for the rest of his merchandise. What other catalogs do with shiny photographs, catchy color names, and rural locations, Peterman does by translating the aura of rumbling through tun-
nels on the Orient Express to a pair of Edwardian-style slippers. It's a
tour de force of branding and Seinfeld knows it.

✳ *PREMODERN BRANDING À LA GLOOMSTERS*

While *Seinfeld* clearly has fun sending up Mr. Peterman (who himself
has fun traveling down to the bank), such has not always been the response in American culture. The idea that we wear a car like clothing,
drink the advertising not the beer, and prefer the story to the slippers
seemed to the sociologists of the late 1940s and 1950s proof that capitalism had gone bonkers. How could rational Americans, who had en-
dured the pangs of the Depression and wartime shortfalls, be so easily
led astray by the nonsense of branding? To this first generation of postwar critics, the peacetime surplus that brought on an unprecedented
flow of branded goods and the concomitant advertising was addling

modern consciousness. Focusing on the seeming illogic of branding more than on its insight into human yearning and aspiration, scholars like David Riesman, aided by Reuel Denney and Nathan Glazer, argued in books like *The Lonely Crowd* that we were being led astray, pulled against our "better instincts." Surely something must be wrong with the Edenic consumer to be believing the promises of Madison Avenue serpents.

Such interpretations that cast the consumer into the role of innocent victim were well received. They became bestsellers. *The Organization Man, The Man in the Grey Flannel Suit, The Status Seekers,* and especially *The Hidden Persuaders, The Want Makers,* and *The Affluent Society* became must-reads to a generation profoundly confused about a fundamental shift in consumption. The irrationality of buying the brand not the product was explained by such concepts as keeping up with the Joneses, subliminal suggestion, or simply, corporate interests infantalizing innocent consumers. Business bullies were picking on us. We were not just being led into temptation, we were being shoved.

But for those of us who grew up in the 1960s branding had already become second nature. Almost everything we consume is store-bought, packaged, stamped, branded. With the exception of the voluntary simplifiers and the back-to-the-landers, most of us have uncritically accepted the mediated life. Instead of seeing the process as degrading to human reason, we tend to see it as exchanging time for money. Why go to the Greasy Spoon where you might have a good burger, when you know exactly what is under the Golden Arches?[5]

Critics often used to talk about the consumer as if she, and increasingly he, were dolts. They shouldn't. According to research by BBDO, the international advertising agency, nearly two thirds of consumers worldwide know there are "no relevant or discernible differences" between rival brands across a broad range of products ("Shootout at

---

5. While one might think that as the relative cost of a shopper's time increased, there would be a greater demand for stores that offered higher levels of service in customer assistance, such has not been the case. Brands have proliferated and full-service retailing establishments have shrunk. Clearly what has happened is that consumers economize on time by purchasing brandname products. They patronize stores that essentially step aside and leave the brands alone. How ironic that the retail store that initially conspired with branding because it meant it could dispense with selling staff now finds that it is being dispensed with.

the Checkout" 69). They are right, of course. Technological advances in manufacturing have raised the quality of most goods and made it easier for competitors to copy one another's innovations—which are, anyway, typically minor and increasingly rare.

The consumer also knows that as goods have become less unique they have become bewilderingly abundant. Each year about 16,000 new products (including extensions of familiar names to new products) are introduced in America. This is happening all over the world, albeit at a slower rate. There are now 200 brands of breakfast cereal in America, 220 types of cigarettes in Holland, and 100 perfumes in Argentina. This torrent of brands, and the advertising avalanche that comes with it, has led to an interesting paradox. Perceptions of product parity are highest in markets like the United States, Western Europe, and Japan, where product proliferation is widest. It is lowest in those cultures with few interchangeable products. In other words, the more knowledgeable you are about branding, the more brands you get, and the less reason to believe in branding.[6]

✳ *THE GOLDEN AGE OF BRANDS*

We are living in the Golden Age of Brands. If the man on the street and the woman in the grocery store do not know this, they should ask their stockbroker. Thinking branded products were immune to economic swings, Wall Street has fallen in love with companies that can produce and maintain them. The principle of "What's in a name? A 50 percent markup" is powering one of the greatest bull markets of modern time.[7]

---

6. Of course, in the cultures like our own where brand consciousness is intense, branding easily turns to contrived parody. The faded Levi's, the rusted-out Volvo, the frayed Brooks Brothers shirt become a mode of subversion, a way of saying "I do not comply." However, even noncompliance is done via brands.
7. This love affair with strong brands started in the 1960s with the conglomeration of often dissimilar businesses. Companies with names like Transamerica, United Technologies, and Gulf+Western were supposedly the wave of the future. Who cared if golf balls and elevators were under the same corporate umbrella as whiskey and brassieres? The process accelerated in the 1980s as the leveraged "take outs" again removed brands from single companies and placed them in huge multinational corporations.

It used to be thought that brands, like humans, had lifetimes. They—to use Dr. Johnson's famous description of human vanity—"rose, shone, evaporated and fell." But no longer. Like the Energizer bunny, the Golden Arches, the Coke can, the Marlboro man can travel anywhere, anytime, to anybody. Some brands seem to have achieved what humans could only covet: eternal life.

Kohlberg Kravis Roberts paid $25 billion for RJR Nabisco (more than double its book value); Philip Morris bought Kraft for $12.9 billion (four times book value) and Nestlé spent $4.5 billion for Rowntree (five times). These seemingly outrageous multiples were based on the thinking that once a brand was established, the only way its price would move was up. After all, creating consumer loyalty meant retail price had become less significant. If the customer was buying the brand not the product, he or she didn't focus on what the underlying product was worth, but rather on how much association with the myth was worth.

By exploiting that supposed loyalty to famous names with price hikes well in excess of inflation, firms such as Kellogg, Gillette, and Heinz increased profits by 15 percent a year. By the beginning of the 1990s, shares in America's package-food firms were trading at a 30 percent premium in relation to Standard & Poor's 500-stock index. As could be predicted, there were even mutual funds established that held only companies that produced branded products. In the bull market of the late 1990s, nothing has changed. The companies managing worldwide brands are still charging ahead of the pack.

Why are these brands so powerful? Some years ago two researchers, one from Harvard and the other from Smith-Barney, a brokerage house, examined cosmetic preferences to develop a method for measuring how much extra consumers are willing to pay for the efficiency and sta-

---

The prevailing belief was that worldwide brands could be more efficiently marketed with worldwide advertising and worldwide packaging. As I write this, the current trend seems to be for the host company to sell off or job out manufacturing facilities while devoting itself to marketing. So Sara Lee Corp. lets someone else make sausages, briefcases, socks, shoe polish, and frosted cakes, while the home office nurtures the Champion, Playtex, Hanes, and Hillshire Farms brandnames. Like Nike, they will stitch the logo to products fabricated by others.

tus promised by branding (cited in Meyers 1995). The researchers started with *Consumer Reports* tests of the quality of lipsticks, mascaras, eye shadows, and face cleansers. The tests measured ease of use and removal, durability, smell, effect on skin, and similar qualities. Then they compared market surveys of the buying patterns of more than twelve thousand women who use these products.

What they found was that women used each of these products differently. The cosmetic use was sometimes secondary. For instance, lipsticks are often taken out in public, in the presence of other women. So fancy brands like Chanel, which come in elegant packages that can be spotted at a glance from a distance, command a premium price. Mascaras and eye shadows are less likely to be flashed around, so differences in packaging and branding of these products are less pronounced. Facial cleansers, in contrast, which are likely to reside in the bathroom medicine cabinet and be seen only by the occasional snoopy guest, have the lowest profit margins of branded cosmetics.

More interesting still, when the researchers compared the cost differences among these different cosmetics, they found that visibility of container *not* end use was the prime determinant. As expected, lipstick—the cosmetic most likely to be applied in public—attracts the most status buying and the greatest disparity between production cost and retail price. So at $2.26, a stick of Flame Glow costs nearly $19 an ounce. At $14.50 for a stick of Chanel that's a third smaller than Flame Glow, the higher priced lipstick is selling for $181 an ounce. Clearly, the appeal of lipstick brands rises with price, even though *Consumer Reports* found little difference among brands.

David Ogilvy, the famous advertising man, once said, "The consumer is no fool, she is your wife." Yet, it would seem that the lipstick study indicates P.T. Barnum's "a fool born every minute" is more appropriate. But what is being bought is time, not in the sense of the clock on the wall but in the sense of what it takes you to present the self you want to put forward. What is being bought is place, prestige, comfort, security, confidence, purpose, meaning. Forget the lipstick; what you apply is the brand.

This phenomenon is not limited to women buying cosmetics. Observe men buying cars, beer, or stereo equipment and you will see that we willingly set aside reason for the pleasures of association, aspiration, and self-applied status therapy. As they say in Detroit, you drive the nameplate. The dissociation of sensibility, which T. S. Eliot so confidently claimed was the hallmark of modern life, returns to a unity in the consuming life. Reason and passion unite in the metaphysics of the brand.

✳ *THE VOODOO OF BRANDING*

That the enchantment of the world should be achieved by willing conspiracies on both sides of commercial transactions seems so vulgar, so profane, so American at its worst. How awful that the real poets of modern life, those who attempt to manipulate and rearrange the signs of reality, are in marketing departments of large corporations and in large advertising agencies. Yet this is as self-evident as it is melancholy. We had better pay these "hierophants of unapprended inspiration," as Shelley called all those who try to arrange meaning for the rest of us, their due.

When you listen to marketing men speak, you might think you were in the company of Miltonic poets. They talk as if they know what they are doing—vindicating the ways of the market to man. They take marketing seriously in part because it is not enough to sell a product, the more difficult selling job is to convince the client to spend millions of dollars on something that can't really be measured. True, much of what they call research is ridiculous. Albert Lasker, founder of what is now Foote, Cone & Belding, said ad research is "something that tells you that a jackass has two ears"; and Ogilvy said it "functions as the lamp post to the drunk." Still, agencies know more about audiences than anyone else.[8] Marketers may well be the unacknowledged legislators of the world. They write much of the current code that links desire and yearning to the commercial world around us.

We manage desire, they say to their clients, not just products. And to sell the sponsors on their expertise they have a lexicon full of cant words surrounding the touchstone brand. So where they used to talk of brand loyalty, they now have concepts like brand equity—subdivided into brand value (the bottom line) and brand meaning (common percep-

---

178

↻

8. For instance, if we trust Dick Morris, the Clinton administration was run by focus groups constituted along well-established lines. It may not make for great government but it does get politicians re-elected.

tion). Brand meaning, in turn, is now divided into brand saliency (what used to be brand awareness), brand associations (the perceived characteristics of the brand, the images with which it is associated), brand personality (the type of human characteristics with which the brand is endowed), and even brand proposition (what to expect from consuming the brand). One West coast ad agency even claims they understand brand soul. Much of this is self-serving mumbo jumbo, to be sure, but just as Eskimos announce the centrality of snow by having some thirty descriptive words for puffs of frozen water, so the vocabulary explosion shows the primacy of branding.

✳ BRAND EXTENSION

Of all the recent developments in branding the most interesting is called brand extension. Like cloning, which it resembles in vocabulary and technique, brand extension is asexual reproduction. It is also magical. Once you have a brand personality established you simply take a bit of its DNA spirit and insert it into a different but analogous product. Once the audience is gathered, brand parthenogenesis takes place.

A few years ago, brand extension, the pushing out of goods from a home base, was thought to be one of the immutable advantages of branding. So Oreo cookies move sideways to become Oreo ice cream; Coke becomes Cherry Coke, then Diet Cherry Coke; Camel appears as Camel Filters, then as Camel Filters 100s; Tide in powder form becomes Liquid Tide; or Miller Beer brews Miller Lite, then Miller Ice. Eddie Bauer was originally a human being, then a clothing store, then an edition of a Ford Explorer, then a travel agency, then a sofa. Caterpillar, which makes earth-moving equipment, licenses its name for a work shoe. Jack Daniels markets a barbecue sauce. Clearly, the producer can shortcut the introduction costs of new goods by such piggybacking.

For some names this process does seem unstoppable. Whether they are automobiles, wristwatches, writing instruments, or sunglasses, all Porsche items supposedly express the Porsche "legend," and can be so identified. Most, if not all, consumers do not buy a Porsche wristwatch because it is a good and reliable watch, but because it reminds them of the brand legend and all it may stand for: precision engineering, sporty look, sophisticated design, German origin, etc. Likewise, Ferrari expects to make some $30 million in a few years by licensing its name

➤   Oreo brand extensions in 1991. (RJR Nabisco, photo by Barbara T. Weilbacher)

for such objects as ties, shirts, caps, watches, and even golf bags. The fact that almost no one can afford the cars only increases the allure of the brand.

But for other brands, extension is a dead end. Think only of the rousing failure of Kodak Floppy Disks, Milky Way Ice Cream, Arm & Hammer antiperspirant, or Life Savers Gum, all conceived and planned by the Masters of Marketing. The surest thing that can be said of brand extension is that it is usually a crap shoot.

★ **THE CENTRALITY OF LUXURY AND THE ASSOCIATION WITH ART**

More than other products, luxury items are clearly bought for what they mean, not for what they are. One sees the dynamics of brand association at work in the marketing of big-ticket objects, and it is here at the extreme, as it were, that we see how central commercialism is in organizing our lives. The luxury brand today func-

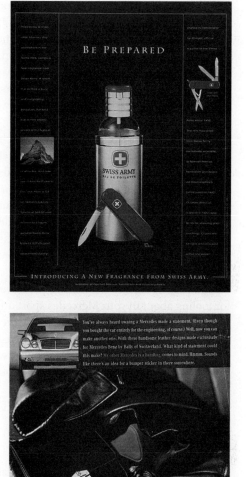

➤ Brands extended a bit far from home base: Swiss Army cologne and Mercedes-Benz handbags. (1990s)

tions as sumptuary laws once did by separating the exotic from the ordinary, the extravagant from the essential. In a culture in which family name, pew placement, educational affiliation, accent, and club membership count for little, brand accumulation becomes the marker of status by default. It is really all we have left. Wearing or displaying such a trumped-up luxury badge may not be the open sesame to social acceptance, but it is often the only security in a world sprung loose from traditional standards of judgment.

Thanks to the rise of trademarked merchandise and the licensing of designer names, the modern consumer can display desired rank in many simple ways. Anybody who can read can pick out a Rolex oyster or a Cartier tank watch. Who can't decode a Jaguar? Is there anyone on Wall Street who doesn't know how an Armani suit hangs? Admittedly, it might be easier and perhaps still more democratic just to have one's sense of self tastefully embroidered across the backs of nicely tailored jackets, but that is not the path we've taken. However, we've taken one close to it.

You may be hooted at wearing your overpriced Polo shirt, mocked for tooling about in your Mercedes sport utility vehicle, snickered at for falling over in your Gucci loafers, hectored for smoking your ersatz Cuban Double Coronas, but you will at least have the comfort of knowing that somewhere, some copywriter has written (maybe even tongue-in-cheek) a line or two assuring you that you have arrived. In a sense, in the way we live now, you have.

✳ THE RENAISSANCE AND BRANDING

Clearly, this phenomenon is not new. In fact, the beginnings of brand association can be seen in the Renaissance as individual families started to buy and display works of recognized artists as a way of displaying prominence. Read Vasari's *Lives of the Most Eminent Architects, Painters, & Sculptors* (1550) or Lisa Jardine's *Worldly Goods: A New History of the Renaissance* (1996) and you will see that artists started signing their names to what had been generic ecclesiastical objects as soon as the demand for such signed goods became a hallmark of displaying the owners' prominence.

Better yet, read Robert Browning's nineteenth-century poetry about Renaissance collectors and you will see that the urge to associate with certified objects is a hallmark of a new dynamic culture. In fact, Browning detailed the phenomenon not because he was so much interested in the Renaissance, but because he was trying to understand his own time. The modern captains of Victorian industry were acting much like the Florentine business families in wanting association with certified value. The endowed chair, the named library, the museum room were memorial opportunities for a new class of merchant prince eager to make sure Shelley's Ozymandias was mistaken.

Browning knew that members of the Medici, Strozzi, or Riccardi families often appeared in works of art because they paid to be included. Botticelli's several Magi portrayals include "messages" from his Florentine sponsors. "Wink, wink," they seem to be saying from the canvas, "look who is important." So Browning's Duke in *My Last Duchess*, or the church businessmen in *The Bishop Orders His Tomb at Saint Praxed's Church, Fra Lippo Lippi,* or *Andrea del Sarto* all repeat the same motif. The protagonists' enthusiasm in holding certified objects of art is a validation of self-worth. It arises from a yearning deep inside that still compels us to isolate items of aggrandizement, *and* then aggressively put them on display as ours. "Look on my works, ye Mighty, and despair!" is a powerful imprecation indeed.

In the sixteenth century, for the first time objects could be produced in collectible quantities so that a new class of recently affluent men could collect, sequester, and then show them off. We still know the names of the luxury brands of the Renaissance—Giotto, da Vinci, Botticelli, Michaelangelo—because they are still the premier luxury brands lusted after by the super rich. We call them by a special name—art—but they really are also the forerunners of display brands.

We are little different from our early-modern ancestors. Clearly, this desire is not really connected to materialism, but to human yearning. The market for luxury goods, begun in sixteenth-century Italy, has encompassed the world. The McKinsey Corporation, which studies this kind of consumption, estimates that in just the last twenty years, the market for luxury goods has grown to an estimated $70 billion and that the demand is indeed worldwide.

The dominant paradox for this explosion of luxury brands is not that human beings are crass, it is that they are idealistic. They don't want things, they want meaning. Luxury brands carry meaning very efficiently. That is part of why they cost more. Often this meaning seems hopelessly recondite to someone out of the culture. If you were a visitor from a distant galaxy could you ever distinguish between such parity products as dungarees from Guess, Gloria Vanderbilt, or Calvin Klein? How could you know that Cadillac, BMW, Lexus, and Jaguar have entirely different brand personalities?

The luxury product has more *personality* than the run-of-the-mill consumable. Who can tell the difference between Coke and Pepsi, Luckies and Camels, Budweiser and Miller? It is difficult to make distinctions between the ordinary. But you should know at once the difference between Rolex and Timex. Even though they keep the same time, they keep different company. Luxury goods exist to temporarily remove the blur. They say unequivocally, "I have made it. I have arrived."

✳ HOW MUCH DO WE COMMONERS KNOW ABOUT LUXURY GOODS? PLENTY

Some years ago, the most comprehensive study of upper-level consumption was undertaken in the United States by the International Research Institute on Social Change (RISC). RISC is a consultancy group funded by multinational companies, based in Switzerland, and active in seventeen of the world's major markets. RISC took a representative sample of the U.S. population (aged 15 years and over) and interviewed them each fall. The study is still going on and its findings are occasionally made public (Dubois and Paternault).

In total, three thousand people were interviewed in person at home using a combination of self-completed and face-to-face questions. Respondents were asked about their acquisition habits and feelings relative to a set of thirty-four luxury brands. This "home" list was developed on the basis of answers obtained from an unaided awareness test. A wide variety of sectors are represented—perfume, jewelry, fashion, leather goods, alcoholic beverages, stereo equipment, and the like. Here is the list alphabetically ordered:

1. Armani	13. Givenchy	25. Omega
2. Laura Ashley	14. Gorham	26. Oscar de la Renta
3. Bang & Olufsen	15. Gucci	27. Remy Martin
4. Bulgari	16. Guerlain	28. Revlon
5. Pierre Cardin	17. Hermes	29. Rolex
6. Cartier	18. Lacoste	30. Shiseido
7. Chanel	19. Lancôme	31. Louis Vuitton
8. Chivas Regal	20. Lanvin	32. Waterford
9. Christofle	21. Estée Lauder	33. Waterman
10. Daum	22. Ralph Lauren	34. Yves Saint-Laurent
11. Christian Dior	23. Lenox	
12. Dunhill	24. Mont Blanc	

The list was generated by equilibrating three criteria: aided awareness (which brands do you know by name?); recent purchase (what have you bought in the last two years?); and "dream value" (imagine that you are given the possibility of choosing a beautiful present because you won a contest—which would you choose?). On the basis of these categories, the respondents were asked which of the five brands they would like the best.

If Anglo-American culture showed the world *how* to expand and colonize using trade, then the most obvious thing that this list

➤ Royalty shilling: King Edward for pianos (1910).

shows is that the French showed *what* to trade. The audience-created list contains about as many French as non-French brands, which is consistent with the estimated 50 percent market share enjoyed by French brandnames in the worldwide luxury market.

While the awareness and purchase indicators used in generating this list are rather standard, the dream value measure merits additional comment for it is the key to understanding the importance of branded luxury. When consumers are asked to describe their spontaneous associations with the concept of luxury, the theme of "dream" almost inevitably emerges. In the world of luxury brands, here's how it goes: awareness feeds dream, purchase makes dream come true, purchase redirects dreams to the next object, and so forth. This is the essence of the paradoxical nature of the marketing of luxury goods: the spirit of Tantalus lives deep in the human breast, always reaching. We are drawn not so much to inevitable disappointment (although that often happens), but away from melancholy angst.

The International Research Institute on Social Change does not have the temerity to evaluate the nature of human desire for luxury, but I'll

"IT'S HARDER THAN
outrunning the paparazzi."

"IT'S HARDER THAN
seeing yourself in a three-way mirror."

"It's the hardest thing in the world.
STAYING ON A DIET."

Sarah, The Duchess of York

Sarah, Duchess of York, for Weight Watchers.

have a go at it. Once we are fed and sheltered and sexually productive, our needs cease to be biological and culture begins. Luxury objects get value not from production as much as from consumption. Who is buying the object often becomes more important than how it is made. The consumers who are most important are naturally those who seem to have resolved problems. They "have it all"—wealth, power, youth, and of course, most obvious in advertising, sexual attractiveness. Such people used to be those who wielded economic, political, military, or even ecclesiastical power. Now we have a new class of aspirational lifestyle, the pure confection of dream value—the celebrity.

In the way we live now, the celebrity is crucial to generating aura for branded products. Having a famous person displaying your product means that the thing *must* have special meaning. Advertisers first exploited this in the Depression when cigarette companies and soap manufacturers found that picturing some minor European royalty consuming your brand was sufficient to make it desirable to others. This still works, which is why movie stars and athletic heroes have become the royalty of our times.

✳ THE DESIGNER AS BRAND

If you look at the famous brandnames according to RISC, you will see that the designer has jumped loose from being the maker and has become the celebrity. Isolating the designer started in Western cultures when stamping the name of the coachmaker or candlestick maker was a way of establishing trademark. But the modern transformation is something different. The name of the celebrity endorser is not the user, not even the supposed manufacturer, but rather the holder of the famous name. Armani, Lacoste, Laura Ashley, Lanvin, Estée Lauder, Cartier, Ralph Lauren, Pierre Cardin, Chanel, Christofle, Oscar de la Renta, Christian Dior, Dunhill, Givenchy, Louis Vuitton, Gucci, Guerlain, Hermes, and Yves Saint-Laurent are names to conjure with not so much because we can associate them with their original product but because they have entered a dream world. If we can hang on to a piece of their personal treasure, it will grant us safe passage to social prominence. Their brands are what we have for graven images, religious relics, images that passeth all understanding.

Clearly, what is determinative is that the designer is perceived not as a specific person (very often he or she is long dead) but as magical dust that can be sprinkled around. In fact, invoking the designer on the product works best when there is no known "home" product, but only a known aura. One can see this process at warp speed in the success of the now publicly traded Ralph Lauren Inc. Mr. Lauren markets not a product but a "look." This look, a variety of ersatz English colonial upper crust, can be branded on almost anything—sheets, shirts, shoes, sweatpants, sofas, sunglasses. The key is that all parts of the brand constellation can be quickly decoded. His advertising often neglects the actual product to concentrate on the old-money objects that surround it. The product of Polo is patina.

My favorite Lauren ad is a two-page layout of the crushed white gravel in a driveway leading to a baronial estate. Nothing else is shown. You can almost hear the sound of your invisible Rolls-Royce as you motor up the driveway in your nouveau, old-style Ralph Lauren outfit.[9]

✳ WHEN BRANDS MISBEHAVE

Branding seems so simple. It's not. Like celebrities, with which they share many similarities, brands will occasionally go AWOL. Think only of Apple computers, Oldsmobile, or Kodak. When you think of how branding works you can see where problems can arise. The marketplace is indeed Darwinian, "red in tooth and claw," in profit and loss. A brand should follow you through the stages of your life. So what happens if you take an abrupt turn? You can quickly grow away from a brand. Look in your closet for proof.

Occasionally producers take an abrupt turn. On April 2, 1993, Philip Morris, fearful that its premium brands of cigarettes were losing market share to no-name competitors (one of which was even called Generic),

---

9. Perhaps the height of this kind of brand consciousness is the Gucci string bikini. While the usual middle-aged Gucci consumer certainly is not going to waddle down the beach in one of them, they are foregrounded in every Gucci store window. The clasp that holds the G-string together is the Gucci "G." Admittedly more advertising gimmick than consumer product, the string allows the wearer to be little more than the designer's insignia. There is no you (or, perhaps nothing other than you) to get in the way of the brand. Kmart could not carry this off even though a "K" might be more sensible engineering.

slashed its prices. Madison Avenue groaned. Wall Street wailed. In one day, investors not only wiped $13.4 billion off Philip Morris's stock market value but also dumped shares in scores of other consumer-goods firms. RJR Nabisco, Procter & Gamble, Coca-Cola, Pepsico, Quaker Oats, and Gillette were all bludgeoned by traders convinced that the explosive profit growth once delivered by branded standard-bearers was a thing of the past.

"Marlboro Friday" is a day that will live in infamy in market culture because brand management was supposed to defend against exactly this. From a producer's point of view one of the reasons to build brands was that you would *never* have to cut prices. Alas, it seemed that given a choice between lower price and brand loyalty, loyalty lost. Prices fell. Brands could crumble quickly. Worse yet, in this case, it was the producer who caved.

But what happens if brands go under not because the consumer loses interest, or because the producer panics, but because the retail environment somehow changes? From the storekeeper's point of view, branding should be a shortcut so he can reduce selling staff and let the consumer reach for the product. What this really means, however, is that discount retailers can cannibalize the value of cooperative advertising and pocket the difference. Wal-Mart, for instance, does relatively little product advertising, carries only name brands at lower prices than the other retailers, and makes its money by bickering with the producer for lower bulk rates. Your local electronics store, which helps advertise Sony televisions, is also creating value for the product at the discounter. Little wonder Sears threw in the towel and created Sears' Brand Central.

Other threats abound. Remember the appearance of "generics," or store brands, so popular in the 1970s when inflation was soaring? They posed the possibility that the cash nexus might well overwhelm brand loyalty. Upscale department stores like Saks, Nordstrom, and Barney's have been able to push in-house brands, but the real battle is raging below.

Witness the grocery store. So far the national producers are still calling the shots. But their days may be numbered. Store brands have not been recognized as having equal value, as is the case in Western Europe and England, because the American storekeeper still has too little control over what is on the shelf. As long as Procter & Gamble, Kellogg, Philip Morris, Colgate-Palmolive, Gillette, Campbell's, Nestlé, Unilever, and RJR Nabisco are adjusting the store mix, coddling certain products until they find an audience, they can retard the generic attack and literally shunt it aside.[10]

To protect themselves, most big branded-goods manufacturers have started making generic products on the sly. Usually they stick to products in which they do not have a dominant brand. So Heinz is the biggest own-label soup maker; Ralston Purina the biggest in cereals. Some firms have resisted: in European markets Kellogg emblazons its boxes with the slogan "We don't make cereal for anyone else." But Kellogg is in the minority. Even Campbell's Soup, one of the last to hold out, has started making off-brand goods—but not soups.

With the introduction of more efficient inventory methods, the balance of power may shift back to the retailer. The Universal Product Code and the optical scanner mean that the storekeeper can finally tell the manufacturer what brands are moving through the store. Certain national brands like Camay, Chun King and La Choy, Michelob, Miller High Life, Prell, and Sanka are in distress not because the producer is cutting them loose or because the consumer is not buying them but because the retailer thinks he can do better with other products. Every night, as the chain grocery stores download the data of the day, the retailer is getting the freshest FMCG information and can reassert control of the aisles. One wag has recently suggested that most FMCG companies' advertising budgets now would be better spent bribing the forty or so retailing executives who now decide what gets onto most of the shelves and be done with it.

---

10. The English developed a different system that made generics more accessible. Their trade-promotion system is not as byzantine as America's because the supermarket holds most of the shelf power. Pioneering retailers such as Britain's J. Sainsbury and Canada's Loblaw have long grabbed big market shares with their private brands. What rattles brand managers now is the surge in store brands in places such as Spain and France, and in products like cigarettes and detergent that were once thought immune to them. Own-labeled and generic products now account for more than 20 percent of sales in some European supermarkets. Once the American consumer knows that most shampoos are made by two or three manufacturers and that they are essentially interchangeable, and if money becomes tight, the store brand may finally make a comeback.

✳ *THE CASE OF PRELL*

The king of branding FMCGS is still Procter & Gamble. P&G has constructed an empire based on the methodical, plodding, never-say-die
approach to selling. Because they usually do so well, it is instructive to
observe them when they don't.[11] Have a look at Prell shampoo.

What could be simpler than hair? The taming and branding of hair
has become central to the modern sense of self and is a crucial marker
of lifestyle. While we may not be able to name the various looks (butch,
slicked-back, crew, comb-over for men, flip, bubble, pixie, shag, page-
boy, bighair, beehive, twist, bob, bouffant, or cropped for women, and
ponytail and afro for both), we recognize that since early adolescence we
have spent much time obsessing about it. And well we should, for hair
is one of the few places where we can work our will on our "presentation of self." The wonderful thing is that it grows back, and the terrible
thing is that, for some of us, it doesn't.

But no matter how we fix it, it has to be washed. Dirty hair stinks. In
the early twentieth century, soap and shampoo were separated. The
premier brands of shampoo in the 1950s were Prell, Breck, and White
Rain. Then in the 1960s, shampoo and conditioner divided. Like cells,
these products keep dividing, colonizing new epidermal and marketing
terrain.[12]

---

11. Some critics question how savvy P&G really is. If P&G really knew brand-
    ing, would they have slashed the wholesale prices of about 70 percent of
    their products and eliminated most discounts to retailers in mid-1996?
    The whole point of branding is that you never have to lower your prices
    because the customer, not your retailer, is loyal. P&G claimed that "every-
    day low prices" was an attempt to reward customers' loyalties, but many
    suspected that this was more an act of brand exasperation than anything
    else. Retailers that relied heavily on promotions and cooperative adver-
    tising were furious. Some even denied shelf space to P&G products.
    Worse, rivals such as Unilever and Colgate-Palmolive stepped in with
    generous deals of their own.

12. Observe just one small aspect of shampoo geography. A few years
    ago one of the most popular associational claims for shampoo was its
    similarity to horsehair cleaner. Horses had lots of hair, women who
    tend horses tend to have long hair, so why not use the animal product on

Stand in the shampoo aisle for a minute and you will appreciate the deep magical meaning of hair. How else to explain such baffling ingredients as watercress, sage, jasmine, kiwi, mango, coconut, grapefruit, strawberry, apple, chamomile, and papaya? They sound delicious, to be sure, but are we really interested in eating hair? Add to this mix exotic ingredients like kukui nut, awapuhi, mura-mura, tucoma, cassava, jojoba, gingko, nettle, St. John's wort, and hair becomes more then just a mane or a meal; it becomes a rooftop garden.

If choosing a shampoo these days can be something of a consumer ordeal, observe P&G's problems with the old standby Prell. This was *the* shampoo of the 1950s, unisex and for all ages—the ultimate brand. Even though Prell still ranks among the top twenty brands, it has been steadily losing market share to newer and more exciting brands. What did P&G do? First they changed the product, then they changed it back again.

As I write this, P&G is now re-reintroducing the original green version. For reasons hard to explain but clearly having to do with the "don't just stand there, do something!" mentality of brand managers, in late 1991 P&G replaced the green stuff with a reformulated blue variety. A horrendous mistake! Now a campaign by Leo Burnett trumpets: "Green is back! The original formula you've always loved." Only in advertising could the relationship between shampoo and shampooer be characterized as "lover come home." As P&G has been rudely reminded, there is often a bond between a brand and consumers that mimics marriage. When it breaks, erstwhile lovers turn combative. Is there any emotion to compare with unrequited love?

Worse than changing the color, P&G changed the packaging. Customers had learned to associate green shampoo with the sensuous see-through container (which looked remarkably like a Coke bottle), but P&G was pouring it into generic cylinders.[13] When you now look at the

---

humans? Mane & Tail, formulated for huge equines, was soon used by smaller humans at home. This horse shampoo, however, proved too atavistic for the mass market so an imitator, just for humans, called Magical Mane was marketed. This shampoo "gives you that magical thoroughbred shine." You can sparkle just like a silky victor of the Kentucky Derby.

13. That initial package was designed by Donald Deskey, an unacknowledged genius of consumer forms. Deskey also designed the package for Crest toothpaste when that product was introduced in the 1950s (and which P&G wisely has kept its hands off), as well as package designs for Aqua

◌

shampoo aisle you see these two products in different packages stacked side by side, called by the same names, P&G's rendition of putting Old Coke (Coke Classic) on the same shelf as New Coke (Coke II). We all know how that turned out.

Both Prells are now languishing. It seems that you can improve a brand (Prell has had eight "key improvements" since inception in 1947), you can add stuff to a brand (Prell has smelled three different ways), you can fool around with the price of the brand (P&G has gone to "everyday low prices" with Prell), you can change the container (Prell has done this a number of times with tube and hourglass bottle), but you cannot, *must not*, ever say that the brand you saw on Tuesday has now become entirely something different on Wednesday.[14]

Pavlov's rule of branding: extend the brand, if you must, but don't brand the same product twice. Or if you do, don't get caught. If in doubt, observe the Cadillac division of General Motors. A few years ago, everyone knew that the Cadillac Cimarron was just a frumped-up version of the Chevrolet Cavalier "econocar." Goodbye, Cimarron. Has Cadillac learned? Only if we don't see that the domestic Caddy Catera that zigs is pretty much the same as the European Opel Omega that zags.

✳ THE MODERN FAMILIES OF MAN ARE BRANDED IN LATE ADOLESCENCE

Every day I see clusters of students who pass before me in class. From behind the lectern they all look very much the same. But inside this class of coevals are discrete lines dividing and subdividing the athletes from the frat members, from the grinds, from the party animals, from the curious onlookers, from the freaks, from the back-row Baptists, from the Xers. Just as our society is a mosaic of social types (yuppies,

---

Velva, Gleem toothpaste, Jif peanut butter, Bounty towels, and Cheer and Oxydol laundry soaps. Deskey also designed the dazzling interiors of Radio City Music Hall.

14. Although this is only anecdotal, it was about the same time that Prell was being entirely rebranded that my daughters swore to me that the reason I was balding was a result of my using Prell. They were not alone in repeating this bit of urban folklore. Certainly it makes some sense. Your father uses an old-fashioned shampoo, your father is growing bald, ergo, the shampoo is a deforesting agent.

church ladies, rednecks, suits, boomers) who change and evolve over time, so too every modern subgroup like my college students is split into discrete consumption communities. What makes these kids different, however, is that they are the number one focus of almost every marketer. You cannot find a major advertising agency that does not have a special department dedicated to "getting under their radar."

Because the undergraduate population is one that is relatively confined and very potent in the marketplace (some $20 billion a year and access to a whole lot more), they are an ideal population to calibrate the force of branding. They are also interesting because so much of their consumption is anticipatory. In other words, they are orienting themselves to entering a variety of postgraduation niches that will hold them for years to come.

Basil Englis and Michael Solomon, professors of marketing in the School of Business at Rutgers University, wanted to show how tightly college students cluster around brand knowledge. They drew samples from undergraduate business majors at their institution and presented them with forty cards, each containing a description of one PRIZM cluster. These clusters, as we saw in chapter 1, are consumption communities that have coherent purchasing habits. They know each other by sharing brands.

The professors sifted the clusters to make four groups—lifestyles, if you will—representative of undergraduate society. They were: Young Suburbia, Money & Brains, Smalltown Downtown, and Middle America. Then they gathered images of objects from four product categories (automobiles, magazines/newspapers, toiletries, and alcoholic beverages) that fit into each group. The students were asked to put the various images together into coherent packets and to state their current proximity to, or desire to be part of, each group in the future.

Next, they were asked to sort the cards into four piles, or categories, defined as: "These people are very similar to how I would like to be" (aspirational group); "These people are very similar to how I currently see myself" (occupied group); "These people are very similar to how I would not like to be" (avoidance group); "These people have no meaning for me; I don't feel strongly about wanting to be like or not wanting to be like them" (irrelevant group).

As might be expected the Money & Brains cluster was the most popular aspirational niche. What was not expected was how specific and knowledgeable the students were about the possessions they did not have but knew they needed to be included. When asked what brand of automobile they would drive, here's what they said: BMWs (53.6 percent), Mercedes (50.7), Cadillacs (30.4), Volvos (23.2), Porsches (21.7), Acuras (17.4), and Jaguars (15.9). They knew what they wanted to read: travel magazines (21.7 percent), *Vogue* (21.7), *Business Week* (20.3), *Fortune* (17.9), and *GQ* (15.9). Again, this is not what they did read, but what they took to be the reading material of the desired group. What they were actually reading (or so they said) were *Forbes, Barron's, The New Yorker,* and *Gourmet,* so they were well on their way to brand closure. No mention of *Rolling Stone, Playboy, Spin,* or *Details* for this group. They certainly knew what to drink: Heineken beer (33.3 percent), expensive wines (26.1), scotch (18.8), champagne (17.4), and Beck's beer (15). They also knew what to sprinkle on their bodies: Polo (27.5 percent), Obsession (15.9), and Drakkar (15.9).

What the professors found was not just that birds of a feather had already started to flock together but that these young birds already knew what flock to shy away from. They were not ashamed of smoking, for instance, but of smoking the wrong brand. These kids were already stocking the humidor. Their prime avoidance group corresponded to the Smalltown Downtown cluster in the PRIZM scheme. The Money & Brainers knew a lot about these Smalltowners. They knew about the favored pickup trucks, Chevys (23.2 percent) and Fords (18.8). They knew that this group reads *People* (30.4 percent), *Sports Illustrated* (26.1), *TV Guide* (24.6), *Wrestling* (21.7), fishing magazines (20.3), and the *National Enquirer* (18.8). Budweiser was seen as the most preferred beer for this group (59.4 percent), followed by Miller (24.6), and Coors (18.8). Essentially, the Money & Brainers had learned not just what to buy but what to shun (or at least what to say to avoid). As chefs say, what is sent back to the kitchen is often more important that what is eaten.

Such shared knowledge is the basis of culture. This insight was, after all, the basis of a liberal arts education. John Henry Newman and Matthew Arnold argued for state-supported education precisely because cultural literacy meant social cohesion. No one argued that it was important to know algebraic functions or Latin etymologies or what constitutes a sonnet because such knowledge allows us to solve important social problems. We learn such matters because cultural literacy is the basis of how to speak to each other, how we develop a bond of shared history and commonality. This is the secular religion of the liberal arts and sciences.

In the postmodern world we have, it seems, exchanged knowledge of history and science (a knowledge of production) for knowledge of brands and how brands interlock to form coherent social patterns (a knowledge of consumption). Buy this and *don't* buy that has replaced make/learn this and *don't* make/learn that. After all, in our couch culture, everyone is a consumer, not everyone is a worker.

There are clear ramifications to such a culture. A producer culture focuses on the independent self of the worker: *self*-help, *self*-discipline, *self*-respect, *self*-control, *self*-reliance, *self*-interest. Responsibility is situated in the individual. Can he get to work? A consumer culture, however, focuses on community. Fit in, don't stand out, be cool, chill out. The standard of judgment becomes personality, the ability to interact effectively with others, to win their affection and admiration—to merge in with others of the same lifestyle. Can he buy the right brands?

Brands perforce become one of the shoehorns that slide up into designated spots. You are not what you make, you are what you buy. Don't like who you are? Buy different brands. Shop for a new lifestyle. In the older culture, aspirations to material comfort were sharply restricted by the limited capacity of the economy to produce. In the modern world, much greater material satisfactions lie within the range of even those of modest means. Hence a producer culture becomes a consumer culture, a hoarding culture becomes a surplus culture, a work culture becomes a therapeutic culture. And what you buy becomes more important than what you make.

This is all quite glib, to be sure, but it is already part of what we take for granted. Gross generalization that it is, we have gone from an "ought" culture, where superego was central—where there were rules for everything from how to commence courtship to how to tip the porter—to a "want" culture—where entitlement to branded objects, or at least, the wherewithal to buy such objects, is a given. At the center of this consumer-based world is always the object; the object is known to us by the brand; and we now turn to how we put the brands together, namely, to the world of fashion.

6

The Function of Fashion
in an Age of Individualism

*"Don't follow me! Don't follow anyone! Think for yourselves! . . . You are all
individuals!" says Graham Chapman as Brian, the mistaken messiah, ex-
horting a crowd of devotees.*

*"Yes, Master, we are all individuals. We are all individuals. We are all indi-
viduals," the crowd replies in perfect unison.*

—Monty Python's *Life of Brian,* 1979

ONE of the dominant myths of consumer culture is that we are each
separate individuals and we express this separateness by what
we choose to buy. We treasure freedom of choice no matter how inap-
propriate or how mythic. Of course, at the checkout line, branding re-
futes that notion. While we may think we are freely consuming goods
according to individual desire, we are really gathering them in bundles.
Or, to be more accurate, while we think we are acting as the result of individual choice we are really passing through stages, "brandscapes,"
layers of consumption, in which we are creating new, supposedly improved, versions of ourselves. Ironically, the bar codes are on us.

Although we may not recognize how sensitive we are to brand
choices in our own lives, we are certainly aware when we watch stereotypes in the mass media. But are the images that we see on television,
for instance, accurate? They don't have to be. That's the beauty part. For
example, how many members of the audience watching *Beverly Hills,
90210* have directly experienced the lifestyle of an affluent Southern

California teenager? So long as fictional choices are congruent with audience expectations, the image groups will be accepted by the audience. As a result, most viewers may now think of the 90210 lifestyle as involving trips to the health spa, wearing midriff-exposing t-shirts, and driving a BMW convertible. One could have as easily been watching *Dallas* or *Cheers*, for the "truth" about a lifestyle category may be less important than its "mass-mediated" image (i.e., its "reality" as conveyed by mass media depictions) and the social connotations it has for the audience/consumer.

As long as the images *fit*, the audience gets the picture. In fact, it is the expectation of, and pleasure in, the formation of an imaginative construct that is the basis of much modern entertainment. Since the plots are redundant, the excitement is discovering how other people use the same branded objects that we too may be able to buy. If we can't buy the exact brand, we can perhaps afford the knock-off. What critics of consumption see as the layering of the repressive hegemony over unformed imaginations is instead the pleasure of fill in the dots. It is how we exercise not just knowledge, but also a sense of shared community. "Can you believe how cool Kelly looked in Dylan's Porsche!?" our daughter asks her school chums the morning after *90210*. This knowledge— what they have for reading Trollope—is their cultural literacy; and this they share with glee.

✳ THE DIDEROT EFFECT

The insight into the joys of perceiving how commercial stuff fits together was not noted first by a modern Marxist, an academic sociologist, or a window shopper, but by a late seventeenth-century essayist— Denis Diderot. In an essay, *Regrets on Parting With My Old Dressing Gown*, the French philosopher explores what was to become a modern condition. As he looks up from his desk and glances around at his study he notices it has been transformed by mysterious forces. It was once crowded, humble, chaotic, and happy. Now it is now elegant, organized, and a little grim. What's happened? Diderot suspects the cause of the transformation is right before his eyes. It is his new dressing gown. A week after he began to wear it, it occurred to him that his shabby desk was not quite up to standard. He got a shiny new one. Then the tapestry on the wall seemed a little threadbare and new curtains had to be found. Gradually, the entire contents of the study were replaced. Why?

Not because he wanted a new study but because he needed a sense of coherence, a sense that nothing was out of place, a sense of a center.

In modern marketing this is known not as the "Diderot effect" but as creating a consumption "constellation," entering a brandscape, conforming to a fashion. No matter what it is called, the pleasure and the pain remain the same. Achieving that sense of completeness that constitutes a set of symbolically related consumption activities is, in that linguistic barbarism of our time, to create a lifestyle. A lifestyle is an emblematic display of coherent brands. In psychobabble it represents being "centered."

This is why buying simple-seeming objects can be so complex. What kind of tie I wear, what kind of car I drive, what kind of gin I drink—all need to fit. No plaids with checks, please. The dissonance I feel when a branded consumable is out of place will cause me to go back and reformat not just that decision, but others as well. I want to be fashionable, to fit in.

What Denis Diderot knew was that things not only fit together but also are tied to a hub. In his case, the centering object was a dressing gown. But it could be anything. For example, not only do my shoes have to match my socks and even my tie, but they also have to match my eyeglasses. Bass Weejuns may go with my khaki pants, but they definitely do not go with my Armani suit and my Bolle sunglasses (just kidding). Certainly one unstudied aspect of fashion is object avoidance, keeping *away* from the Joneses. Avoidance is more complex than being mistaken "for one of them." If I have to buy something else, or I have to start purchasing an entire new system of accessories, I will be anxious, a fashion victim.

When this consumption of brands inside set boundaries is elaborated, it becomes a "look," a fashion. And creating fashion is what defines the modern self. Diderot could not have known how dressing the self—the microcosm created by the individual and the macrocosm created by vast groups consuming similar objects—was to become the basis of modern culture. But it certainly has. For instance, look at the difficult passages of life like adolescence, courtship, first job, marriage, raising children, demonstrating success, or even retirement, and you will see that they require entire ensembles of matching goods. "Am I ready for the sport utility vehicle?" asks the modern Prufrock, not "Do I want kids?"

If I had to isolate one item of dress that encapsulates the fashion process, it would be the black windbreakers I used to see my male students wear. If I asked them if they were fashion-conscious, they would usually deny it, but here they were wearing a jacket with a little label flapping on the chest pocket. The label said "Members Only," and this easily legible flag appeared over the heart pocket in the same place the alligator used to reside, or where the polo pony eternally gallops. The jacket, part of a family of goods that includes ties, luggage, footwear, and cosmetics, was made in China for a New York company named Aris. The Members Only label hangs off all these products. Rather like the ambiguous bumper stickers of the "My God isn't dead, sorry about yours" (I'm saved, you're not) type, this announcement of contrived status didn't seem to register as ironic with the wearer. The claim of exclusivity is viewed only as a shopper's choice. Still, the admission that this is, after all, the goal of fashion may be refreshing, if also slightly jarring, not to the wearer but to the onlooker.

✳ FASHION CULTURE

We much prefer the word "culture" to "fashion" because we think that culture is somehow enduring and fashion is transient. Culture is "the best that has been thought and said" for all times, and fashion is whatever is being thought and said this week. Or, to extend further: culture is male; fashion female. Culture is English, fashion French. Culture is high, fashion low. Culture is aesthetic, fashion vulgar. Culture me, fashion you.

The image that most people would associate with fashion would be the runway, the so-called catwalk, down which helplessly emaciated and obscenely overpaid women (girls, really) wear the hopelessly expensive follies of often effeminate men. True, this is an aspect of fashion, an aspect as instructive as it is out of date. In the old days when the rich set the tone for fashion, selling your couture to tastemaking bluenoses would allow you to sell the rest of your line as ready-to-wear to the wannabes.

No more. In fact, the runway show and the kind of fashion it implies is now a favorite butt of postmodern ridicule. When Andrew Logan did his "Alternative Miss World" Contests in the 1970s and Susanne Bartsch did her "Voguing" balls in the 1980s, one could see that haute couture was being sent up. Now it has been hijacked. Performance "artist" Kembra Pfahler recently dragged herself down the runway with blue-dyed skin, blackened teeth, and bowling balls strapped to her feet. The fashion world was not as much horrified as melancholy. They knew what was going on. And what of the amazing rise of RuPaul and the blasé acceptance of drag as a way to sell accessories (such as M.A.C., a major cosmetics line distributed by Estée Lauder, no less). Clearly, all these subversions show that in the way we live now, the runway literally is a dead end.[1]

Fashion—this kind of haute fashion—is indeed in disarray. To understand why, one need only follow the money. Fortunes are not to be made selling to the rich, but to the middle class, and not to the old but to the young. Kids are the only ones with sufficient disposable time and money to pay attention and be concerned about style. When teenagers control fashion, every fringe—be it hippies, mods, punks, or grunge—is assimilated quicksilver fast into the system. Rich ladies take to the hills. Little wonder that couture has been relegated to the back sections of the newspaper while kidculture is front page. Just look at the average age of the models in *GQ* or *Vogue* today, and look at what activities the models are pretending to be engaged in. Then have a look at what was happening in the pages of *Esquire* or *Harper's Bazaar* back in the 1950s.

Why should high fashion have fallen so low? Why is it now such a joke while only thirty years ago it was taken so seriously? To be sure nothing so reflects our envy, insecurity, and snobbishness as directly as fashion. Fashion is how we get ourselves up, how we make do, how we attempt to fit in, how we brand ourselves; and certainly we are a little embarrassed about its power. Could it be that we know that fashion of all sorts, not high culture, is a dependable barometer of the times? So, of course, fashion makes us uneasy. Fashion really *is* important.

---

1. If the postmodern derision of runway fashion is not enough of a sign of calcification, then note the three places where high fashion is ending up—in the museum, at the auction house, and in the classroom. Each week one sees the opening of a major show on this or that couturier occurring at the premier cultural centers like the Costume Institute of the Met, the Victoria and Albert Museum in London, or the New York Public Library, of all places. At the same time the fashion photograph is center stage at the Whitney and elsewhere. Sotheby's and Christie's both have had recent sales of discarded finery, not just from English royalty, but from private collectors like Catherine Deneuve and Jacqueline de Ribes. Academic courses are offered in the history and sociology of haute couture in Ivy league schools thanks in large part to the rise of Women's Studies and its need to find "texts" to study. Meanwhile, over at *The New Yorker*, former editor Tina Brown ran annual issues dedicated to fashion.

It is profound in its superficiality. At some level, we know how thoroughly what we wear shows what we are. Fashion is packaging and we are inside it. We may have left adolescence, but adolescent anxiety is still with us.

We are not the first to have sneered at fashion and the fashionable. Looking *down* at fashion is what self-conscious, educated people have been doing for centuries. That sneering is because educated people intensely dislike the idea that surface is depth, that form is content, that packages are more than containers. It is profoundly demoralizing for many to consider the profundity of the material world. "Be wary of all enterprises that require new clothes," wrote the sage of Walden Pond. Worse yet is the realization that most new clothes are delivered and advertised and branded by commercial interests that care not at all for what is being created. What they care about is making money, not making fashion.

Take a trip into your closet and you soon realize that this is where you have lived through various lives. For me the tie-dyed τ-shirt, the engineer boots, the interview suit, the bow ties, the pointy Italian shoes, the Nehru jacket, the polyester bell bottoms, the double-knit jump suit (okay, just checking) are mute testament to my trying on of selves. They are not just clothes, they are entrails of my self. All I have to do is look at one object and I remember the constellation that swirled around it. When I bought them I was very serious. Such ensembles are called outfits for a reason. They are literally how we fit our insides out.[2]

---

2. A generation ago, the closet was stable and reflected changes in body size. The modern closet is huge—often a walk-in and sit-down experience— and reflects deeper cultural changes. How to explain the large modern closet? Here are a few theories from recent anthropology.

Chaos Theory: there is no single determinate unifying my closet, rather the overdetermination of whimsical choice.

Electronic Explanation: fashion's variety and its myriad interpretations are an outgrowth of the electronic technological revolution; images have passed before me and I gathered them up.

Gender Tension: as feminism has increased the variety of selves for women, men have gone along for the ride.

While I don't know what's going on in my closet, I do know this: that stuff comes a lot closer to what I'm really thinking and feeling than what I'm admitting to.

⇧

No wonder fashion is frightening. Once we realize that the closet is only a small part of the husking of modern selfhood, the prospect is more daunting. Fashion is face. In fact, before the advent of vegetable-oil soap that was cheap enough so that we could wash repeatedly during the day, faces stunk. We now soap them twice a day. Add to this for men the daily shave, thanks to King Gillette and his safety razor, and "dressing the face" becomes a diurnal chore. For a while I was a Bay Rum man, then an Old Spice Man, then Aqua Velva, and so on. Now I go it alone. There is now an aftershave called Score which advertises that it is built of pheromones. You can't buy Score in stores—too dangerous; use an 800 number instead. For women, of course, making a face can become almost a part-time job. Not only do they have to remove a face, they then have to re-create it all anew. Just as clothing is called rags along Seventh Avenue, cosmetics are called paint for a reason.

We comfort ourselves that this is being done to us, that we are fashion victims, that "they" are making us uncomfortable, anxious, but deep down we know differently. We like the shedding and refashioning process. We can make ourselves fresh every day; not the fountain of youth, to be sure, but the principle is the same.

✳ A BRIEF HISTORY OF FASHION

What made fashioning the self possible was shopping. Shopping depends on a surplus of goods. Machines made surpluses. Essentially this is why fashion really becomes a modern popular concern, an industrial concern. Diderot was a man of considerable means. He could afford to refashion himself. Few others could. A generation later thousands could do the same, then millions followed. Moralists and preachers of earlier eras had condemned fashion as overreaching individualism. Only royalty was exempt. For them fashion was a function of control. We do this, you don't. Saint John Baptist de la Salle wrote in his seventh-century treatise *Rules of Christian Manners and Civility* that "singularity in dress is ridiculous: in fact, it is generally looked upon as proof that the mind is somewhat deranged" (in De Witt 2). No one today would take such a stand. Fashion is one of the ways we can assert ourselves, fit in, stand out, be rebellious, conform, break loose.

Just as the allure of fashion now drives youth of all classes to the malls of America, the allure of fashion drove the French bourgeoisie to Paris. In fact, it helped create the bourgeoisie. By the early nineteenth century, traditional tailors who had made entire ensembles were giving way to the specialists. There were hat makers, pants makers, jacket makers, and then this whole process was supercharged by the application of machinery that produced specialty items en masse. As clothes stalls grew into fancy-goods stores, and then, in the 1850s, department stores, so new retail innovations followed. In 1852 Le Bon Marché, the first real department store, opened its doors in Paris with fixed prices, free entry, and an increasingly wide choice of goods. For the first time, the ordinary consumer could put different pieces of clothing together, just the way the courtesans did.

✴ THE DEMIMONDAINE

Along the way, gender got separated from sex, and keeping up with fashion became women's work. If you look at pre-nineteenth-century portrait painting you will see that fashion was clearly the province of men. But then, with the Industrial Revolution, something happened. To get fashion to "work," a new and very delicate system had to evolve. A fashion class had to be found, willing to show off and even flaunt new style. Today, this is found along the edges of adolescent culture such as with grunge, punk, hip-hop, and the rest. But in the world of our great-grandparents the role of being daring was played by the demimondaine. She was the "other woman," the younger, sexier, risk-taking woman who would become institutionalized as the mistress. Named after a character in a play of the same name by the younger Alexander Dumas, the demimondaine was a keystone in the fashion industry. Immoral, flashy, given to display, and deeply conscious of money, she was the perfect clotheshorse. On her shapely back, fads could be fashioned, styles made manifest, and shopping for a style could begin in earnest.

The demimondaine, not the couturiers, made Paris the fashion capital of the world. Without her, "women of refinement," who have always been slightly afraid of the demands of fashion, could not know what was vulgar, aka exciting, aka sexy. From here the iron rule of modern fashion evolved: what fashion abhors as vulgarity today becomes stylish tomorrow. And one step further, in Oscar Wilde's elegant expansion, "It is only the modern that ever becomes old-fashioned."

Ironically, perhaps, the dressing of these young women made the first designer brandnames as haute couture was born. Without them, and their sense of changing styles, Monsieurs Boucicaut, Cognacq, and Jaluzot, respectively the founders of Bon Marché, Samaritaine, and Printemps, could never have succeeded with the merchandising of a never-ending flow of shifting styles. Retailers did not create desire, however comforting it may be to think, but they certainly harvested it.

✳ THE DESIGN AS BRAND: SUIT UP

Fashion messages used to come in nice complementary branded packages. You can still see the aura of this earlier world in the desire of Gucci (and his customers) to stamp his G, or Chanel her C, or Ralph Lauren his tiny polo player, or Lacoste his alligator. Like a work of poetry, fashion accessories rhymed. The shoes rhymed with the belt, the blouse with the scarf, the skirt with the jacket, and so on. In the modern world of television, you just connect the dots. You try to line up the Gs, Cs, polo players, or alligators and, voilà, you are set to go out in style.

This was called a look, as in Dior's "New Look," for instance. For a decade after World War II, Dior reigned over the world of fashion with emphatically tiny waists and vast and sumptuous full skirts. I grew up looking at these clothes. Now they are at the Met. They still inspire vehement, even militant, pleasure or horror. They are so controlled and coherent and unlike anything you see around us now. They do indeed seem built, as the designer Geoffrey Beene has said, to transform female torsos into pedestals. If you look at advertising of the 1950s you can see that not only were women looking *like* pedestals, they were often pictured *on* pedestals.

Dior's dresses were suits of armor. The male counterpart was the gray flannel suit. This uniform hung around for years covering Cary Grant and becoming a metaphor of ambiguous conformity with the film, *The Man in the Gray Flannel Suit*. Sold at Brooks Brothers, Paul Stuart, and J. Press, it gave Madison Avenue a bad name. We now use the word "suits" as a metonym of scorn. Yet, a generation ago, when fashion was still coherent, the suit was king. You wanted to wear one. I remember my first suit. Although my mother took me to buy pants and sport coats, my father took time off from the office to buy me the suit. Say what you will, the suit caught a postwar longing to reassert control. It was a return to tradition and enduring values. Suit up. No dress-down Fridays. Men in black (or at least gray). Suiting was serious and so rebelling against it was almost preordained.

✳ *THE FASHION PHOTOGRAPH: HOW WE SEE WHAT TO BE*

No innovations have been more central to the branding of fashion, especially to the spreading of designer fashion, than the photograph and
the medium in which it travels, the fashion magazine. Like the department store window with which it shares many similarities, the magazine photograph fixes objects for public delectation. It shows you not
just what to see, but how to see it. Like the store window, the glossy,
highly reflective paper of the monthly fashion magazine allows you to
see yourself reflected in the world it promises. Window shopping for
the self, daydreaming. A fashion plate is not just an image of style, but
a literal layout to be reproduced over skin—your skin.

So central to the process of fashion is the photograph that we know
the names of photographers (Newton, Avedon, Leibovitz) as well as we
know the names of the magazines (*Vogue, Harper's Bazaar, Elle*) as well
as we know the names of the models (Crawford, Campbell, Evange-
lista), as well as we know the names of the designers (Armani, Klein,
Lauren, Versace, Gaultier, Lagerfeld). If you want cultural literacy, here
it is. We may not wear the clothes, but we know the fashion. And we
know it because the photo didn't just stop the style and hold it in its
tracks, it made fashion an aide-memoire. The photograph made fashion into art and vice versa.

Who now disputes that fashion photography is an art? Who would
have thought so a generation ago? More intriguing still is that commercial photography is almost completely interleaved with the art photo. I
daresay that most viewers could not tell the difference between a high-
cult photograph by the late Robert Mapplethorpe and those homoerotic
shots that Calvin Klein uses to advertise his Obsession body care products. In one recent example, for instance, the Klein ad is spread over
two pages. The black-and-white image is a close-up of a male torso.
There's no head or face to make the portrait individual. It shows only
an anonymous naked body, almost down to the groin. Needless to say,
had the body been female, cries of mutilation and dehumanization
would have been heard. But, shh, please, this is art. This image fairly
drips in the sensual delight Mapplethorpe took in the male physique.

While Robert Mapplethorpe seems to be on one side of the divide
(art) and Calvin Klein on the other (commerce), it is now simply impossible to tell if Annie Leibovitz or Irving Penn are on the payroll when
they open and close the shutter, or are doing it for "art."

But that's no longer the point. The point is who cares? We may not, but the sponsor does. That's why such commercial photos have the shutterbug's name prominently displayed at the side just like the signature of a painter. That's why when the *New York Times Magazine* runs its weekly fashion section or its special fashion issues for men and women, it is always done in arty style. This can't just be about clothes, don't you know. And because it's "art," this is the only place the *Times* doesn't have to be politically correct, and it's not. In these fashion pages we see young women pictured in ways that the editorial page writers would certainly never countenance.

Here the case of Richard Avedon may be instructive. Avedon is a first-rate fashion photographer who started his career doing layouts for *Harper's Bazaar,* graduated to the advertising campaigns of Revlon and Calvin Klein, and then jumped the tracks to produce "art" images. His famous art portraits, however, are not of everyday folks but of celebrities like Marilyn Monroe, Audrey Hepburn, Charlie Chaplin, and George Wallace. And these celebrities are not shot in the Bachrach or Karsh style but in the high-gloss style of look-at-me fashion. They are shrill. Attributes are magnified; skin pores the size of craters.

How do we know this is art? Because he has also photographed coal miners, asylum inmates, and drifters. More importantly, *The New Yorker,* the arbiter of mid-cult intellectual fashion, gives Mr. Avedon almost weekly space, announcing him in boldface in the table of contents as simply "Avedon" (as if he were as important as Dior or Armani). And when the Whitney Museum of American Art arranged a retrospective of his work they called it: "Richard Avedon: Evidence 1944–1994." Evidence of what? Of art, of course. If we miss the point, the self-serving catalog aka press release helps us out. Mr. Avedon is "a major figure in postwar American art," we are told on a number of occasions.

To really see how fashion photography has brought the transgressive extremes into the mainstream under the rubric of art, leaf through *Fashion: Photography of the Nineties* (Nickerson 1996). Here, with no distracting copy, are the raw images that merchandizers thought would attract the attention of target audiences. And what a collection of images it is! Images of abuse, addiction, pain, angst, mutilation. Even the most forgiving viewer will conclude that modern fashion is brutal. Nothing airbrushed here. No images of airy elegance. Fashion is taking its cues from the world of the disaffected, the unkempt, the struggling, the battered, the bruised; in short, from adolescents. My favorites: a photo of a

THE ART OF AVEDON

©Richard Avedon, China Machado, 1965

Richard Avedon's photographs first appeared in Harper's Bazaar. Fifty years later, they appear at the Whitney.
Harper's Bazaar has helped make possible "Richard Avedon: Evidence 1944-1994".
A major retrospective at the Whitney Museum of American Art, on view through June 26, 1994.

BAZAAR
fashion's new testament

➤   Richard Avedon, an artist not a commercial photographer, has a show at the Whitney Museum
sponsored by Kodak and *Harper's Bazaar* (1994).

limp penis protruding from a pile of clothes, a young man peering up
the vagina of a headless woman, and an American gothic portrait in
which the female is holding the penis of her compatriot while both gaze
off to different horizons.

✸ FROM SKIN TO WALL: THE FASHIONING OF HOME AS SELF

Before we return to explain how the polarities of fashion got reversed
from flow-down to bubble-up, let's acknowledge fashion's place in two
separate areas: home decor and food preparation.

As we have seen, in the last few decades the power of commercial
branding has rapidly moved outward from the face (Cover Girl cosmetics to make you into the literal cover image of a fashion magazine), to
the body (Maidenform, body by Jake), to the choice of vehicle (the Bill
Blass edition of the Lincoln, the Eddie Bauer Jeep), and now even to the
inside of the house (Martha Stewart and Ralph Lauren both have lines
of designer house paint). A generation ago few people knew the names
of interior designers. Yet today the names of Martha Stewart, Laura
Ashley, and Ralph Lauren are like next-door neighbors. In fact, entire
"looks" of branded design stuff can give your house a unique personality, to match your own.

Take an abstract concept, for instance, like homeyness. The progenitor of the homey is the English country home. This look has recently
taken on aspects of a franchise, complete with numerous accessories.
We all know it by heart. Homey is warm (orange, gold, green, brown);
physical (wood, stone, brick, nothing plastic please); detailed (bay windows, beamed ceilings, dark wainscotting, joyful fireplaces, shutters,
porches, small paned windows, small front door); fabricked (floral); fur-
nished (in wood only) and filled with paddywhack images of personal
significance (silver framed pictures of family and pets, tattered books).

Just look at the ads in *The New Yorker* or the *New York Times Magazine*. Homey is on every other page. The English home look is informal,
cluttered, humble, comfy, unpretentious, reassuring, riskless. Every
form moves inward to the secure and successful and protected self:
low ceilings, small windows, ivy on outside walls, magazines on tables,
overhanging roof, awnings, hardback books, reading lights, circles of
chairs—warm and comfy. You can almost scratch and sniff this look. It
smells of good cooking. You can almost taste it. What is that smell? Is
it bread, coffee, or bacon cooking? No, it's Thanksgiving turkey.

Homeyness is a cultural construction and, as such, it can be prefabricated and then merchandised. Home sweet home is now as easy to construct as is the family crest. You send in your check and you receive by return mail a coat of arms. Laura Ashley or Ralph Lauren can assemble it, bric by bric, giving you either the feminine or masculine flavor. Generating this look is the basis of retail empires.[3]

Just take a walk up Madison Avenue and look in the shop windows. Interior house design is just an extension of exterior body display. So here we have the elegant shops of Ralph Lauren, Calvin Klein, Versace, Armani, Joseph, and even Gucci that carry everything from clothing to glassware. Fashion plays no favorites, however. What was once the preserve of the clients of "Sister" Parish (1910–1994), doyenne of English-style decorators in America, is now available down at your local Ethan Allen furniture store and is being delivered by the truckload stamped with the Martha Stewart name down at Kmart.

✳ TWO ALL-BEEF PATTIES: THE FASHION OF FOOD

Just as the stuff of home life has become branded with trademarked names and logos, so too has the staff of life. Although gustatory fashion really takes hold at the upper reaches of the market (wines, four-star restaurants, and specific delicacies like truffles), the substructure is remarkably similar. What is there that we eat that is not branded? Fruits are branded or stickered (Sunkist oranges, Dole bananas), vegetables are sold by place (California lettuce, Florida tomatoes, Idaho potatoes) and, of course, anything in a package has already been marked and named. The general rule of thumb (hopefully not the butcher's—after all, it was packaging that kept his thumb off the scale) is that the minute you can package a foodstuff, you can double the price. A tomato in a can is worth two in the hand, literally.

The exception sometimes proves the rule. Why has there been no na-

---

3. The reigning King of Clutter is the Prince of Chintz, Mario Buatta. You see his homeyness all over the place. Buatta has become a kind of patina on internal living space. He is partially responsible for all those dog portraits, chocolate pots, floral prints, trophies, tea caddies, cat needlepoints, tartan throws, saddles, bronze stags, Queen Anne tapestries, Georgian wine coolers, and all those stuffed things Americans consider English. When you go into a living room and you see all those table tops covered with silver photo frames and ersatz souvenirs, you know Buatta has been there before you.

tional brand of milk? Although the milk processors have had powerful ads touting the fluid ("Milk Does a Body Good," "Every Body Needs Milk," "Had Milk?" and the clever milk mustache), we may have to wait until our association with milk becomes more complex before it can be branded. It is simply too bland, too much like, well, too much like milk.[4] But look at what happens to milk made dangerous. Ice cream comes in national brands. From the phony named Häagen-Dazs to the phony righteous Ben & Jerry's, here at last we have a milk product acting like a caffeinated cola or a domestic beer—becoming fashionable.

The same process occurs in reverse along the roadside. The rise of fast food first depended on the branding of otherwise generic eats. The hamburger qua hamburger has all but disappeared. As they say, "A hamburger by any other name costs twice as much" and the Whopper, the Big Mac, or Dave's DeLuxe is proof. We know fast food by heart. We even know the ingredients. Ask anyone of my generation what it takes to make a Big Mac and you will see how deep the shared knowledge of commercial life really is. In case you've forgotten, here's the blueprint for 530 total calories and 28 grams of fat. Feel free to sing along: two all-beef patties, special sauce, lettuce, cheese, pickles and onions on a sesame-seed bun. Want cultural literacy, Professor Hirsch? Here it is.

Slow food works the other way around. Dining out is a special occasion, signifying extravagance, intimacy, or an expense account. It is difficult to brand but susceptible to fashionable tastes. Only true foodies can appreciate the distinctions Ruth Reichl and Daniel Puzo point out. Fast food, on the other hand, depends on branding. The food critics are your kids in the back seat and often what they want is not the meal but the prizes. Look around you, however, and you can see slow being made into fast as "in-between food" like Mexican (Taco Bell), Italian (Olive Garden), Japanese (Benihana), and various steak houses (Outback Steakhouse) are moving into branded territory.

Increasingly, social scientists have turned their attention to the world of consumption (and away from the world of production), because

---

4. The milk aisle is one of the few places where generics have moved in first and still dominate. Chain food stores initially captured sales from doorstep deliveries and then provided a range of healthier products in the form of skimmed and semi-skimmed milks as store brands. Most milk sales lose money, however. They are loss leaders sold to entice customers to buy other stuff, branded stuff.

consumption so clearly defines individual and social identity today. You are not your work, you are your purchases—not what goes *out* from the self but what comes *in*. For food, this is summarized in the catch-phrase, "you are what you eat," just as you are what you wear, what you drive, where you holiday, and so forth. The aphorism about being what we eat is a provocative distortion of the more palatable claim of the nineteenth-century French gourmet Brillat-Savarin: "Tell me what you eat and I will tell you what you are." Brillat-Savarin was making a claim for social status; we now interpret his words to denote social understanding.

For instance, while we are not much interested in milk, the fluid we really associate with lifestyle and fashion is beer. Beer is the product that made not Milwaukee but Madison Avenue famous. Beer succeeded (cigarettes a close second) because advertisers could claim associations that had nothing to do with the specific brand. The first pioneer was the redoubtable Claude Hopkins, famed wordsmith of Lord & Thomas, who asserted in the 1930s that the Schlitz company "steam-cleaned" its bottles. He knew perfectly well that all breweries did the same. But he pointed out a deep truth, which is that in matters of consumption no one cares much about the truth. Schlitz sales soared. Perception *is* reality. Schlitz was *clean* beer. You are clean to drink it. In the way we live now, you buy the beer that fits your lifestyle; it is a fashion statement, a taste that shows your good taste, an accessory.

Hopkins stumbled onto what was to be called the Unique Selling Proposition, and usp is now omnipresent. Because most people cannot distinguish the taste of "their" beer from other domestic brews, making a claim, albeit outrageous, is crucial. The object is to stake out and own certain emotional territory of target audiences. Or at least try to.

Of course, in most beer ads the usp is directed to sexual success. Buy the beer, become attractive, lure the girl. Ditto cigarettes. Smoke the weed, get the love object. But again the claim can move into distant areas. Marlboro "owns" the cowboy lifestyle, Virginia Slims attempts to own not just the woman's movement but slim looks, Parliament owns risky elegance, Camel is for real men in jeans, and so on.

✳ SELL-THROUGH TO FASHION

212

⟳ USP can be applied to such far-flung objects as actual pieces of clothing. As cigarettes and beer have been pulled off the low shelf and placed out of the reach of the kiddies, marketers have quit selling the products

➤ Called "sell-through," this is how to market cigarettes in a hostile environment. Sell the accessories. (R.J. Reynolds Tobacco Co., 1994)

and started selling the fashion. In fact, fashion has become the prime USP of cigarettes and beer.

In marketing this is called sell-through or continuity selling. Cigarette companies *have* to advertise to youngsters. Of course they deny this, but one of the central rules of marketing is that you always pitch to those who have not yet make their brand choices. So, for instance, if you look at ads for products like Revlon's Loving Care, you will see the models are nowhere near the age of graying hair. They are way too young. Why? The cosmetic companies know that you set the brand preference way before you expect the consumption. So too with cigarettes and beer.[5]

---

5. Although both industries will cross their hearts and hope to die in claiming they are only interested in brand switchers (and they will even do this to Congress on national TV), when you see campaigns like Joe Camel or see Miller logos plastered all over drag racers, you know better.

To get around the obvious problems of targeting the kiddies, the beer and cigarette behemoths (many of them are cocooned in conglomerates like Philip Morris and RJR Nabisco) have taken to selling fashionable clothing as an extension of their host product. So there is Joe Camel, wry and scrotal, on a windbreaker. Or here is a Marlboro patch on the book bag (called a climber pak, however, to drag a red herring over the trail), or the Budweiser emblem on jogging pants. No one seems to care about the appropriateness of the fashion statement; what is being sold is association with style.

✳ GET READY, GET SET, SURGE!

What started as a way for dangerous goods to circumvent public censure and possible government interference has blossomed into a surging new direction for marketers. In fact, look at how Coke is marketing Surge, its new competition for Pepsi's Mountain Dew. Surge is a greenish-yellow citrus drink high in calories, caffeine, and maltodextrin, an energy booster common in sports drinks. Alas, jumpiness is both the claim and the problem. You could tout Surge for what it is, as did Jolt cola a few years ago. But remember this is the Coca-Cola Company, not some renegade bottler. So Surge has been promoted with the usual print, radio, and Internet spots as well as direct mail advertising. But, as any college teacher can tell you, it was also given free to some million students, just the way cigarettes used to be back in the 1960s.

That's where fashion designer Al Abayan comes in. Abayan designed the funky, hip, urban streetwear line 1X2 and was commissioned to design the outfit the promoters of Surge wear while handing out samples of the soda on college campuses. To match the drink, Abayan designed a waterproof, three-quarter length, zip-up windbreaker in a melony green color. The jacket is vinyl on the inside and nylon on the outside, laminated together for warmth, and carries 3M's waterproof silver reflective tape on the sleeves and on the center of the back collar. I know all this because the young man who was giving free samples of Surge was also eager to explain his fashionable uniform. The front of the jacket features the red, lime green, and black Surge logo, which resembles a splash of liquid. The coat even has an accessory, a beanie with embroidered logo and some black, see-through plastic goggles. Now, you tell me, what has this outfit got to do with a pep-up sugar drink? Nothing. What it has to do with is fashion, style, and association.

Now observe the Surge television ads in which we see rag-tag teams of youngsters wearing their stormy weather garb to "Go For the Surge," or, in the company's caffeinated slogan, "Feed the Rush." In one version we see a tribe of ratty GenXers climbing up a mudpile to reach for the Surge at the top. In another, the group of stalwarts has taken to rolling down a hill inside fifty-gallon barrels to capture the Surge. In each spot they are all wearing the nifty outdoor gear necessary for such brainless endeavors.[6]

✳ HOW FASHION WORKS IN THE WAY WE LIVE NOW: DIFFUSION THEORY

Clearly what is happening is that fashion is up for grabs. In the eighteenth century, fashion flowed from the court to the courtesans; then in the nineteenth century from the designers to the demimondaine; now fashion is flowing from all over, especially up from the street. The only truths that have remained constant are that imputing *intent* to fashion is a tricky business, and that while fashion may be a visual art, and while it may be deep social commentary, it is primarily a way to manufacture difference and to sell new stuff. Just as movie makers make movies to make money, fashion designers make clothing for much the same reason. Call them auteurs if you want, call them couturiers if you must, but if they want to succeed they need to be called credit worthy by their bankers.

The great shift in fashion is how style is spread around. Let's return to my favorite text of modern consciousness, *Seinfeld*. On October 6, 1994, an episode titled "The Pledge" focused on the subject of the communication of style, fad, and fashion. Elaine sees the insufferably pompous Mr. Pitt eating a Snickers bar with his fork. She tells curious George, who then casually uses his silverware to eat candy in the Yankees board room. Soon Yankee execs are using their forks, then the players start doing it, and finally, full circle, at Monk's Cafe, the coffee

6. Clearly, Chicago-based ad agency Leo Burnett has the eXtreme sports theme of Mountain Dew in mind. In these Mountain Dew commercials the hell-bent peewees come flying at us on snowboards, skateboards, skydiving boards, and anything else that will literally get them over the top and into our faces. Alas, the Burnett agency did not know of certain copyrights; the name "Surge" and "Feed the Rush" had been claimed by three other companies, most touchingly by Babson Bros., a maker of Surge milking machines.

shop hangout, Elaine sees everyone eating Almond Joys with knives and M&Ms with spoons. She yells out: "What's the matter with you people. Are you mad?"

They are not, of course. They are simply participating in what is known as "diffusion theory." How are things adopted as standards? How is etiquette communicated? How do we know what to say, wear, behave? How does fashion flow? The first scholarly research centered on not candy in Manhattan or clothing in Paris but hybrid seed corn in Greene County, Iowa. In the 1930s a superior corn was available but not adopted by any of the 250 farmers in the county. Only a few planted it in 1933; then 1934 there were 16; then 25, then 21 more; in the next year 36; and the following year 61. After that the rate of acceptance dwindled—46, 14, three, until by 1941 all but two farmers studied were using new seed. No one knows why the diffusion works in this balloon-like bell curve, but it does.

Marketers claim to be able to isolate various groups calling them, by turns, Innovators, Early Adopters, Early Majority, Late Majority, and finally, the Laggards. The entire process is sometimes called trickle down, but that does not account for the systolic pulse that moves like a rabbit through the python. There is nothing new about the process. Supposedly, Josiah Wedgwood used this emulation-based technique when launching his china in the 1750s. First supply the fashion leaders, in this case, the crowned heads of Europe, and the inexorable inflating of the fashion bubble will occur. Sometimes the names of the consumption clusters change, but the inflation-deflation pulse remains constant.

Each broad social group, the theory goes, will have—now in hipper lingo—Purists, a handful of people who create the fashion; Style Leaders, who pick up on it first; Early Adaptors, who crave recognition by the Style Leaders; Happy Compromisers, who know they're not Style Leaders but know what's "in" and what they want from it; and the Unsophisticated, who dress up, dress funky, but probably get things six months too late. In the seed corn scenario made urban, these late-comers—fresh from the farm, as it were—can only watch as one bandwagon after another goes over the horizon.

✳ *FASHION TRICKLE—FIRST DOWN, THEN SIDEWAYS, NOW UP*

What separates the way we live now from earlier times is that the style leaders tend to be younger than the style followers. Once kids were the only ones with sufficient disposable time and money to consume, once advertisers realized that you sell to those who have not made brand choices, and once television became the primary medium of learning, trickle *down* reversed directions and became bubble *up*. As youth gradually captured the machinery of consumption *and* the delivery of entertainment, groundswells passed through commercial culture. What started in the 1920s, chronicled by Fitzgerald as the defining aspect of the Jazz Age, has become the norm: upper and lower crusts sprung unpluggable leaks.

Never underestimate television. In print/magazine culture you show a picture of a debutante or royal beauty puffing on your cigarette, or washing with your soap, and social aspiration does the job of inflating the diffusion bubble. With movies, so much the better, simply insert a movie star. But television is different. It is programmed by those who don't care about diffusion theory, and this audience doesn't know top from bottom. As *Seinfeld* showed, the changes now jump all over the place. George is not the usual avatar of fashion.

To be sure, modern fashion has always been willing to absorb sideways influence, the look of the street. Where would high fashion be without prostitutes and perverts? Think only of how successfully the cosmetic industry adopted the facepaint and lipstick of street walkers. Where do you think short skirts and four-inch stilettos come from if not from the red-light district? Over the last thirty years, fashion designers have also spent many hours in the fetishist's closet. How else to account for all the corsets, pointy bras, rubber macintoshes, frilly underwear, leather and latex gear, body rings, and tattoos? These appropriations have been so masterly that most trendy dressers who have adopted them have no idea about the fetishistic roots of their fashion. Meanwhile, there are doubtless fetishists running around fretting that their magical objects have been drained of their magical power.[7]

---

7. Look at Madonna's predilection for wearing Jean Paul Gaultier bustiers and wearing underwear as outerware, Michelle Pfeiffer's dominatrix getup in *Batman,* or RuPaul's platform shoes, and you will see how successfully S&M gear has jumped off the runway. An entire industry currently commodifies fetishism, to wit: Vivienne Westwood, Claude Montana, Thierry Mugler, Versace. In addition, you can see it bubbling up weekly into bourgeois discourse by looking at the "Fashions of the Times" section in the *New York Times Magazine.*

Fashion diffusion went down, sideways, but rarely up. At least not until recently—until television became the primary site of consciousness, and advertising the primary communicator of culture. A decade or so ago, if you had picked up any fashion magazine, you would have read how some fashion pundit was claiming that styles were being set somewhere or other. If not Paris, it was London or New York. The one place never mentioned was right in front of us: the downtown street, the barrio, and the slum. Now the people making fashion statements are the ones who used to be outside fashion. Counterculture has been mainstreamed: the conquest of cool.

✳ THE T-SHIRT AS EXEMPLUM OF WHAT'S HAPPENING

Consider the humble T-shirt. Two generations ago it was part of the working-class uniform.[8] Who can forget the uproar following Clark Gable's epochal unveiling in *It Happened One Night* (1934). He was *not* wearing an undershirt. How daring! But even worse was that by the 1950s the T-shirt started to hang around with the wrong crowd. It became the uniform of the anxious adolescent outlaw, worn by sensitive hoods and motorcyclists (Marlon Brando in the 1953 film *The Wild One* and James Dean in *Rebel Without a Cause*), usually accessorized with a dangling cigarette and a leather jacket. How dangerous! When Tennessee Williams's play, *A Streetcar Named Desire*, premiered in New York City, Marlon Brando's white T-shirt took top billing.

The T was next appropriated by the hippies. With bell-bottom pants and tie-dyed Ts, they offered another brand of anarchy. Not long after, T-shirts were catapulted to high style by the likes of Jackie Kennedy

---

8. The origins of the T-shirt go back to the long-tailed shirt that eighteenth-century soldiers tied diaperlike between their legs. By the Spanish-American War, this had advanced to the elbow- and hip-length undershirt worn beneath regulation jumpers by American sailors. At the start of the twentieth century, so the story goes, Queen Victoria ordered her soldiers to sew arms on their slingshot undergarments so she wouldn't have to see the underarm hair revealed when they saluted her. The U.S. Navy made the next fashion statement. It adopted a crewneck, short-sleeved, white cotton T-shirt as part of the standard-issue uniform in 1913. By the start of World War II the rest of the services had followed suit.

Onassis, who was spotted wearing T-shirts during the 1970s. Diffusion theory taking hold. By the 1980s, Don Johnson put T-shirts into the male mainstream of style when he sported them with jackets on *Miami Vice*. In a generation the short-sleeved cotton undershirt had gone from extreme hot to extreme cool.

The T-shirt is an apt example of how branding works with fashion once the fashion bubble is inflated. While the T-shirt never lost its democratic flair, designers understood its allure. In the words of Giorgio Armani: "Under a T-shirt, the beautiful bust of a woman or the handsome chest of a man are sculpted and desirable without becoming vulgar." He continues, writing in the Introduction to *The White T*, "And then, I love the T-shirt as an anti-status symbol, putting rich and poor on the same level in a sheath of white cotton that cancels the distinctions of caste" (Harris 13). Given such an observation, it was inevitable that designers would attempt to brand the object with their emblematic stamp—the T-shirt with the interlocking C and K, or the Polo pony, or DKNY.[9]

✳ ENTER THE GAP

Meanwhile, the Gap latched on to the T-shirt. Ironically, the success of the Gap's one-time branding of the T-shirt can be seen by the backlash and resurgence. Gap attire and advertising became the butt of jokes. Gap marketing attempted to position the T as a "classic," along with khakis and broadcloth shirts. To GenXers, anything classic is the cross to the vampire. They want anything but. By the time Douglas Coupland, author of the book *Generation X* and one of his peers' favorite spokesmen, made public his unwillingness to appear in a Gap ad, the diffusion bubble had burst.[10] High culture was not in an uproar, sideways culture did not care, it was the kids who balked.

9. Incidentally, you can see this process happening in reverse with the Levi Strauss campaign. They are now advertising their nondesigner jeans as having been worn by designers. Hence the billboards show only the Levi's tag and the headline "Calvin Wore Them," or "Tommy Wore Them," or "Ralph Wore Them" (referring to Messrs. Klein, Hilfiger, and Lauren, respectively).

10. Opened in 1969, Gap once offered the epitome of cool, with basic T-shirts and pants that looked like designer clothing without the arrogance—no

Commercial culture responded. Mock ads with headlines like "Jeffrey Dahmer wore khakis" appeared in 'zines. Closer to the mainstream, on ABC's popular *Ellen,* comic Ellen DeGeneres, reaching for the ultimate putdown, tagged her navy- and khaki-clad neighbors "gaps." The reference may pass me by, but it is picked up by the only demographic sector that counts. On NBC's *Saturday Night Live,* a recurring skit has actors mocking Gap's valley girl-like sales clerks. The Gap was learning the first law of cool: nothing defeats like success.

Who knows, the Gap T may go the way of the zoot suit, another up-from-below fashion style. But wait, not so fast. As I write this, the Gap is repositioning the T as part of a retro swing culture in a series of exuberant dance ads. And the zoot suit, which featured the tarp-on-a-stick shape, is currently on its way back *up*. Not as a suit, mind you—that would be asking too much—but as a style. As a suit, the zoot had wide, padded shoulders, narrow cuffs, baggy, high-waisted trousers, and a long, draped jacket. The exaggerated fashion fad blasted away an era of conformity and became a uniform for swinging hipsters of the 1940s. Like hip-hop fashion of today, zoot is an eye-popping style that is loose-fitting enough for dancing and sloppy enough to upset Mom. No wonder young men are wandering around with their pants riding at half-mast, making Dan Aykroyd's refrigerator repairman into a fashion plate. Now, that's cool.

✳ BUBBLE-UP CULTURE: YOUTH WILL BE SERVED

The street with all its raucous noise has triumphed over the salon with its hushed calm. In retrospect, a century hence, the T-shirt and baggy pants will not be seen as anomalies, but as the wave of change. Since

fancy labels, logos, or inflated price tags. Gap boomed to 892 stores as its apparel became the uniform of the middle class and the middle-aged. In 1992, about 90 percent of teens said Gap clothes were "cool," in Leo Burnett Co.'s biannual "What's hot among kids" survey. But that fell to 83 percent the next summer, to 75 percent in winter 1993, and to 66 percent in the two most recent polls—diffusion in reverse. In the "coolest brands" category, a 1996 Teenage Research Unlimited survey showed Nike, Guess, and Levi's beating Gap (Duff 6).

the 1960s, the primary fashion plates are no longer in store windows or in glossy magazines, but in entertainment.

And entertainment is driven by a carnival culture carried inside the television loop. How long is the line in front of this show? asks the carnival barker in charge of programming for NBC. As we know all too well, this carnival is programmed to a demographic niche of twelve- to thirty-year-olds, so of course, getting to them is the primary preoccupation of our culture. It is not that we worship youth; it is that youth (and all it en-

➤ Be an individual, paint your toes mildew. (Urban Decay, 1998)

tails about consumption) has become the financial center of our culture.

Little wonder then that the phenomenon of "granny dumping" occurs in all modern media. Why program to people who are uncooperative to the claims of advertising? The success of first ABC and now Fox has shown the commercial viability of mining younger and younger audiences. Little wonder that the major news magazines are being dumbed down (have you looked at *Time* recently?); that the now-in-living-color *New York Times* has added special sections on entertainment and "living"; that movies are filled with explosions and car chases; that Stephen King and Harlequin Romances sell more than all the first novelists each year put together times ten; that the millimeter-thin World Wide Web is growing like loam; that the evening television news looks exactly like *Current Affair* and *Inside Edition,* and, well, you know the rest of this dreary litany.

In this context, little wonder that the trends in fashion since the 1960s have followed the kiddies. Remember fashion's first rule: make money. From the hippies to the mods to the punks to grunge, the magnetic poles of what is fashionable have been shifted downward. The whole concept of taboo, so central to adolescence and to the avant-garde, has been commodified and exploited so often that its path has become predictable. Once you put a ring in your nose, the eyelid, lip, nipple, genitals are sure to follow.

To wit: A few years ago teenage girls in punk and rap clubs started to wear nail varnish and lipstick in black and shades of dark blue. Look at the models in *Harper's Bazaar.* Now look at the ads. One from a delightfully named company, Urban Decay, has lipstick, nail polish, and rouge with names like Plague, Bruise, Rat, Roach, Pigeon, and Asphyxia for young ladies—and Uzi and Asphalt for their young escorts.

Of course, such fashion is jarring to the eye, sometimes shocking, sometimes offensive. It receives attention because it is designed to surprise. Right this way to the freak show. Generating frisson is the allure of the midway. Carnival shock is the stable of midcult fashion.

✳ GETTING TO YOUR SELF BEFORE THEY DO: THE FASHION OF SELF-BRANDING

In fashion, individualism has been colonized by corporate interests. As counterculture has been mainstreamed, the truly rebellious, like the fetishists, have found themselves either locked out or penned in. When *Lollapalooza,* the music fair of GenX, is sponsored by Sony and Time Warner, you know there is little frontier left. Rather than be branded by the "phallocentric hegemonic corporate culture," many adolescents have taken to doing it to themselves—literally. Walk down any street in the Western hemisphere and what you see as style is a startling reaction to style itself. The height of chic is cool, and nothing is more cool than to look poor, downtrodden, and beyond style.

Body piercing, scarification, nose rings, lip rings, unmentionable-places rings, plus that old standby, tattooing, are not so much the signs of rebellion as of the colonization of the only personal space left. Quick! Brand yourself before the worldwide conglomerated package goods company headquartered somewhere out in the American Midwest does it for you.

This kind of self-customizing is stunning, literally. It is on the edge. The epidermis, which the ancient Romans branded as punishment for disobedience (a stigma, literally a brand), has come full circle with self-stigmatization. In a world where secondhand smoke, sugar, saccharin, and asbestos are the hobgoblins, in a culture that spends part of its energy telling kids how great they are and the rest saying there is no room for them at the inn, in a commercial world in which adolescents can drive the car, but only down to the clotted mall, it is not unreasonable that youngsters should turn to such rites of self-imposed initiation. Where is the risk of danger in a world of air bags, training wheels, and curbs on all sidewalks? Such self-branding seems to say "been there, done nothing, don't care, on my own."

So fashion returns to its primal core: skin decoration. To the kids who are so savvy about the colonization of their space by industrial interests, perhaps there is really no place to go but to the literal edge, their own soft skin. After all, if fashion statements are being instantly co-opted by Ralph, Donna, Calvin, Tommy, and Giorgio the only personal thing you have left is your own personal thing. When Mercedes-Benz runs an ad in which they have burned their small logo into the face of Marilyn Monroe to appear as a birthmark and then titled the piece "Glamour," you have to move fast to make your own way.

So if you are a boy you pierce an ear; which ear was important years ago but now any ear will do. Then you test your resolve. How much of a statement do you want to make? A pierced nose, lip, bellybutton, nipple, or genital? A bone through the eyebrow? One of the latest teen

idols, a member of the Spice Girls, has a metal stud through her tongue. In a recent Calvin Klein jeans advertisement one model has studs poked through her cheeks. "Gimme my space," say Jason and Jennifer. "I need to be myself. The body is my temple. Double-dare you to do the same."

Almost a third of my students are pierced. Many of them are also tattooed. A few are even scarified with body burns. No one yet has a cicatrice, where metal shapes are inserted below the skin, but I guess it's coming. Is it too insane to imagine that some kid will stretch the bottom lip so you could fit a Marilyn Manson CD in it? Who knows?

Nose rings and tattoos: the cultural complexities of self-branding. (Postum in 1944 and Mercedes-Benz in 1998)

✴ A RALPH LAUREN AD

In 1979 Dick Hebdige, an English academic at the Center for Contemporary Cultural Studies at the University of Birmingham, wrote what was to be the prescient book about the influence of fashion from below, *Subculture: The Meaning of Style*. His book took youth subgroups seriously just as the great inversion of fashion was about to occur. Hebdige's categories were ones we find self-evident today, although in different guises: teddy boys (excluded and temperamentally detached from the respectable working class, but uncompromisingly proletarian and xenophobic); mods (lower-class dandies, obsessed with the small details of dress); skinheads (aggressively proletarian, puritanical and chauvinist); Rastafarians (the most political grouping, a style that proclaimed unequivocally the alienation felt by many young black Britons); and punks (inhabitants of nameless housing projects, anonymous slums, blank, expressionless, rootless).

Hebdige attempted to sum up the moods, needs, and desires of British youth as reflected in the fashion statements they chose to make. Was he on target? Have a look at this two-page, side-by-side ad from Ralph Lauren appearing in the *New York Times Magazine* and tell me he did not see what was coming. The current upside down fashion clearly had put down its roots decades ago.

Ralph Lauren is no fool. Like Calvin Klein, Tommy Hilfiger, Giorgio Armani, Donatella Versace, Donna Karan, and a number of other household words who now have, or are planning, stores on Madison Avenue, he is merchandiser first, then a designer. You cannot look at these images without thinking that the dapper and debonair designer Lauren must have cringed as the merchandiser Lauren took over. That

➤ Dress for success à la Ralph Lauren. Side by side full pages. (*New York Times Magazine*, February 16, 1997)

beat-up Vespa, symbol of the ancient battle between Mods and Rockers of the 1960s in London, that African skirt and those Rasti wrist/ankle bracelets, that plaid overshirt and horizontal striped undershirt, that shoulder-length hair and day-old beard—my, my, is this really the audience for Mr. Lauren's chest-protecting Polo pony?

And what of petulant Junior to the right? Has he spent too much time prepping at St. Grottlesex, or what? Maybe this kid used to get into Yale, but no longer. Now he's off to the local community college. He presents the layered look borrowed from a Westport drunk: madras pants, seersucker suit jacket, cotton T-shirt, broadcloth dress shirt, wool cricket sweater, bandana as handkerchief, and that tie, that hat, that look! Goodness me, this is so "bad" that Mr. Lauren, the merchandiser, must really be with it.

✳ CHILL OUT: SLANG, SWAGGER, AND SAGGING JEANS

Both Mr. Laurens had better get with it or Tommy Hilfiger will eat their lunch. Mr. Hilfiger has not just acknowledged the upside down nature of contemporary fashion, he has exploited it, sometimes ruthlessly. After all, Mr. Hilfiger seems to reason, if inner city youths will kill for a $70 pair of sneakers or a $200 jacket with athletic insignia, you might just as well go along for the ride. While white kids in Greenwich are ho-humming the layered look, these inner city kids really care about fashion. "I'd kill to wear that" and "a look to die for" are no idle praise.

Mr. Hilfiger has made the "urban homeboy" look au courant in the burbs by picking up 'hood fashion, sticking his name on it, and returning it to the street, gratis. He even has the chutzpah to call giving his branded clothing to the poor "giving something back." It might be better understood as very savvy marketing.

"The Look," which Mr. Hilfiger has merchandized, is a favorite of street rappers. It essentially consists of oversized shirts worn over pants lopped down to the thighs showing BVDs with an elastic band peeking out that reads "Tommy Hilfiger." Calvin Klein was the first to colonize this space, inching ever closer to branding the groin. The dropped drawers recontextualize not just the floppy zoot suit but also prison style where no belt means that everything has to slop down the back. Like prison-made denim, which passed through the fashion radar a few years ago, associating with the enforced outré is now fashion conformity.

But Hilfiger has done more. As a savvy merchant, he has supported various rap groups with clothing ensembles and artistic subventions. Just as athletes get free branded sportswear to take onto the playing fields, so city toughs get free clothing to make statements in the street. For this tax-deductible contribution, Mr. Hilfiger has been memorialized in rap lyrics. Here are a few:

> Tommy Hill was my nigga
> and others couldn't figga
> how me and Hilfiga
> used to move through with vigga —Q-Tip on Mobb Deep's "Drink Away the Pain"

> Fuck rap hip hop for me off top
> Lo wears and Tommy Hill frily shit with a knot
> The witty unpredictable live shit
> Drive by shit
> Do or die shit —Chef Raekwon, "Criminology"

This crossover synergy works. It sells *schmatte* ebonically. When Snoop Doggy Dogg, a rap artist who had been a "long-time friend" of Mr. Hilfiger, appeared on *Saturday Night Live* with a Hilfiger shirt, the shirt was sold out across the country the next day. Who cares that Mr. Dogg—not a paragon of probity—had been tangled up in a drive-by shooting, found with a loaded gun in his car, and convicted of various misdemeanors not untypical of a certain segment of Los Angeles youth? What is important is that he is speaking to us not from on high but from down low. Is he ever.

Meanwhile, Mr. Hilfiger, who lives the high life in British Tudor splendor in Greenwich with his wife, four kids, eight servants, and three groundskeepers, keeps in close contact with the street. The other street, Wall Street, is also impressed, making his stock one of the high fliers of recent times. He is certainly not the only one upstairs cashing in on what is happening down below. Topsy-turvy is the norm. Look at Benetton's cynical exploitation of poverty and political correctness, with which it self-righteously condemns capitalism while selling what? Colored sweaters. Or what about all-time favorite Calvin Klein, whose relentless cruising of the outré envelope passes close to the man/boy love association, anorexia, pedophilia, bestiality, and, well, whatever is naughty.

I'm not ranting about the carnivalization of culture here (well, okay, just a bit) as much as I am trying to show how the energy fields of style, taste, fashion, fad, vogue, and all the stuff that makes common consciousness is moving *up*, not *down*. Scrawny Kate Moss is a top model; heroin chic becomes a fashion; and "gangsta" rap sells insignia-heavy garments not just because the swagger of the street is clearly more explosive than the life of the salon but also because it is cool, chillingly cool. As Thomas Frank has recently shown in *The Conquest of Cool,* business culture has become counterculture. Consumerism is hip. With no gates, let alone gatekeepers, what do you expect?

✳ *UNIQUE INDIVIDUALS IN CLUSTER GROUPS*

In marketing jargon this appropriation/exploitation is called reverse marketing or sell-back. You go to the street to find what is cool, change it a tad to make it seem slightly original, slap on your brand, and return to sender in the street. From there you push it upward to where the big money is—at the mall.

As might be expected, the growth in advertising research has been in the proliferation of professional trendspotters, wavemakers, or coolhunters. These people, often kids themselves, scour the streets looking for the surging foam of a new wave. What will it be? Hush Puppy shoes, Mountain Dew, retro peacoats, orange spiked hair, Econoline vans, ska music, gothic games, facepaint, heroin, raves? What about Brooks Brothers blue shirts, J. Press sportcoats, silk rep ties, wingtips, gray flannels? Who knows and, in a sense, who cares? The objects of current desire are not important. The hot-handed users are. They show the future fashion.

To find these hot hands a new band of snitches has sprung up. They no longer depend on focus groups. They watch not the catwalks in Paris but the back alleys of Austin. They lurk in San Francisco, Seattle, Chicago, New York, and Los Angeles, attempting to construct a taxonomy of taste they can resell to their clients. Remember, ad agencies have two selling jobs to do. First, they must sell their clients on the fact that they know what they are doing and are worth trusting with millions of dollars. Second (and less important), they have to try to sell the client's product. So they hover in chatrooms on the World Wide Web; attend music industry parties, art openings, and poetry readings; visit fashion showrooms and trade shows; and drink lots of strong coffee. Following the footsteps of Faith Popcorn, these researchers (primarily young women who are more trusted by the kids) produce reports of life in the skateboard lane.[11]

---

11. It is perhaps a sign of how we live now that a popular method of observation is to send coolhunters out with videocams to record conversations of delight or disgust. Old-style research won't work because the kids can't fill out questionnaires and are also hard to interview because of articulation

In expensive reports with names like "MindTrends," the "L Report," and the "Hot Sheet," these consulting companies with conservative names like Teen-Age Research Unlimited, the Zandl Group, and Roper Starch Worldwide tattletale back to the fifty-year-old Man at the Agency about what is going to be moving. It has not yet become fashion. It will.

One of the most interesting reports comes from a group called Sputnik (they are spies, get it) which publishes "MindTrends." Sputnik services big-time clients like Pepsico, J.C. Penney, North Face, Reebok, Levi Strauss, to name a few. In keeping with the Zeitgeist of colonizing the fringe by making it alternative (as in alternative music, alternative beauty colors, alternative lifestyles, alternative solutions), Sputnik relabels Generation X the "Alternative Generation."

So here, named and described according to Sputnik (and my own classroom experience), are the subcultures churning at the edge of Alternative Generation (Lopiano-Misdom and De Luca 29-45). Don't be upset if by the time you read this the groups have evaporated—that's just the point.

1. **Club Kids:** These kids live at night flitting between clubs and hence have affinity for all those things that go bump in the night. Most are female. When I see them in my classes they are looking a little peaked, bodies pierced, tattooed, sometimes with black lipstick and nails. When they come up to see me after class it is almost never about the course material but because I once wrote some books on horror literature and movies. These kids like all kinds of stuff from the beyond, like cartoony versions of vampires, space aliens, fetishists, and cross-dressers. They watch a lot of the Fox channel shows like *X-Files*. Their fashion tastes run to vinyl clothing, boots, weird cosmetics, and revivals of anything outré like platform shoes. They get to the cutting edge first. Although they are the second largest group after Hip Hop, the Club Kids have the biggest fashion input. They like to look and be seen. They understand Dennis Rodman.

2. **The Speed Generation:** Mostly boys who sit in the back row, these sports enthusiasts like skateboarding and mountain biking (they even bring these bikes to class), wear a combination of techno and 1970s retro fashion, and drink Surge. These are the young who define themselves by their energy and dedication to "eXtreme sports"—motorcycling, mountain cycling, snowboarding, surfboarding, skate-

⇧ ───────────

problems. Best method? Just give the camera to the kids—they know what to record.

boarding, and so on. They watch a lot of ESPN2. They may sleep in my classes but they are caffeinated elsewhere. Their fashion interest runs to jeans, T-shirts, which should be printed with images from children's cartoons, and everpresent, backward-worn baseball caps.

3. **The Collective Intellect:** Bookish, vegetarian neo-beats, these kids are more concerned with social issues than fashion, forging a look that is a combination of mod, techno, and hippie styles. They sit in the front row. Will this be on the test? they ask. The Collective Intellect is the more educated and cultured fringe. They like 1950s retro home decoration, avant-garde films, good books, as well as beatnik fashions—all of which means they spend money. These young people drive beat-up old cars and anticipate a more limited Armageddon than the Hip Hoppers and Speedos. They are very curious about what it was like to be in college during the Vietnam War.

4. **Soldiers for Culture:** Like the above, except they tend to be more multiethnic and spiritual. The Soldiers for Culture are the new-age beatniks crowding the coffee bars of the big cities. They may be vegetarians and believe in boycotting animal-derived products. They like to buy sneakers made from fake suede instead of leather. You never mention the importance of animal research or that such activity might benefit them. Watch your language around them, they care passionately and are politically correct. Don't try to tell them that multiculturalism is often limited to just a few cultures, hardly multi.

5. **The Hip Hop Nation:** The largest and best-known group, which embraces both preppy and techno fashions. Designer clothing, retro shoes, and track suits are favored. They are the biggest spenders and music is central to consumption. Many of them want to earn a living from the pop music industry, and all of them try to look as if they do. Rap music came from this culture. The established badge of the falling-down, baggy jeans is on the way out, however. Often at sales or secondhand shops, they are now buying Chanel, Gucci, Versace, Donna Karan, Ralph Lauren, Calvin Klein, and Tommy Hilfiger. They then put these clothes together with care into an oversized ensemble. Like others of their generation, they like the ersatz. An older Hip Hopper wants to be noticed drinking dry martinis while eating fast food from the strip mall chains. Choice of car is critical: they are on their way to buying a sport utility wagon, but don't tell them.

While Sputnik's taxonomy is refreshingly canty, each competing consulting group has its own labeling system. For some reason, each seems

to consist of about five subgroups of unique individuals who cluster together in fashion tribes. So here is the pattern outlined by the Zandl
Group: (1) Noisy Boys: rap and metal music enthusiasts; (2) Glamour
Girls: ultrafeminine, into relationships and fashion; 3) New Tradition-
als: conservatives, with understated tastes; and (4) Bohemians: alternative, underground culture.[12]

I mention all these various groups because, although these consul-
tants have a vested interest in producing what seems to be unique observations, they are highly redundant. What unifies them is that for the
first time in Western culture, the center of fashion gravity has clearly
shifted. These kids, not their parents, are powering change. They run
the carnival. What comes down the catwalk is judged not by the likes of
Diana Vreeland but by those just entering adulthood.

One sees this everywhere. Movies are driven by blockbusters, and
blockbusters are films viewed by repeat viewers, and those viewers are
clearly the kids. Television is programmed not for middle-aged "brand
dumpers" but for those who have not even chosen a brand. Even books,
long a refuge for the contemplative if not literate, are driven by the
popular tastes of those who think reading is watching words on TV.
So why should fashion be different? It is not that the gatekeepers
fell asleep; it is that the money trail so clearly leads to those with disposable time and income. And where much of that money changes hands
is down at the mall.

---

12. We are not alone. The British, who love social taxonomies, have their own
    bubble-up graph put together by Right of Admission Reserved (ROAR), an
    enormous study of youth attitudes, funded by ad agencies, newspapers,
    radio stations and commercial television stations. The study ran over five
    months from August 1995 to January 1996. Thousands of fifteen- to
    twenty-four-year-olds were interviewed about their consumption habits,
    their jobs, their incomes, and their loves and hates and hopes and dreams.
    It was the largest and most comprehensive research study into the youth
    market ever. Here's what they found: (1) Bill and Ted—this group has
    three passions in life: music, music, and music; (2) Conservative Career-
    ists—the English equivalent of yuppies; (3) Moral Fibers—they excel at
    their studies, are good at games, say "no" to drugs; (4) Blairites—English
    Clintonians, politically correct and proud of it; (5) New Modernists—
    artistic, principled, trendy, and not yet graduated; (6) Corporate Club-
    bers—East Enders living for the weekend; and (7) Adolescent Angst—
    those having a hard time with the opposite sex, adolescence, and devel-
    oping taste, so they play lots of computer games (Armstrong features).

7

Enough Talk

Let's Shop!

Because you see the main thing today is—shopping. Years ago a person, if he was unhappy, didn't know what to do with himself—he'd go to church, start a revolution—something. Today you're unhappy? Can't figure it out? What is the salvation? Go shopping.

—Arthur Miller, *The Price*, 1968

✳ *I TRY A LITTLE CHRISTMAS SHOPPING*

It is just before 7:00 A.M. on the Friday after Thanksgiving and I am standing at one of the side entrances to the Crabtree Mall in Raleigh, North Carolina. The police are guarding the door and people are streaming in from all over like ants waiting for the picnic to begin. Crabtree Mall is located on the western side of Raleigh down in a flood plain with gentle hills rising from all sides. Everything drains down to here. From where I stand you can watch the cars and buses, headlights still on, descending those hills to the mall. Although I usually hate to shop at any mall and always hate to Christmas shop, I am not here to criticize. I intend to follow people around for a day. Surrogate shopping.

Most of my early rising compatriots are white-haired females, many hunched over, some with canes. They have come with bags on their shoulders. A few have gotten dressed up in Christmas red and are wearing "Christmas: Bring It On!" type outfits. A few wear Santa hats with long red pompoms. Other shoppers have sweatshirts with the names of stores like Banana Republic or Timberland on their fronts. No kids are here; too early. One woman is pushing a baby stroller, but the baby is nowhere to be seen. Another one has an airport luggage carrier. As far as I can see I am the only rogue male. What few men there are, are with their wives. We jostle at the entrance and then at exactly 7:30 the doors of Chartres swing open and we rush inside.

The mall has a grandiose interior—everything is way too big. Although many newer malls attempt to re-create the look of ye olde downtown complete with streets and pretend streetlights, Crabtree's theme seems to be shiny stuff piled on shiny stuff. The place is literally hung with outsized Christmas tree ornaments. Escalators go up the middle apse, giving a view of the three stories of brimming display spilling out from the stores onto the walkway. Huge balloons, hung by steel cables, seem to float from the ceiling.

In the very center of the lower level is Santa and "Santaland." Old Saint Nick sits in a most uncomfortable wingback chair that is clearly set up for photos, as it has reflecting screens all around it. He sits alone—it's too early. Over his head is a store catalog and descriptive map so the jolly old fellow can point out to Junior's mom where to go. For a long time Santa does no business, then suddenly in early afternoon it goes like gangbusters. Perhaps diffusion theory can explain why kids will either line up for hours to meet Santa, or ignore him.

Each store seems to have made an effort to produce an interior to go with the pretend window that fronts the walkway. So the Great Outdoor Provision Co. is made to look like a gold-mining store complete with a raw wood creaking floor. Victoria's Secret looks like a whorehouse. The computer store looks like an old Univac with whirring noises and big screens playing endless diagrams. The athletic stores look like locker rooms, with banners announcing "Team Pride" and "Go Team." Not so the Lady Foot Locker; it looks just like a shoe store. Treasure Isle sells jewelry and appears to be something from the South Seas. Pier 1 Imports looks like . . . you guessed it, a pier filled with off-loaded stuff, as does The Bombay Company. The Tinder Box is a giant humidor. The Warner Bros. Studio Store is misnamed, however. It doesn't look like a studio office. It resembles The Disney Store down the way. Both have huge cartoon figures out front—Daffy Duck, Bugs Bunny, Mickey and Minnie—just like the gods outside a Greek temple. Athletic Attic isn't, but Nordic Track looks like an infomercial gym, and Abercrombie & Fitch is a men's smoking club. Only the Gap and J. Crew are holdouts.

They are minimalists to the *nth,* no window displays, merchandise piled up on simple display counters.

The only crowded store in the early morning is the Hallmark Card Store. I pop in but can't stay long because it reeks of patchouli. At a big display near the window is a clutch of shoppers. I think the attention might be on cute Christmas cards, but instead it is cards called "Between You and Me." Serious people, mostly women, were examining the inventory. Here is what they are considering: "I Still Believe in Our Love," "Loving Me Isn't Always Easy," "God Meant Us to be Special Friends," "We'll Make It Through," "Please Give Me a Second Chance," "Please Forgive Me for Being Moody," and my favorite, which is also well read, "Mother—We Have So Much in Common." Perhaps these early shoppers are not as happy as they seem.

Many stores have Christmas signs and decorations in their faux windows announcing "Share the Joy." I'm not sure why these stores need glass in the windows since everything is hermetically sealed, but the glass does provide a sense of separation and a place to hang seasonal stuff.[1] And the windows allow a variation of POP (point of purchase) signage. A touching sign in the Lerner New York store under a misty picture of a young lady clearly in the throes of the Voluntary Simplicity movement says, "I Wish for a Little Simplicity."

While there is no music in the walkways, there is music and plenty of it inside the individual stores. One store, 'Tis The Season, is filled with predecorated trees all complete and ready to take home. Christmas carols are blaring. I can't stay long. I try to figure out if each store has a different Muzak theme, but it is an aural blur. The sounds are of Christmas music all right, but I don't recognize any of the tunes. At the Music Box Company they promise to "give musical memories," but they play the same canned stuff.

On the corner of the mall are the ubiquitous anchor stores— Hecht's, Sears, Hudson Belk, and—what everyone is very proud of

---

1. As nineteenth-century merchants found, a glass window allows the viewer to be reflected among the things for sale, while at the same time placing the things at a distance. Distance is important because it seems to say that this is valuable, behind glass, yet at arm's length. Glass countertops revolutionized retailing. Glass also inhibited the rising tide of Victorian shoppers whose arms reached, lifted, and shoved merchandise under coats.

and wants to tell me about—the new Lord & Taylor. Inside these stores are perky young women hawking not just free samples of awful-smelling stuff, but store-specific credit card applications. "Fill it out and get a free gift."

About 9:30 African American women start to appear. Kids come with them. Soon couples appear—I see the first men by themselves. I'm busily taking notes, and I notice many of the women are doing it too. Clearly, they are working up a future shopping list.

I like touching things and the mall is a toucher's paradise. "Touch our Velveteen Collection" says The Campagnie Internationale. At Brooks Brothers I am encouraged to touch the Egyptian cotton shirts. In The Disney Store a young lady asks if I would like to touch a stuffed Dalmatian, as they have hundreds to advertise the release of the non-cartoon version of 101 Dalmatians. At The Comfort Zone I can get my feet massaged, touched by professionals.

In the center of the three decks that make up the mall are numerous vendors of specialty items that all have the "personal touch." This must be very close to what the ancient marketplace was like: stalls and street vendors. Here you can get a baseball hat with granny's name on it from Custom Caps. Or you can have a picture of yourself transferred onto a sweatshirt. Here is where the "World's Best Dad," "Sports Mom," and "Granny's Catch" shirts come from. And what of wearing this down your front: "God Made Moms and It Was Good; God Made Little Sis and It Was Better; God Made Grandmas and It Was Awesome!"?

Many of the little tucked-in shops have "Accessories" in their names like Claire's Accessories, which gives the impression that their stuff goes with other stuff. But I can't imagine how most of their stuff goes with anything. You can accessorize elsewhere. At A Natural Nail you can get "therapeutic pedicuring" as well as acrylic, silk, or gel nails. At Bee Natural you find what bees make, and at The Herb Shop are herbs. Imagine Victoria sells big earrings and large pins. Impostors Copy copycats jewelry. Watch out for Tiny Treats, though; they may be misnamed. At El Kisosito you buy trinkets and at Nautical Hangups you get T-shirts with maps. Beanbag Nation, County Seat, Moondance Gallery, and a place to get your family crest, called Historic Research, are all in this street bazaar. I appreciated Tamera's Unique Expressions. Tamera was selling "creative" rubber stamps. You can also get your ears pierced at four separate locations, my favorites named Afterthoughts and The Piercing Pagoda. Clearly, this is the place where the central rites of passage are performed on our children. No tattoo artists in this mall, not yet.

Many stores have to do with body decoration. There is Hair to Go, which sells wigs; The Body Shop, which sells everything organic for your body; the Polaroid Face Place, where you get your picture taken; and one called Glamour Shots, which allows you to choose a self: Romantic, Professional, Glamorous, Fun, or Elegant. First you get decorated as a beauty queen, a movie star, or a glamourpuss, with special wigs, clothing, and face paint. Then you have a videocam test just like a screen test to see what part fits you best. Finally, the photo session. Although the store advertises that they will do this for $14.95, it is really much more expensive. It would have cost me almost $150 to give my wife a few pictures of me as a roughneck roustabout.

I spent a lot of my time in a store called Successories, taking a pause from my labors and thinking about my life. Successories sells accessories for those on the way up. I think it's for men, or for women who want to buy something they think men will like. I was initially much taken with the welcome mat out front. It said, "You Can't Spell Success Without U" and there was a note in the window, "Looking For People to Join Our Team." What their "Success Team" does is sell "Posters, Passion, Priorities, and Champions," or at least that is what the signs said. There were plenty of quotation books titled *Power of Goals, Quest for Success,* or *Go Get It.* There was a special shrine for Dale Carnegie's *Think and Grow Rich.* Lesser shrines were for Tom Peters and Deepak Chopra, M.D. (P.A.?).

In Successories, pictures and plaques of Vince Lombardi approximate those of Christ in Florentine churches. There was a statue of a football with this inscription: "If you don't pick up the ball and run with it, someone else will." A generic ball says, "The one who complains about the way the ball bounces is likely the one who dropped it." And another: "When you control the ball, you control the score." Golfers also are in the Successories crosshairs. They can buy pictures of impossible tee shots to improbable greens with the titles *Focus,* or *Perseverance,* or the heroic *Make It Happen.* Even Tiger Woods could not make one of the shots: teeing off from a skyscraper and landing on an island green far from shore.

I also spent time at The Nature Company and the Museum Company. The Nature Company has pithy sayings carved on stones, deerhead weather vanes, flocks of ducks on things, plastic tyrannosauruses, moose pajamas, and reams of notices proclaiming how a percent of their profits "goes back to nature." Ditto the Museum Company. The Museum Company even has a plaque on the entrance proclaiming:

> Because museums play a unique role in preserving mankind's great cultural achievements, we encourage you to visit and support your favorite museum. For our part, the Museum Company is committed to dedicating a share of our profits to museums.

They make their profits by selling Michelangelo's *David* in Christmas garb, a *Mona Lisa* stamp pad, *Venus De Milo* on a paperweight, Queen Nefertiti as magnetic note pad, Degas-illustrated handbags, and numerous plastic and plaster reproductions of nameless classical statuary with labels such as "Eternal Love" or "L'Amour." There are even freestanding collections: The Greco-Roman Collection of Jewelry, The Middle Eastern Collection, and the Russian, Celtic, and African collections. Personally, I can't stand any place that sells those painfully cute photographs of Weimaraners by William Wegman, so I was happy to get out in a hurry.

By noon cellphoners appear at the mall. Power shoppers step aside. These are power people. I imagine the cellphoners are receiving instructions from home base. Women now appear wearing long formal skirts. Their clothes say, "This is important and social and I'm serious about it." Now there are dads with their kids in tow, divorced dads by the looks of it because they are looking confused. Or are they buying presents for mom? Knee-knockers are now appearing in strollers. Teenage girls in twosomes, then packs of them, materialize. Teenage boys? Not many.

The mall police are now out in force. The serious shoppers from early morning have gone and so perhaps it is time for the serious shoplifters. The security force has radios, handcuffs, huge shiny badges, shoulder patches that announce "Security Officer," polished black shoes, canisters that look menacing (Mace?), but thankfully, no sidearms. Like most everything else, they are clearly on display.

Way in the back of the mall is the Food Court where many exhausted consumers are huddled down over a little fat and sugar. The Steak Escape is popular. There are cookie stores all over selling for one dollar what look to be something you might find in a bag of Pecan Sandies. Clearly eating at the mall must never interfere with more important consumption.

Back in the mall, the kids are starting to cry. Some are yelling. Tempers are short. MOMMY! I WANT TO GO HOME! NOW! I knew what the tyke meant. By 3:00 P.M., I am exhausted. But I keep at it. I go to the Village Gallery to get a little picker-upper of art culture. After all, what was it Yeats said about *this* country not being for old men? Surely there will be surcease at a store that "Cares For The Finer Things." At this Byzantium they are having a special show of The Scandia Collection. There are no golden birds singing to the lords and ladies, but instead, lots of plastic and porcelain animals, mostly dogs. There are also more angels here than in the Sistine Chapel and more pre-Raphaelite swooning maidens than Rossetti ever imagined.

By late afternoon I am beyond exhausted. I exit to Red Deck parking section 2F, but I cannot find my car. It is on the Blue Deck. A few other shoppers seem to have also lost their way. This shopping day, the day after Thanksgiving, has been designated as "Buy Nothing Day" by a Canadian group that publishes the heroically optimistic *Adbusters* magazine. They are trying to tamp down shopping frenzy and remove the "driven" from consumer-driven. Good luck!

✳ THE ACT OF SHOPPING

What I had observed in Raleigh's Crabtree Mall might well be the central act of social behavior in the way we live now. Evolutionary biologists tell us that if something feels good it is often because at one time the activity provided protection. So we still have a taste for fats and sweets because at one time loading up on calories and fats would tide us over periods of famine. Furthermore the taste of sweetness tells us that fruit is ripe and digestible. Taste is also a sign that we have the necessary enzymes to process what is ingested. We don't have a taste for tree bark, but beavers do. Presumably, they can't digest apples.

So maybe loading up, not on carbohydrates but on disposable merchandise, protected us in earlier times from inevitable scarcity. We share the fable of the grasshopper and the ant with our children for a reason. Ants protect themselves and, who knows, they may actually enjoy the process of laying up against shortage. Watch monkeys furiously stockpiling green bananas and then hording them until the fruit passes ripeness to decay, and you may appreciate how much of primate behavior is dedicated to stockpiling.

Don't ask if it makes sense. Look around at the oversized refrigerators and garage freezers and you will see that the idea of putting stuff away is powerful. Or better yet, observe the success of Sam's Club or Costco where you have to buy in bulk, often needless bulk, and you will see that there is something more in buying twenty frozen Cornish hens than just saving money.

Evolutionary explanations aside, for many consumers shopping in itself is satisfying and fun. That is why so many of the women in Raleigh were specially dressed for it. Shopping is a predictable and bounded experience filled with "May I help you?" and small successes. Like people who traveled to bazaars hundreds of years ago, we go to see and be seen, to touch and feel new and interesting merchandise, and, naturally, to buy and cart home. Certainly one of the explanations of what has proven the most cataclysmic change of the late twentieth century—the fall of state-managed markets—is that the pleasure of shopping trumps intellectual concepts of inequitable distribution. If shopping were sensible we would all be at home reading *Consumer Reports* and all buying the same stuff by mail. After a while, even Amazon.com may lose some of its allure.

Of all the freedoms demanded by Central Europe in the 1980s— freedom of individual speech, freedom of religion, freedom of assembly, freedom of the press—the most cauterizing was the freedom to shop. Here is a joke told in Berlin as the Wall was falling down: Q: How can you tell the difference between East and West Berliners? A: The West Berliner enters a shop and says, "I want . . . " The East Berliner enters a shop and asks, "Do you have . . . ?" When the Berlin Wall finally came down where did East Berliners head first? You know where.[2]

One of the reasons that Eastern Europe was so quick to fall is that they had been softened up by Western advertising. They were ready to buy. What with dish antennas and Sky TV, they had unknowingly been shopping all along—just not completing the circuit. Clearly, they

---

2. Western European countries have been chary about permitting enclosed malls to be built on the outskirts of town. They realize that they must protect downtowns for the tourists, even if it means higher prices for the locals. Not so for Eastern Europeans. In the East, malls are multiplying just as they did in this country a generation ago. The Polus Center in Budapest is the largest enclosed mall in Europe, with almost half a million square feet of retail space. Budapest already has two other megamalls.

had been forced to spend an inordinate percent of time in the pre-purchasing mode. Like missiles roaring for the minute before liftoff, they sat at the launching pad quietly rumbling for most of the twentieth century. The rest of us, however, were airborne, heading out to the distant galaxy of Stuff.

✳ *WHY A NATION OF SHOPPERS? DISPOSABLE TIME NOT JUST INCOME*

If the act of shopping can be quantified into search, purchase, post-purchase letdown, and renewed search, so too can the participants be separated. Although there have been many taxonomies, one of the most revealing was put together by William J. McDonald, a Professor of Marketing at Hofstra University. Instead of looking at purchases, McDonald used a standard Time Structure Questionnaire (TSQ) that measures the extent to which respondents perceive their use of time as structured and purposeful. Here are the three categories he found:

1. **Routine Managers** (50.7 percent) specialize in time management through a daily routine of activities. This involves efficient organization and a moderate sense of purpose. RMs report spending about 3.1 hours per week shopping, with 0.3 search, 2.6 purchase, and 0.2 post-purchase hours. Most RMs are moms.

2. **Aimless Wanderers** (37.1 percent) have the lowest overall time perceptions score profile. They have the lowest scores on a sense of purpose, are the least organized and routine oriented, and appear less efficient at organizing their time during daily activities. And they report spending the most time shopping at 8.2 hours per week, with the majority in search at 4.1 hours and the remainder in purchase and post-purchase, 3.3 and 0.8 hours respectively. As you might imagine most of the AWs are young.

3. **Purposeful Organizers** (12.3 percent) have a strong sense of purpose in their daily lives. They are also effective organizers who accomplish goals and complete tasks and are routine oriented. This group reports spending the least amount of time shopping, 2.5 hours per week, including 0.1 search, 2.3 purchase, and 0.1 post-purchase hours. These are the infamous power shoppers: have a list, eat before shopping, wear comfortable shoes, drape purse across chest instead of off shoulder, buy straw hats in February. They are the Ninja warriors of the mall.

✳ *THE HEDONIC VALUE OF SHOPPING*

There are other ways to describe the shopping experience aside from the decision-making process and time consumption. It's either fun or it's a chore. Of course when professors of marketing have at this explanation, the terms have to change. Like professors of humanities, the first thing to go is language. Having fun becomes the "heuristics of hedonic excitement" and not having fun is expressed as "utilitarian ex-

American Retailing
coming Sunday, April 6

 ➤ "I shop therefore I am." The *New York Times Magazine* announces a special issue for shoppers. (February 16, 1997, p. 20)

periential activity."[3] But whatever you call it, we all know what they mean. There is a sunny side of shopping and—as we are reminded daily by Marxist academics, Voluntary Simplifiers, and environmental gloomsters—a dark side, a very dark side. Those women I saw at Crabtree Mall, those women in celebratory outfits looking like Lucy and Ethel, were clearly enjoying the act. Later in the afternoon I could see the other species, as it were—and certainly they come out during the last days before Christmas—looking like they had just been jump-kicked by Bruce Lee.

Clearly, we oscillate between *homo ludens* and *homo emptor*. Sometimes it's just a party, sometimes all business. Often, it's both. The festive part of shopping is overlooked by cultural pessimists. While we know the truth of such statements as "people buy so they can shop, not shop so they can buy," or that "the purchase of goods may be incidental to the experience of shopping," it is not so clear why this should be. Just what is it that makes shopping fun for so many? Why do we spend so much time so inefficiently? The answer is not as simple as it seems. The pleasure in shopping is only tangentially linked to consumption.

✳ SHOPPING FOR PLEASURE

When focus groups of shoppers are queried, here are some of the reasons certain people crave what many others cannot stomach. Shopping entails the joy of going into a safe spot filled with things to look at where they are treated deferentially. Although no one has hooked up a turbo lie detector to a shopper out for fun, if they did, the machine would register increased arousal, heightened involvement, perceived freedom, and fantasy fulfillment. Not for nothing were early department stores called lands of enchantment and dream palaces. You are Queen for a Day, or at least an hour, or at least until the bill comes due. Escapism is

---

3. Here's the way marketing professors make the fun/nonfun distinction: "A general view of value recognizing both (1) a utilitarian outcome resulting from some type of conscious pursuit of an intended consequence and (2) an outcome related more to spontaneous hedonic responses captures a basic duality of rewards for much human behavior. It reflects the distinction between performing an act 'to get something' as opposed to doing it because 'you love it.'" Whew! (Babin, Darden, Griffen 644).

clearly part of the allure of shopping and this is why malls are often out-
fitted with the trappings of exotic mystery.[4]

If the pleasures of shopping are not tied just to consumption, they
are certainly tied to the joy of looking—scopophilia. Blind people do
not enjoy going to the mall; the reverberating sounds are confusing.
Sighted people are enthralled, especially children. The ritualized exchange between spectator and salesperson gives all the pre-purchase
power to the viewer. When they say, "May I show you something?" or
"What would you like to see?" you need only say, "Just looking."

This ritualized interchange gives the initial power to the shopper.
The moment the purchase occurs, however, the charade is over and the
salesperson is off to tend another. You *look* elsewhere. Not for nothing
is the central trope of shopping the store window—window shopping.
For the recreational shopper the mall simply allows window shopping without the discomfort of being separated from the objects, but
the process is the same. Dream, look, enter, touch, buy, exit, dream.

Happy shoppers often describe themselves as "a kid in a candy
store," loving to look and shop "because of the little kid in me," and de-
lighted over becoming immersed in a store "that wasn't a run of the mill
kind of store." Sometimes a focus group respondent has the candor to
go the next step beyond reviving childish pleasure: "I enjoy shopping
when it helps me forget my problems." Indeed "retail therapy" is so
widespread that a 1990 poll for Virginia Slims by the Roper Organization found that 60 percent of American women say they often or sometimes shop to relieve stress (Krier 1). Only two stress-relieving activities
ranked higher: watching television (77 percent), and talking on the telephone (65 percent).

By no means is this recharging sensation divorced from purchase,
but it does not necessarily depend on it. We approach the moment of
purchase in a zigzag fashion. The analogy for shopping may be game-
playing. Although the sport allows the player to concentrate and give

---

4. No one would deny that large malls are reminiscent of cathedrals, offering
aspiration, comfort, security, reassurance, and a certain anonymity. Ira
Zepp argues even further in *The New Religious Image of Urban America:
The Mall as Ceremonial Center* that malls are filled with fountains and flowing water, symbols of regeneration, for a reason. Malls are patterned on re-
capturing the lost innocence of Eden. Redemption in a box. Perhaps.

oneself over to the game, there is always irregular movement toward the goal. In sports the goal is winning, while in shopping it is finding the bargain. This may explain why shopping is so often talked about to peers. "You can't believe what I paid . . . " is the other side of "Pardon me for asking, but what did you pay?" Sometimes the bargain is foregrounded so that it seems to trump the other sensory pleasures. What you bought is the bargain, not just the object. You scored.[5]

The gloating of goal-making, fist-pumping, and high-fiving is at the heart of bargain shopping. The omnipresent discount mall along the interstates, the "factory store" with "rock-bottom prices," or the fine frenzy of a Filene's basement commodifies the pleasure. We are not the first to find joy in this process. Ironically, our ancestors were savvier. They made bargains *before* goods made it to market. The word "forestall" means to buy goods before they reach the stall, literally. Forestalling was considered unscrupulous by other shopowners and such practices were often illegal. But that these practices took place, that they were clearly pleasurable to those who participated, and that they were considered immoral, especially to the Puritans, shows how deep-seated the pleasure of being there first to get the bargain really is.[6]

---

5. We even acknowledge scoring bargains in our calendar. We keep time not by vegetative cycles but rather by periods of discounted prices—bargains for all. So there are after-Christmas sales, Washington's birthday sales, Easter sales, and so forth throughout the year. A shopper even knows what the sales center around: when sheets go on sale, when to buy refrigerators, etc. The formalization of sales, as a way to guarantee the bargain, is the retailer's unacknowledged testament to what shopping/scoring is about.

6. Sometimes we take pleasure in what might be called afterstalling, the buying of goods almost used up. A step past usual purchase time is found at the Salvation Army Thrift Store and the Flea Market (the etymology explains the merchandise, but Stolen Goods Market is often more like it), and the omnipresent weekend yard sales. Here you see some of the most awful stuff—stuff that really can have no conceivable use such as old cans and worthless trinkets. You also see a class of diehard shoppers who go from stranger's front yard to stranger's garage to stranger's backyard with the enthusiasm of ancient explorers. When you ask them, as I have, why this kind of shopping, you find out that they are not just buying stuff. Their task is consumption of almost worn-out objects, to be sure, but it is also consumption of privacy, of how others live, voyeurism.

The idea that shopping could be entertainment is hardly new. In fact, in one of the more peculiar coincidences, it was Frances Trollope, mother of Anthony, who saw it all coming. She conceived of a new kind of store, a bazaar, she called it. She even hoped to open one in, of all places, Cincinnati, Ohio. She knew about the format of enclosing shops in an arcade from London. She had seen fashionable people flock to the Soho Bazaar, the Baker Street Bazaar, and the Pantheon Bazaar in Oxford Street. Such bazaars were essentially large buildings with stalls and open counters ranging on both sides of long passages on several different floors. But Mrs. Trollope envisioned more. Her bazaar would include a coffeehouse, an art gallery, a ballroom, and even an orchestra all under one roof. Although her idea never found reality, the insight that a store could offer a link to the world of amusement, that it could offer pleasure along the way, was indeed a prefiguring of what would find fruition in the magical worlds of Monsieur Boucicaut, A. T. Stewart, John Wanamaker, Stanley Marcus, and the show that is currently playing down in the mall.

In November 1994 *Consumer Reports* published a special issue on shopping. What they found from a fifty thousand-plus readers survey was that more than a third of those who completed its 1993 annual questionnaire said they considered shopping their hobby. Clearly the split occurs along gender lines. A majority of men (53 percent) and nearly a third of women (30 percent) described themselves as "shopaphobes" who want to make a speedy exit from the store. Men and women typically pursue very different shopping strategies; women visit many more stores on a shopping trip than men do, and more women than men say they enjoy the experience. Since most of what is bought is branded merchandise, this gender divide can also be explained in terms of the obvious. Men prefer brandnames to get it over with quick. Women use brands to create relationships, to be social, to be creative, and hence the affiliations are longer lasting.[7]

---

7. Men also tend to go shopping for an object like a pair of pants and so once the purchase is made, the event is over. American women don't need an excuse to go shopping. Given a free afternoon, *Consumer Reports* found that one in four women would spend it shopping, whether needing to buy something or not. Two of every five women would rather shop than catch a movie or take a nap. Clearly shopping for them is entertainment. Little wonder shopping centers have the look of amusement parks and stores look like magical emporia.

※ TRAVEL SHOPPING

For a key to the festive aspect of shopping, look at how we spend our vacation time. The *Wall Street Journal* reports that one of the hottest vacations for time-starved couples is a night at the mall motel or the city hotel followed by weekend shopping (Nelson B1). Called a "spree" in the trade, it's a package deal with the discounted rooms bundled in

➢ The *New York Times* goes tripping: "Shopping the World." (Travel section, April 5, 1998)

with retail discounts at local stores. The Maxwell Hotel in San Francisco even features a spree with free $25 gift certificates on the pillow instead of mints, free foot massages for weary shoppers, and a bronze statue of a female shopper in the lobby to make it all seem elegant and a little wink-wink ironic.

Those with more than spree time go farther from home and call it traveling. We go somewhere different, exotic, and foreign, not just to see new things, but to buy them and truck them home. Glance through any travel magazine and you will see foreign climes touted for bargain hunting. On cruise ships there are shopping seminars prior to entering new ports of call. In fact, there are complete packaged tours dedicated only to shopping. After all, the souvenir is more than just an aide-memoire, more than just a conversation piece, and more than just a trinket. It is proof positive that you have been somewhere important, are someone special for having been there, and can legitimately claim affiliation.

In the travel trade there are five leisure areas that can be merchandised to a client: sport, foreign culture, socializing, exploratory trips, and shopping. In the travel agency jargon, shopping is known as a "long-burst activity" because an entire journey can be organized around it. Not only are trips sold on the basis of specific stuff to be bought along the way, but there is an ancillary activity to increase the enjoyment. Before you go, you read a shopping guide.

One of the most popular of these guides is a series called *Born-to-Shop*. These books, written by Suzy Gershman, provide insight into the allure of consumption as the organizing principle of making meaning. Travel is by nature chaotic, shopping by nature is coherent.

The *Born-to-Shop* series, which includes guides to Britain, London, Italy, Mexico, New York, New England, Paris, Hong Kong, and Moscow among others, doesn't offer just a list of shops, but detailed strategies for charging your way successfully across a foreign landscape. Ms. Gershman and her minions detail the procedure:

> The first step to a successful shopping experience is to go to a museum and familiarize yourself with the art of the place you're going. To shop well, you have to have a general knowledge of the very best of everything that's to be found locally. Then you have a lot of research to do, to find out what's made there and what the best buys are supposed to be. What people often forget is how many competing demands there are on your time when traveling, so show up ready to go. You can't expect to get into town and see big signs that say "This Way to the Cute." So

> by the time you land, you should have already familiarized yourself
> with the layout of the city you're visiting, drawn up lists of what you
> want to buy and shops you want to visit grouped according to neigh-
> borhood. (in Lobrano, feature)

As you can see, this kind of serious souvenir shopping is not easy.
You do homework first. You need to follow the rules. The most important of Suzy Gershman's rules is the "Moscow Rule of Shopping": If you
see something you like, buy it immediately. Pounce. You're often wrong
if you think you'll come back to shop later, or if you do, it might be gone.
Another rule: follow your instincts. Ask yourself, is this an item you
can't live without, even if you are overpaying tremendously? If the
answer is yes, buy it now. Don't worry about post-decision dissonance.
Remember, you are traveling (not shopping), so the anxiety rules are
suspended.

Gershman's guides are not only chock-full of how-to-move-around
information, they also provide a context to show that the act of buying
is central to travel. Here she is in Mexico:

> Cortes took about two years to make his way to Teotihuacan, so the
> Spanish colonial period is traditionally dated from 1521. Yet the looting
> and the craving for local goods began the day Spanish boots set down
> on Mexican soil. And while Cortes introduced many Spanish arts and
> crafts to the country, he was really on a buying trip for the king of
> Spain. After all, this was before Bloomingdale's and El Corte Ingles. (21)

By mimicking the acts of conquest, you become not a browser but an
explorer, not a tourist but a traveler, not shopping for stuff but hunting
for treasure. Like stout Balboa, you too are silent upon a peak in tourista
heights.

✳ SHOPPING SICKNESSES: BUY TOO MUCH, STEAL THE REST

The best way to appreciate the hedonic power of shopping is to observe
it when it goes haywire, when it gets separated from the social and entertainment context, when the romance of travel is removed and consumption is tied directly to loading up on things. Victims of this mis-
prision are, on one hand, the "shopaholic," and on the other, the klep-
tomaniac. The former can't stop taking and paying, and the latter just
keeps taking without paying. For various reasons, the attractions of the
material world trump the forces of repression. Shopping for those so

afflicted is not entertainment, not wish fulfillment, not escapism but mania.

The more interesting for our purposes is the shopaholic because she simply extends the process over the edge. What a victim class! Powerless power shoppers. They are only doing what they are told. They read advertising without irony. They are told, "just do it," and they do. Alas, in dreary reality their affliction is not so benign. Shopaholics plot the shortest routes to malls, pore over catalogs during coffee breaks, greet store sales help—and security guards—by name. Even when they browse with friends, they can be secretly prowling for purchases. Often they sneak back to make a "hit." Out on a spending spree, they pick out items in a euphoric daze, so many of their purchases make little sense. When queried, shopaholics often say a major attraction is that salespeople are deferential and attentive. They say, "May I help you?" and the shopaholic says, "You bet."[8]

Of course, we don't mention the word "disease" when discussing the manic shopaholics of yore like Peggy Guggenheim, Electra Havemeyer Webb, William Randolph Hearst, or Russell Sage. They are "collectors." Nor do we think that Andy Warhol and his huge collections of knickknacks, the Duke and Duchess of Windsor with their pug dog trinkets, Jacqueline Kennedy Onassis and her boxes of stuff, or Ivana Trump and her closets of designer outfits are in need of a twelve-step detox process. Jay Gatsby, with his hundreds of shirts, is not a member of Shopaholics Anonymous.

No, with the exception of Imelda Marcos and her 2,400 pairs of shoes, the pathology is invoked when it afflicts the middle class. We have a different term—deadbeats—for those who are in the lower classes. And for a reason. The shopaholic is "one of us" who is simply tapped out. If only the credit card companies would stop sending those unsolicited cards with such large credit limits! In the nineteenth century it was not the banks but the stores that were to blame. Think only of Mme. Bovary or Sister Carrie. In our it-can't-be-your-fault culture, the plastic card with the magnetic strip takes the rap. That charge card is to the shopaholic what a bottle is to the alcoholic; the swipe replaces the swig.

As might be expected, compulsive shoppers are predisposed to other

250

8. To a considerable degree, this modern condition is the result of depersonalized transactions and availability of easy credit. While no figures exist on debt run up by compulsive spenders, the Federal Reserve Board says that credit card debt in toto is now almost $600 billion.

disorders including depression, substance abuse, and particularly other
impulse control disorders, such as eating disorders. According to ad-
dictologists (yes, they exist!), the shopaholic is a substance abuser
and the substance is money in the form of credit. The compulsive shopper has one disadvantage over other substance abusers, especially the
alcoholic or the gambler: in our culture one *has* to spend money, one
doesn't have to drink or wager.

In the lingo of addict specialists, compulsive shopping is more appropriately an *impulsive* control disorder, not a *compulsive* control disorder. Impulsive control behaviors, such as kleptomania, are associated
with some kind of mounting tension because at the time the person
does it, it's compatible with their desire. On the other hand, someone
suffering from a compulsive control disorder doesn't feel comfortable
about the behavior, attempts to resist it, and experiences intrusive
thoughts during the act. Chronic shopping and shoplifting are not at all
like chronic handwashing.

There is a growing scientific belief that such addictions may have a
genetic or chemical base. Any behavior that involves pleasurable activity
may be physically addictive, and this may be a key to understanding the
power of shopping. We understand that alcoholics seem to have a genetic
propensity for a certain kind of pleasure most of us can absorb only in
moderation. Ditto shoppers. Scientists have found much higher occur-
rence in alcoholics than nonalcoholics of a pleasure-seeking receptor
gene linked to the reward area of the brain. Studies of this gene, the D2
dopamine receptor, suggest that certain individuals are simply more
susceptible to addiction—not just alcoholism, but any activity that gives
a certain amount of pleasure. If so, this implies that the act of shopping,
like consuming intoxicants, is based on extending an extant desire.[9]

The counseling community has not been thrilled to see their busi-

251

---

9. We accept affliction as disease when a drug appears to lessen its effect. In a
kind of modern application of Occam's razor, we assume that if a chemical takes it away, a chemical must have brought it on. So it is not happenstance that just as compulsive shopping has been officially certified as a
distinct malady in the latest edition of psychiatric disorders—*The Diagnos-
tic and Statistical Manual*—a new class of drugs, called ssris, or serotonin
re-uptake inhibitors, have come on the market. Luvox (fluvoxamine ma-
leate), a medication commonly used to treat depression and obsessive-
compulsive disorder, does seem to inhibit the urge to get to the mall ASAP.
Hence, the best antidote for the ads announcing a big sale down at Sears
may be a few pills of Prozac or Zoloft.

ness go up in Prozac. They are convinced, and they have almost convinced the large insurance companies, that shopaholics are victims of loveless and/or molested childhoods. Their argument: if the child comes into maturation with a feeling of emptiness, of impotence, of low self-esteem, she may shop her way into esteem. Hence the roots of compulsive shopping lie in unresolved childhood problems. People whose parents withheld attention and affection or set impossible standards may feel driven to purchase power, control, and prestige. Read the literature on compulsive shopping and you will find that the usual statistic cited is that half of the furious shoppers were molested as teenagers. But, then again, read the literature for any of the modern addictions (what used to be known as bad habits or weakness of will power) and you will find that childhood molestation is almost always the culprit.

No matter, the cure is always the same. If the victim is insured, plenty of counseling is coming up. Here's what you do, according to Marilee Zdenek of Encino, California, who leads detox seminars for shoppers (Marks 1): (1) Set aside fifteen to thirty minutes when you won't be disturbed. Use relaxation techniques to help you enter a dreamlike state, such as deep-breathing exercises, meditation, biofeedback, or simply listen to relaxing music in a darkened room. (2) Create a constructive daydream by imagining yourself buying one of those expensive gifts. Feel your pleasure in buying the gift. Imagine the experience of giving it. Go deeply into that daydream. Then experience your feelings when the bills arrive. Let yourself feel the anxiety. Take your time. Then imagine buying a thoughtful, but less expensive gift—perhaps one that expresses a more sensitive awareness of the other person's needs and your own creativity. (3) Now evaluate your feelings about the dream. Do you still want to buy the extravagant gift? Of course not. Now get your insurance company to pay the counselor.

I dilate on both the pharmaceutical and counseling "cures" because they indicate that, Marxist and Puritan naysayers notwithstanding, the desire to consume is deep and abiding. We have not been tricked into desire. We have led ourselves into temptation because there is something so pleasurable about it. Like other behavior carried to excess, gathering stuff may even have had evolutionary rewards. It is well to remember that such behavior only becomes a sickness, an addiction, an affliction, when your debits exceed your credits.[10]

10. I admit it is hard to take this affliction seriously. In fact, this view is shared in popular culture where the over-the-top shopper is usually a target of

✳ *THE HOME SHOPPING NETWORK AS SCIENTIFIC LABORATORY*

In this regard it may be instructive to observe one of the more insight-ful rituals on television—not the feel-good comraderie of detox but the baby steps of learning how to buy beyond your means. The shopping channels inadvertently provide information about the therapeutic nature of consumption. Just as in normal life, here in tubeland some 10 percent of the viewers have a serious problem coordinating desire with income. Nothing in American life is quite as easy as shopping, and television makes it easier. Watching a shopping channel is like looking at a catalog, except there are such nice salespeople ready to help you turn the page. We see the goods in a home setting and all we have to do is make the purchase with a toll-free number and credit card. Just pick up the phone. Shoppers can recline and buy, simply by punching but-tons and reciting numbers. It's dreamland.

One of the keys to direct selling on television is *not* to kid the cus-tomer into thinking you are *not* selling direct on television. Most selling on network television is like door-to-door selling. The foot must be placed carefully and the commercial interruption is that foot. The home shopping channels, however, are like selling inside the store. The cus-tomer's foot is already at your counter. You have only to close the sale. Clearly many people respond to this interaction with pleasure.

When home shopping addicts are queried they often respond that "Home shopping is very good at what they do; they draw me in. There is continual conversation; it's almost like they speak to me personally." Or, "It's not intellectually stimulating; it's light. It's not like watching CNN where there is this horror story." Or, "I become so enticed by what they're selling it doesn't matter if I need it or whether I have anyone to give it to." A QVC spokesman said that the network doesn't exert undue pressure on viewers to buy, noting that the company backs that asser-tion with a liberal return policy. "We present merchandise in a low-key, soft-sell presentation, and we allow viewers to take their time to place

---

satire. So, for instance, on a recent episode of CBS's *The Nanny,* Fran (Fran Drescher) goes on a feel-good spending spree after hearing that her ex-boyfriend is getting married. Her friends intervene, placing her in a Shoppers Anonymous group where, presumably, she is helped over her affliction. For the shopaholic pathology to have reached the level of primetime sitcom you know it's become the most common of common knowledge. After all, Tammy Faye's been talking about it for years.

an order" (McAleavy B1). He is right. Clearly, for some shoppers this low-key, one-sided exchange is worth the price of consuming ersatz gold chains, zirconium diamonds, radio earmuffs, spray-on vitamins, music box-cum-toilet paper dispensers, and autographed Bibles.

✳ *WHEN LADIES GO A-THIEVING: KLEPTOMANIA*

A generation ago the focus of social concern was not on compulsive purchasing, but on compulsive stealing. Shoplifters had their heyday in the mid-nineteenth century when mounds of machine-made goods were exhibited unprotected on countertops. No one expected ladies— who were, after all, the primary consumers of "store-boughts"—to be thieves. But they soon became so. Again, the scapegoating is interesting to observe. If we now blame advertising and credit cards, our grandparents blamed the counter designers and window dressers for overly tempting displays of merchandise.

To generate the sense of easy availability, department store managers would pile goods on shelves near the store entrance so passersby would think that a cornucopia was just across the threshold. As Emile Zola wrote in *Ladies' Delight,* a common street sight in Paris was the milling of shoppers at the store entrance literally spilling onto the street. "It should seem to people in the street as if a riot were taking place . . . that the shop was bursting with people, when often it was only half-full." Once inside, women were trapped in a glittering Aladdin's cave where everything was easy to touch and the "five-finger discount" hard to resist.

The police records of second-empire Paris abound with details of well-off women, overcome by the richness of it all. "Ravaged by a furious, irresistible need," Zola continues, stealing became for many of these women "a sensual pleasure necessary to existence" (in McDowell feature). So too in America, the daily newspapers were filled with stories of unnamed society dames who were detained by storewalkers (whose secondary job was to escort ladies safely through the emporium so they would not be disturbed by the excitement of goods), embarrassed by management, and bailed out by their ever-solicitous husbands. England was no different. By midcentury "Ladies, Don't Go A-Thieving" was a popular saloon ballad.

Oh, don't we live in curious times,
You scarce could be believing,
When Frenchmen fight and Emperors die

And Ladies go a-thieving.
A beauty of the West End went,
Around a shop she lingers,
And there upon some handkerchiefs
She clapped her pretty fingers.
Into the shop she gently popped;
The world is quite deceiving
When ladies have a notion got
To ramble out a-thieving.

While this may have been a joking matter to the songsters, it was a serious matter for pundits. Why would ladies steal? These were not women who needed goods. They just enjoyed the process, the excitement, the chase, and capture of the forbidden. As was so often the case in high Victorian circles, the answer was soon located in class- and gender-based explanations.

According to some commentators, the orgy of shoplifting was just that. After the foreplay of advertising, women were coddled to the point of orgasm by unctuous salesmen and erotic goods in alluring display. Department stores were theater, to be sure, but the Grand Guignol scenario had a sinister plotline too easily followed by the unwary. Once across the threshold into emporia, women were led down the garden path to inevitable seduction. They were not responsible; they had been led into temptation.

The appearance of male voyeurs, who were found to enjoy watching women shop, seemed to be proof positive that something erotic was occurring downtown. When questioned, these men admitted that they found stimulation in the physical hysteria of the women who, flushed and sweating, pawed the latest materials and frantically toyed with the newest accessories. Occasionally, one of these males would grope a shopper, sometimes one would reveal himself to the entire group, and there were even cases of such men masturbating in crowded department stores. If this is what happened to our stout-hearted men, one could only imagine how dangerous shopping was for our women.

While we may medicalize compulsive shopping as making up for unhappy and molested childhoods, the Victorians were convinced that kleptomania, this new disease for women, was the result of sexual confusion. As Elaine Abelson makes clear in *When Ladies Go A-Thieving: Middle-Class Shoppers in the Victorian Department Store,* when the police and doctor's reports comment on "reflex nervous troubles," they are invariably tied to "womb disease." These women wanted to accumulate, to produce, to procreate. Almost always the attending physician (who was called forth to assure the court that charges should not be pressed) tied the acts to women's physiology. Either she was pregnant (or recently delivered), lactating, ovulating, menstruating, or menopausal. In short, kleptomania was a female reproductive urge run amok.[11]

Alas, today shoplifting has become squalid. Most goods are displayed beneath countertops covered in glass, cameras eternally pan the scene, anything leather that's bigger than a wallet is likely chained or cabled to its rack, and plastic Sensormatic tags, which set off sirens when they get too close to the exits, are stuck on everything. Despite all this technology, stores continue to lose $25 million a day to shoplifters, most of whom are definitely not ladies.[12]

This is not to say that the shoplifter of yore, "one of our customers gone bad," is no more, but only that the compulsion to steal has become dreary. The sex appeal is gone. Even the celebrity shoplifters can't compare to their shopaholic confreres. You can't compare Hedy Lamar with Madonna.

✷ SHOP 'TIL YOU DROP

Although we may steal differently, we still shop the same. The seemingly long trip from the outdoor market, to the sheltered stall, to the arcade of enclosed stalls, to the general store, to the stores around the green, to the downtown department store, to the discount store, to the strip mall, to the stalls inside the modern enclosed mall, to the current breaking off of the stand-alone superstore is really just a small circle. Just look at how closely the Galleria in Houston, Texas resembles the one in Milan, Italy. Compare the Beverly Hills Mall in California with

---

11. Why poor women did not also suffer from "ungratified sexual instinct" is why poor women were not considered "shopaholics." You must be able to afford medical care to be diagnosed as a this- or thataholic and such diagnoses don't come cheap.

12. According to Peter Berlin, executive director of Shoplifters Anonymous, shoplifting has increased 33 percent in the mid-1990s, making it the fastest growing class of larceny in the country. But it is not the respectable ladies who are taking, but rather young drug addicts and professional shoplifters who steal merchandise to resell (in McLaughlin 5).

St. Mark's Square in Venice and then compare St. Mark's Square with the bazaar in Teheran during the Persian empire and you will see a deep continuity in merchandising.

What remains constant in all marketplaces is the central relationship between goods, salesperson, and consumer. Through most of history, the focal point of cities has been the market, a well-designated area where farmers, craftsmen, artisans, entrepreneurs, consumers, and the curious gather to barter, buy, trade, and sell produce, goods, and services, be entertained, socialize, talk politics, and generally indulge themselves in the emerging culture of the period. From Paris to Marrakesh to Calcutta to Hong Kong the great markets of the world have always mixed the buying and selling of disposable objects with the getting and spending of cultural capital.

Every once in a while some innovation appears such as catalog shopping in the early part of this century or Internet shopping of today, and everyone says the ancient marketplace is finally dying. But for all the predictions of imminent demise, there have been few changes. And that is because, as shoplifters and compulsive shoppers know, the market is only tangentially about stuff. For most of us, most of the time, shopping is about consuming meaning, about socializing, about dreaming, about being out and about with others, milling around.

The dominant marketplace for most of the twentieth century has been the department store. Thanks to the entrepreneurial genius of Alexander Stewart, Henry Siegel, Marshall Field, and especially John Wanamaker, these new dream palaces experimented in using color, glass, and light, along with easy credit and free delivery, to entice customers' imaginations and desires. They framed windows on magical worlds viewed by millions in Chicago, Boston, Philadelphia, and New York. These merchants built multilevel stores, organized the interiors into commercial wonderlands, and in so doing, shaped and reflected the evolving relationship between middle-class shoppers and machine-made things.

✳ *BEFORE THE MALL: THE DEPARTMENT STORE*

Electric lights, mirrors, and brightly lit, polished glass showcases gave stores a coruscating atmosphere, one that seemed to live under the eyelids. The only comparable experience was at the local Bijou. Looking at things shining in the dark is always powerful because it is so dreamlike.

In this context, think of film director Victor Fleming's adaptation of

L. Frank Baum's *The Wizard of Oz*. Baum's original fable, written at the turn of the century, clearly reflected a magical paradise "over the rainbow." In fact, while Baum was spinning his fantasy he was earning a livelihood dressing department store windows. His interest in merchandising also led him to found the National Association of Window Trimmers in 1898 and a year later to begin publishing *The Show Window*, the nation's first magazine to describe modern display techniques. Baum knew well that the power of pretend was connected to the pull of commercial objects.

The Yellow Brick Road starts in Munchkinland. This make-believe world is overflowing with commodities, particularly food, jewels, metals, trinkets, and all those miniature people in elf outfits looking like candy. Not by mistake does it look just like a Christmas store window. But Munchkinland is also the starting place for the journey to the magical Emerald City, the literal "city on the hill," the land of adults who run the show. Although the movie version spends more time in the pastoral interludes between Munchkinland and the confrontation with the Wizard, in the book much is made of bright shiny store-bought objects like the ruby slippers. It's not like Kansas, that much is clear.

Dorothy's odyssey is ours, right in line with consumerist culture, an ever-growing belief that "you can have it all" without any psychic or economic pain. You can get a heart, find courage, develop intellect, *and* make your way home not by following Puritan dictates of hard work, but by trusting the magic of the Good Witch Glenda. Wish for it. Dream it. Charge it. You deserve a break today.

✳ *IT'S A MALL WORLD AFTER ALL*

Kansas is in black and white, Oz is in technicolor. Our version of the Land of Oz is the enclosed mall, really just the downtown department store that Baum decorated, flopped on its side, and and set in the suburbs. The color is all on the inside and all electric. The man responsible for tipping over the department store was Victor Gruen, a kindly architect, who designed Southdale Center in the late 1950s in Edina, Minnesota, just outside Minneapolis. By all accounts, Gruen did not know what he was doing. He knew that cold winters and hot summers made enclosure sensible for a cluster of stores. In trying to save money on "conditioning" air for individual stores, he stumbled onto the new marketplace for the end of the twentieth century. For the large enclosed shopping mall (along with the skyscraper) has become one of the few new building types created in our time.[13]

The mall has also been one of the fastest growing architectural forms. The number of such shopping centers in the United States has grown from about three thousand in 1960 to twenty thousand in 1980, to about forty thousand today. There now are more enclosed malls than four-year colleges and television stations, and malls almost outnumber county courthouses. The ungainly structure is the signature form of our age, the Emerald City of post–World War II consumerist culture where Munchkins come by the thousands.

Surveys show that Americans go to shopping centers more often than they go to church, and American teenagers spend more time in malls than anywhere besides school or home. Not everyone is happy about this, naturally. Alan Durning speaks for many when he contends in *How Much Is Enough: The Consumer Society and the Future of the Earth* that these malls are hazardous to our general health. He says we are being suffocated by malls. Americans are so caught up with mallcondo culture that they forget about social, psychological, and spiritual aspirations. Have we heard this plaint before?

Still, naysayers have a point, and you can see it in the names of malls. Almost without fail the mall is named for what it has destroyed. Think about Meadowbrook, Longacre Farm, Twin Oakes, Rosedale, Old Orchard, Northbrook Court, Woodfield, Briarwood, Woodland, Twelve Oaks, and my favorite, Crabtree Valley. It is not that we murder to dissect, or that we kill what we love most. Rather, it is that we insist on memorializing what we destroy with the invocation of what can be no more.

Durning misses the bigger point. People do not destroy nature to erect malls for caprice, nor do they flood into malls just looking for

---

13. The term "mall" is surely as ironic as it is appropriate. The modern mall that has swallowed up countless acres of choice farmland and decimated countless city blocks of retail stores owes its name to a pastoral sport called pall-mall, similar to croquet and popular in eighteenth-century England. The lush fairway where the game was played came to be known as the mall. To a few, "mall" still means any shaded walk or promenade, such as Washington, D.C.'s Mall in the Federal Triangle. For the rest of us a mall is the huge commercial octopus that was once on the edge of town and is now the town center, the town green, the town cathedral. It might also be noted that the word "mall" comes from the same root as "maul."

more silly stuff to consume. They are interested in more profound matters, matters they used to find in church, or in the neighborhood, or in the family. Another researcher, Francesca Turchiano, has concluded in a study for the Center for Retailing Studies at Texas A&M University that almost three-quarters of Americans say they already possess most of the material things they want (Ode 6). So clearly, malls must have some other deeper social purpose.

When you look around at the mall, you can see what people are doing there. When I was at the Crabtree Mall, it was the beginning of the Christmas shopping season and most people were actually engaged in shopping. But if you were to attend the mall on a summer's day, or in late afternoon, you would see a different clientele with different behavior. The people who now swarm the mall are the young. They are the ones most affected by the experience, especially in early adolescence. They are the Munchkins who take seriously what the mall offers. While it looks as if they are loitering, they are moving through the rites of initiation into a consumer society. For them socializing (and dreaming) through store-bought things is a major part of their lives. After all, they are the only ones with sufficient disposable time and money to make shopping worthwhile. In addition, they are also the only ones who need what the mall offers: controlled space. In the reproductive stampede of adolescence, they bound around like so many wildebeests. This is why many of us no longer enjoy going to the mall.

✳ THE MALL AS TEENY-BOPPER TELEVISION

Understandably the people who operate the malls are not entirely thrilled by being hijacked by the kids whose pockets they so love to pick. As with all shopping innovations, the modern double-decker, enclosed mall is a study in demographic and technological shifts gone one step too far. While the mall originally resulted from the convergence of key post–World War II developments—the superhighway, the suburb, and the baby boom—its primary current purpose has become the cruising grounds of teenagers. Along with television, it is a central part of how we raise our children.

When you look at what the mall sells you can see this influence. Youth rules. Stores like the Limited, Benetton, Aeropostale, Gap, and Banana Republic—many of which were once exclusively for urban shoppers, offering such style staples as pre-aged denims, canvas knapsacks, bandana-print shorts, pocket t-shirts, tube skirts, and leggings—

have now become mall stores. They sell stuff to kids. And these kids can buy. According to the International Council of Shopping Centers as gleefully reported in *The Wall Street Journal* (Sebastian A1), the average tyke drops a whopping $38.55 per trip. Better yet, from a retail point of view, these kids, properly branded, will soon move up into more affluent groups.

As might be expected, their homogenized look of branded apparel owes an obvious debt to television. In fact, the mall is as connected to the tube as the department store was linked to the newsprint. Both modern media—mall and pixels—are their own make-believe dream worlds, protected from adverse weather, programmed from far away, and irrevocably dedicated to upping consumption. If "free" television is the most dedicated advertising medium of all times, then the modern mall is the most dedicated distribution medium of all times.

In earlier days, all kinds of extraneous forces got into the downtown shopping experience: churches, governments, civic organizations like men's clubs or woman's auxiliaries, libraries, and various do-gooders. None of that is at the mall. Also missing at the mall is garbage, beggars, hookers, and most pickpockets. Nothing gets into the mall without being checked out, and nothing gets onto television that has not passed the programmer. And the mall owner/programmer/gatekeeper has only one thing on his mind: make money.[14]

The comparison between television and the enclosed malls is felicitous. As William Severini Kowinski has observed in *The Malling of America,* "If you look at people watching television—especially their eyes—they look pretty much like mall shoppers" (340). Just as the programming on television is the bait to get you to bite on the ads, so too the carnival atmosphere, the colorful decorations, the music, the internal architecture that seems so inviting and polite, is designed to funnel you from store to store. Just as you are shunted from program to program during the broadcast day, and from aisle to aisle down at the A&P, so too at the mall you enter often through an anchor store and proceed along the two-sided street of shops into a common area. From

---

14. Notice how malls are embracing television, their coeval medium. Now when you walk through the center court of almost any mall (and sometimes within stores), you'll see clusters of people around small kiosks in which video screens have been embedded. The crowd is usually children and teenagers staring glassily at mall promotions, advertisements, and even music videos. Stop, look, view, and listen—then shop.

this locus with the signature town square done in plastic, you wend your way back along another bazaar into the other anchor stores. Once inside, you can never be private, contemplative, or eccentric.

The various boutique stores, bookstores, bath-and-beyond stores, trinketerias, lingerie stores, and redundant whatnot, are equidistant along the internal causeways just as dairy products, vegetables, cleaning fluids, and pet food are carefully spaced to make you go all around the grocery store. Television programming attempts exactly the same process, leading you from show to show, aisle to aisle, ad to ad, until finally you close your eyes and slumber.

✳ THE MALL AS WALLED CITY

If you were looking for an analogy for the modern mall you would have to go back to the walled cities of Italy and France. Like San Gimingnano or Les Baux de Provence, the mall offers the ancient trifecta of enclosure, protection, and control. The analogy is not with a well-policed downtown but with a small, thoroughly fascist medieval city-state. Your neighborhood suburban fortress has its own rules and private police to enforce them, its own internal public relations department, a tenants' association to handle messy situations, and a hermetically controlled environment as privately run as anything clinging to the hills of Tuscany or Provence.[15]

---

15. In the entire mall and in its constituent franchise outlets, the operative word is control. In the standard legal boilerplate of rental contracts, the malls exercise a degree of control over "the appearance, products and procedures of its businesses" that no downtown can match. The rental agreements have stores making base payments not as a flat fee but on a percent of receipts. Therefore, a store not maintaining traffic will be jettisoned, which is why you will almost always see such a large turnover of stores as low producers are kicked out and new ones introduced. Also, since many of the mall stores are owned by megachains—the Limited, for instance, owns its namesake store plus Express, Lane Bryant, Lerner New York, Limited Too, Victoria's Secret, as well as big chunks of other stores like Abercrombie & Fitch—the analogy is again with the grocery store. As Procter & Gamble has to dicker about what goes where on shelf space, so the retailing giants have to continually readjust the mall mix, often by replacing one of their own stores with another store from inside its conglomerate.

If anything, the mall approaches a totalitarian Eden into which the innocent and the oppressed enter eagerly, lured by the dream of riches. The size and location of each store, the character of its advertising and displays, the hours it keeps, the specific products it sells— all of these and more are decided by the management of the mall. No dirty books, no X-rated arcade games, no pornographic movies, never. The same control from on high is true of the individual franchises. National headquarters decide the design and operation of outlets, the size and cut of french fries, the positioning of jeans racks, the crusts of pizzas, and the placement of stoves and refrigerators. It is just this intense predictability of mall shopping, its combination of stimulation and deprivation, that is among the causes of "mall-aise," a sense of disquiet, disorientation, and even a seasick-like distress some people experience in the mall. Get me outta here! This trip has lasted too long!

Ironically, this "mal de mall" was just the opposite of what Mr. Gruen originally envisioned. His mall was going to be the village green, a unifying antidote to suburban sprawl, a friendly place where people could come together from all parts of town and congregate. The mall now has more in common with the village jail than the village green. When Mr. Gruen retired to Vienna he was a sadly disappointed man. Like Victor Frankenstein he had created a monster. Not only had open ground been subsumed by private interests, but like the Enclosure Acts of the eighteenth century, the process of privatization has led to severe restrictions on public speech and movement. The tragedy of the commons—or in modern terms, the tragedy of the mall—is that the merchandising that goes on is done by huge conglomerates that have as much to do with your local community as a sitcom on television has to do with your next-door neighbor.[16]

---

16. Once in a while a mall will live dangerously and tie its meaning to something other than the repetitious display and retailing of goods. Often this link will be to local history. Think, for instance, of Faneuil Hall Marketplace in Boston, Harborplace in Baltimore, or Ghiradelli Square in San Francisco. Here the commercial construction is thematically coherent. Critics breath a sigh of relief. But more likely your neighborhood mall will dedicate itself to being totally ahistorical (with the exception of its name) so it can go about its business unfettered.

✳ SHUT UP AND SHOP: THE MALL AND SPEECH CODES

Aristotle argued that the public square should be separated from the marketplace so that the free exchange of ideas would not be polluted by the crass exchange of stuff. Presumably, you can't think straight when you are being led into temptation. Oddly enough, 2,300 years later he would be getting his wish. What with the public square becoming an enclosed private mall, speech—any speech—is viewed as an impediment to the uninterrupted flow of commerce.

The courts, however, are taking a different view. From New Jersey to California they have been ruling that since shopping centers have supplanted traditional downtowns, their owners must grant the same speech rights that were once available on the village green. The courts have held that while the mall may be private property, it is so close to being public that distinctions cannot be made.[17]

The real impact of the mall is not on freedom of speech but on freedom of imagination. Just as television has become the center of the family's home entertainment, so too has the mall become not just the after-school playground but also a destination for the entire family. Rand McNally even puts them on its maps; they are trip destinations, just like national parks.

✳ THE MALL OF AMERICA

Any student of modern consumption needs to go to the Mall of America, the country's biggest mall, just outside Minneapolis-St. Paul. The Mall of America is no misnomer. This cathedral of commerce is a 4.2 million-square-foot shopping *and* entertainment center. "Extravaganza" is a better word. Should you go, prepare yourself; you will be re-

---

17. The U.S. Supreme Court has balked from making this a nationwide rule, however, leaving states to decide whether their own constitutions grant broader free-speech protections. Some six states have made some provisions guaranteeing speech protection at private malls. The Court has reassured mall operators that its ruling does not include bullhorns, megaphones, or even a soapbox; it does not include placards, pickets, parades, and demonstrations. What free speech in the mall really means is that someone can pass you a leaflet, if they do it quietly.

peatedly told what can fit inside. To spare you the lecture: 32 Boeing 747 aircrafts, 27 Lincoln Memorials, 34 normal shopping malls, and 78 football fields. Here are some things that are inside: ten men's bathrooms, ten women's and two for either sex, 31,000 live shrubs and trees, 60,000 underground drip spouts. The mall has a seven-acre amusement park with a roller coaster that goes 30 miles an hour on silicone wheels so that shoppers won't be disturbed. There is a miniature golf course. It has its own doctors, dentists, sports bars, police station, ZIP code, and nightclub district with an Australian beach club. There are 14 movie theaters and 46 places to eat. There's a store that sells mounted butterflies and a store with half a basketball court and a boxing ring. There is a giant fantasy factory made of Lego blocks. And there are four "family rooms" with microwave ovens where everyone can go to revive and watch a little TV.

In the mall's center, where in ecclesiastical times one would have found an altar, stands Camp Snoopy, a holding tank for the kids. This mall attracts more visitors each year than the Vatican, more than Mecca, and more than Disneyland and Disney World combined. Many people come on packaged tours and spend the week. This is not a little world made cunningly, but a big world made grossly.[18]

The Mall of America has a cousin north of the border, the West Edmonton Mall. It is by far the world's largest shopping center with, inter alia, a five-acre indoor World Waterpark, an exotic aviary and zoo, a 47-ride indoor amusement park, as well as 53 women's shoe stores, 187 women's fashion stores, 138 places to eat, 11 major anchor stores, 19 optical outlets, two car dealerships, 828 shops and service agencies, more submarines than the Canadian navy, and a floating 80-foot re-

---

18. The Renaissance cathedral was usually owned or managed (if either is anywhere near the correct word) by one of the many mendicant orders like the Franciscans, Dominicans, or Carmelites, all eagerly competing for new contributions to build more worship space. So too, shopping malls are owned by the modern mendicant orders of capitalism. Life insurance companies and banks, traditionally conservative in their investment and loan portfolios, have historically provided the bulk of total capital for shopping centers' long-term mortgages. The principal owner and investor of the Mall of America, however—and here the irony is especially rich—is the Teachers Insurance and Annuity Association of America. My retirement is dependent on Camp Snoopy—a worthy linkage!

production of Columbus's ship, the *Santa Maria*. These malls are more than breathless tributes to commercial excess. They show how intimate the connection between consumption and entertainment has become.[19] If you can't have fun shopping in the world we live in, where can you have it?

19. As might be expected, the mall has become one of the central settings in modern entertainment. Since it is the commercial cave of family life, one would expect to see it in motion pictures. And indeed we do, from *Fast Times at Ridgemont High* to *Clueless* to *Terminator 2*. The target audience may be young (*Mallrats*) or mature (*Scenes From a Mall*). But the best mall movie ever is George Romero's first sequel to *Night of the Living Dead*, called *Dawn of the Dead*. No plot to speak of, thank God. If Romero ever had a plot, the audience would collapse exhausted. *Dawn* is a visual adaptation of Ravel's *Bolero* applied to human relations, this time set in the mall. Here's how it goes. Refugees from the first film's zombie plague are at the Monroeville mall busily shopping away. The zombies, however, have still not been destroyed. A few starved zombies shuffle by looking for food. Much is made about how similar these two groups really are, mindlessly going about their business. Once inside the mall, however, the real zombies have their own shopping style. They don't kill their prey. They pummel them, rip them open, and then turn them into hungry zombies. What we see for almost two hours is emaciated zombies chasing pudgy shoppers around, harvesting their fast-food fresh off the hoof, as we are told, and then making victims into victimizers. In a wonderful crescendo, the assembled zombies even have a gang of mall-marauding Hell's Angels for dessert—finger-licking good, literally.

No work of literary fiction can top *Dawn of the Dead* for its virtuoso treatment of America's love/hate relation with the mall. To be sure, Joyce Carol Oates names one of her early novels *Wonderland* after an early shopping center, Frederick Barthelme sets his short story "Cleo" in a mall, and Bobbie Ann Mason is forever following her characters as they go shopping. Some critics have called this genre "shopping mall realism"—Tom Wolfe calls it "Kmart fiction"—paying tribute to the fact that inside the enclosed, weather-controlled, brightly lit, Muzak-toned environment, many of the daily rituals of modern life occur. Personally, I think a prime contender for best mall-aise description is a book for the kids, *The Berenstain Bears and Too Much Junk Food* by Stan and Jan Berenstain. After too many trips to the mall, the young bears have gotten into the habit of snacking and are now pudgy and out of shape. Mrs. Bear and

✳ THE FALL OF THE MALL

The bloom is now off the flowering mall. It has been estimated that we have 10 percent more mall space than we need. In 1988, 64 malls with more than 400,000 square feet opened nationwide, while in the late 1990s only about four open per year. Many malls have already lost their retail tenants and become low-grade office space. Owners of some struggling establishments are even "de-malling" by removing the roof and creating open-air strip stores. In 1995, *Shopping Centers Today,* an industry publication, took a 180-degree turn. Its December issue carried a story beneath a big headline: "Demalling Becomes a Positive Option."

For a number of reasons malls are fading. First off, most metropolitan areas are now well served by regional malls. In fact, too well served, because today often ringing the mall are the big box stores—the infamous category killers—like Toys "R" Us, Staples, Office Depot, or a free-standing Borders, Barnes & Noble, or Circuit City. The road still goes to the mall, but shoppers get off early. Also, other shopping options have proliferated. Television and computer shopping have joined traditional mail-order catalogs. In addition, malls have gone downtown as part of urban renewal, and ironically promise shoppers the same airless experience they once had out in suburbia. Vertical malls like Manhattan's Trump Tower (a shopping mall for the rich and famous), Citicorp Center (a village square submerged in the city) and Chicago's Water Tower Place and Illinois Center are really department stores with individual departments separated out into different stores.

Another reason for mall atrophy is that the nation's interstate highway system has stopped breaking new ground. In the 1960s, the mall heyday, an average of 2,000 miles a year of interstate highway was opened. It's now down to less than 100 miles a year. In addition, the countrywide department stores, the traditional anchors of regional malls, aren't expanding as much as they used to, choosing instead to put more emphasis on renovating their existing stores. The anchor concept only works when a Sears or Penney's is willing to bet, and bet big, on at least two decades of customer growth.

Dr. Grizzly set them back on a nutritious path. Inescapably preachy, but brightly done, the fable of youth wasting away at the mall is indeed a moral tale for our times.

And finally, let's face it, the mall is boring. What made them attractive, now makes them dull. On the way up, the fact that if you've seen one mall, you've seen them all, works in the mall's favor. A Big Mac in Toledo is a Big Mac in Tupelo. On the way down, however, after too many Big Macs, you look for something new to taste. Malls are yet another victim of the "been there, done that" syndrome.

Worse still, the very trait that made the mall so attractive to the retailer is collapsing. Malls' attempt to police their inner spaces by enforcing curfews and exclusionary rights has been questioned by the courts. Remember that utopian Mall of America, that Cathedral of

➤ Camp Snoopy waits at the Mall of America, Bloomington, Minnesota. (Promotional brochure)

Commerce in Minnesota? Every weekend night at least 2,000 teen-agers gather inside its protected walls. Winter is worse. On a normal weekend winter night some 3,000 teenagers swarm its "streets," disturbing shoppers with chases, jokes, and fights. With art imitating life and vice versa, they drop food, pour drinks, and spit on shoppers from the upper decks, just as their fictional counterparts did in the movie *Mallrats.* When the mall manager attempted to ask unchaper-oned youths to prove that they were at least 16 years old before allow-ing them playspace, the Standard Outraged Groups were outraged. The ACLU made its views clear: the mall manager is not a parent. Robin Meredith, a *New York Times* reporter, interviewed kids outside the mall. They were really upset. Although the kids had already visited the mall twice that week, they told her that the mall management "took away our best shopping days ("Curfew Raises Questions of Rights and Bias" B9).

A paradox for our times is that if mall management were willing to report the levels of criminal behavior occurring in the malls they might substantiate their case for still greater control. But the price of letting such information go public might mean more anxious shoppers. And the primary rule of consumption is that it should never be done on a nervous stomach. So the very atmosphere that makes the malls allur-ing—escapism—also makes them magnets for those who take escap-ing as a way of life—the young and the rowdy. The keepers of the gar-den of consumerist Eden have found that the very walls that were to keep out urban contagion now are the very walls that keep it in.[20]

Then there is the final unmentionable that explains the decline of the mall. The consumer has been, in the jargon of merchandising, maxed out, and not just on credit card limits. Baby boomers simply own most of the material products known to mankind—power drills, wicker

---

20. The malls must maintain a very delicate balance. On one hand, they want Junior to be pulling the levers and punching the control panel over at the arcade. They want him to use the mall for the expensive courtship rituals of adolescence. On the other hand, they don't want him scaring the moms away. Two out of three women already feel at least a little unsafe while shopping, and an equal proportion say they're more fearful now than they were a few years ago, according to a recent national survey of five hundred women conducted by EDK Associates of New York City. As a result, EDK researchers estimated that concerns about personal secu-rity have cost large malls one in four women customers (Morin C5).

furniture, computers, cross trainers—and the only growth area in mall retailing now is jewelry. Even that is drying up. The post–World War II generation that makes up one third of the U.S. population today is simply getting older, and old is bad for most mall sales. Spending priorities have moved away from consumer durables to servicing retirement programs. In fact, if you've looked recently, the conglomerated hospital is behaving suspiciously like the mall.

We are just tuckered out. Maybe it's affluenza. In the storekeeper's jargon, this is called shopper fatigue. On November 13, 1993 the *Wall Street Journal* published the results of a survey concluding that many Americans have lost the get-up-and-go-to-the-mall urge. People who shopped in malls anchored by big department stores spent an average of four hours a month in such malls in 1990, down from twelve hours a decade earlier, and the number of stores visited dropped to three and a half from seven. Admittedly, this may not mean we're spending any less, but that our shopping has become highly focused and dictated by need, rather than a form of entertainment. One in four shoppers never leaves the anchor department store to browse the mall.

By no means am I predicting the end of shopping as we have known it. The predicted future of consumption we are being told every day is on the World Wide Web. Don't bet on it. If there is anything we have learned by observing humans consuming, it is that the least of their concerns is laying up goods. Shopping is far more complex. Along with getting the goods, it is a social activity, an epistemological activity, and even a religious activity. Although the mall may go the way of the medieval cathedral, the passion to find meaning in material, salvation through stuff, will endure.

8

The Liberating Role of Consumption

Sell them their dreams. Sell them what they longed for and hoped for and al-
most despaired of having. Sell them hats by splashing sunlight across them. Sell
them dreams—dreams of country clubs and proms and visions of what might
happen if only. After all, people don't buy things to have things. They buy things
to work for them. They buy hope—hope of what your merchandise will do for
them. Sell them this hope and you won't have to worry about selling them
goods.

—Helen Landon Cass

THESE words were spoken in 1923 by a female radio announcer to a convention of salesmen in Philadelphia. *The Philadelphia Retail Ledger* for June 6th recorded Ms. Cass's invocations with no surrounding explanation (in Leach 298). They were simply noted as a matter of record, not as a startling insight.

There are two ways to read her spiel. You can read it like a melancholy Marxist and see the barely veiled indictment of the selling process. What does she think consumers are: dopes to be duped? What is she selling? Snake oil? Or you can read it like an unrepentant capitalist and see the connection between consuming goods and gathering meaning. The reason producers splash magical promise over their goods is because consumers demand it. Consumers are not sold a bill of goods;

they insist on it. Snake oil to the cynic is often holy water to the eager.[1] What looks like exploiting desire may be fulfilling desire.

How you come down in this matter depends on your estimation of the audience. Does the audience manipulate things to make meaning, or do other people use things to manipulate them? Clearly, this is a variation of "I persuade, you educate, they manipulate," for both points of view are supportable. Let's split the difference and be done with it.

More interesting to me, however, is to wonder why such a statement, so challenging, so revolutionary, so provocative in many respects was, in the early 1920s, so understandable, so acceptable, even so passé that it appears with no gloss. Why is it that when you read the early descriptions of capitalism, all the current bugaboos—advertising, packaging, branding, fashion, and retailing techniques—seem so much better understood?

And why has the consumer—playing an active, albeit usually secondary, part in the consumptive dyad of earlier interpretations—become almost totally listless in our current descriptions? From Thomas Hobbes in the mid-seventeenth century ("As in other things, so in men, not the seller but the buyer determines the price"), to Edwin S. Bingham in the mid-twentieth century ("Consumers with dollars in their pockets are not, by any stretch of the imagination, weak. To the contrary, they are the most merciless, meanest, toughest market disciplinarians I know"), the consumer was seen as participating in the meaning-making of the material world. How and why did the consumer get dumbed down and phased out so quickly? Why has the hypodermic metaphor (false needs injected into a docile populace) become the unchallenged explanation of consumerism?

---

1. In medieval times, halos were often retrofitted over the heads of the saints not because the priests wanted them there but because the parishioners did. In fact, as Leo Steinberg illustrated in *The Sexuality of Christ in Renaissance Art and in Modern Oblivion*, the early church fathers did not even want Christ pictured as human. If He had to be imaged, let it be as a lamb. The congregation, however, insisted that He be pictured as human. If Christ died for us then He should be not a Holy Spirit, but "one of us." Hence the burst of crucifixion images in the Renaissance, images initially fought by the producers, demanded by the consumers, and then universally accepted by both. "Sell them their dreams . . . sell them this hope" did not originate in capitalism, as comforting as it may be to think so.

☀ *NARCISSISTIC IATROGENIC ACADEMIC OBFUSCATION*

I think that much of our current refusal to consider the liberating role of consumption is the result of who has been doing the describing. Since the 1960s, the primary "readers" of the commercial "text" have been the well-tended and -tenured members of the academy. For any number of reasons—the most obvious being their low levels of disposable income, average age and gender, and the fact that these critics are selling a competing product, high-cult (which is also coated with dream values)—the academy has casually passed off as "hegemonic brainwashing" what seems to me, at least, a self-evident truth about human nature. We like having stuff.

In place of the obvious they have substituted an interpretation that they themselves often call *vulgar* Marxism. It is supposedly vulgar in the sense that it is not as sophisticated as the real stuff, but it has enough spin on it to be more appropriately called Marxism *lite*. Go into almost any Cultural Studies course in this country and you will hear the condemnation of consumerism expounded. What we see in the marketplace is the result of the manipulation of the many for the profit of the few. Consumers are led around by the nose. We live in a squirrel cage. Left alone we would read Wordsworth, eat lots of salad, and have meetings to discuss Really Important Subjects.

In Cultural Studies today everything is oppression and we are all victims. In macrocosmic form, the oppression is economic—the "free" market. In microcosmic form, oppression is media—your "free" TV. Here, in the jargon of this downmarket Marxism, is how the system works: the manipulators, aka "the culture industry," attempt to enlarge their hegemony by establishing their ideological base in the hearts and pocketbooks of a weak and demoralized populace. Left alone, we would never desire things (ugh!). They have made us materialistic. But for them we would be spiritual.

To these critics, the masters of industry and their henchmen, the media lords, are predators, and what they do in no way reflects or resolves genuine audience concerns. Just the opposite. The masters of the media collude, striving to infantilize us so that we are docile, anxious, and filled with reified desire. While we may think advertising is just "talking about the product," that packaging just "wraps the object," that retailing is just "trading the product," or that fashion is just "the style of the product," this is not so. That you may think so only proves their power over you. The marginalized among us—the African American, the child, the immigrant, and especially the female—are trapped into this commodifying system, this false consciousness and this fetishism that only the enlightened can correct. David Ogilvy's observation that "The consumer is no fool, she is your wife" is just an example of the repressive tolerance of such a sexist, materialistic culture.

Needless to say, in such a system the only safe place to be is tenured, underpaid, self-defined as marginalized, teaching two days a week for nine months a year, and writing really perceptive social criticism that your colleagues can pretend to read. Or rather, you would be writing such articles if only you could find the time.

✳ *A PERSONAL EXPERIENCE: HOW I BOUGHT MY RED MIATA*

All our wants, beyond those which a very moderate income will supply, are purely imaginary.   —Henry St. John, 1743

Things, as such, become goods as soon as the human mind recognizes them as means suitable for the promotion of human purposes.
                                                          —Carl Menger, 1871

Sometimes it is best to test academic theory against—gasp!—personal experience. When my daughters were little they would go with me to the grocery store. We would start as friends, and before a few aisles had passed we would be at each other's throats. "Gimme this, I want that, can we have these?"—it would go on and on until, by the vegetables, I would lose control and things would degenerate into Kmart Khaos. "No, no, a thousand nos," I would yell at them. "No, you can't have that. No, I won't buy you that." This didn't work, and by the time we had reached the checkout line, they had gotten much of what they had sought.

To stop the demoralizing defeat I tried to teach them about consumption. I developed The Nerminological Laws of Consumption, and I drilled these so-called laws into them so that I could later say, "What Nerminological law have you just broken?" whenever they asked for anything.

Here are the rules. First, isolate the need. Do you need this thing or do you just want it? Don't let *needs* be confused with *wants*. Next, shop around. Check out the competition. Do your research. Third, can you afford this? Check current and anticipated cash flow. And last, once you have decided, can you read the instructions on how to use it properly?

Why buy a toy you can't assemble? The success of such a system was not so much that it was logical but that it took so long to go through that once they had come to the instruction part, we were out the door. I would live to regret my explanation of what goes on in the Land of the Nermies ruled by the inexorable Nerminological Laws.

It happened about ten years ago. I bought a Mazda Miata. This is a snappy little red sports car that twelve-year-old boys really like, but chubby, balding fifty-year-olds usually buy. My daughters like driving it, but better, they like asking me which of the Nerminological Laws I followed when I bought it. Did I need a car when I biked to work? Did I need a car that seats only two? Did I really shop around? Could I afford it on my schoolteacher salary? Did I even know how to drive it properly? If so, why did I brake during cornering instead of accelerating? Could I fix it? Did I even know where the battery was hidden? Clearly, they enjoyed seeing me hoisted by my own petard.

Although this car has given me much pleasure, I still can't figure out exactly why I bought it. I know how to buy stuff. I'm fully mature. I have a 401(k) plan. When I was growing up my parents subscribed to *Consumer Reports,* and I learned how to read all the little bullseye symbols telling you if this was a good deal or a so-so one. So what happened?

I bought the car because of an advertisement. The ad itself is not complex. In fact, it is the standard "product as hero" ad that we have all seen a thousand times. There stage center, lit from behind like a haloed angel, is this thing in your garage. If you are middle-aged, the garage is clearly from your early adolescence, when you were moving out of your room and mixing your toys with the stuff of your parents. But wait! That stuff in the pictured garage is not your dad's stuff—those are not his toys, they are yours. Dad didn't grow up with a whiffle ball, a dart board, the teddy bear, the metronome (aargh!), the dollhouse, that bike.

The maudlin text below the icon makes it clear. All this is/was yours:

> It was one of those summer evenings you wished would never end, and the whole neighborhood turned out to see your new car. You answered a million questions, and everyone sat in the driver's seat. They went home long after sunset.

In an interesting kind of temporal dislocation the "you" is in the past tense. This is the "you" of your childhood, the you who rushed downtown each September to see what the new cars looked like, the you who

For more information call 1-800-424-0202.

It was one of those summer evenings
you wished would never end,
and the whole neighborhood
turned out to see your new car.

You answered a million questions,
and everyone sat in the driver's seat.
They went home long after sunset.

But it was still t-shirt warm
by the time the kids were in bed.
So you came out for one last look.

The Mazda Miata.
Named Automobile of the Year
by Automobile Magazine.

mazda
IT JUST FEELS RIGHT.

∧   "It Just Feels Right" : cue the Beach Boys. (Mazda Miata, 1990) dreamed about getting an MG, an Austin Healey 3000, or maybe a Triumph. It would be red, or maybe English racing green. When someone had a car like that what could you do but just stand there and look at it? There was really nothing you could say.[2]

The last line in the copy pulls the plug. "But it was still T-shirt warm by the time the kids were in bed. So you came out for one last look." The "you" as observer has become the "you" as owner. It's yours now. This missing part of your past, this thing that always belonged to someone else, is yours. Little wonder the car is positioned and lit like a holy relic. It's coming at you. All you have to do is grasp it.

What separates this ad from the usual automotive pitch is its claim on memory. The more usual claim for sports cars is sexual: Get this car, get that girl. So the sports car is usually photographed out in the rugged countryside, the sport himself is young and virile, and the chick by his side just can't stop looking at him. In advertising lingo this is called the aspirational sell: use the product and everyone will see what a real man you are.

What is important about the Miata ad is that there is no one at the wheel and no dreamy chick flapping her lashes at him. This driver's seat is vacant. You've always wanted to sit there. Now you can. Here, as my colleagues might say, is nostalgic onanism.[3]

---

2. I still remember being in the parking lot in Stowe, Vermont at the base of Mt. Mansfield after a day of skiing. Someone from New York City had left his Aston Martin idling while he was in the warming hut. There must have been fifteen teenage boys who stopped in their tracks and just listened to that car. No one dared get near it. It was as holy as any object I had ever seen. Later at Christmas I remember thinking that I could understand how the wise men felt as they beheld the Christ child in Bethlehem. I knew it was sacrilegious to make such a comparison but I also knew it was true.

3. Larry Kapold, executive creative director of Foote, Cone & Belding in Los Angeles, which made the ad, has a slightly different explanation. He says he was able to tease this ad from various focus groups.

> Early on, whenever we'd show a picture of the car to anyone, we'd get one of two reactions. Either, it's beautiful or you know what it reminds me of. . . . We wanted to tap that feeling of a car evoking warm memories without hitting people over the head with something like a 1950s sock-hop. (Goldrich 6)

Although I had "new-car fever" (a common enough strain of affluenza), the object was difficult to consume. Here's why. I teach school. I
wear khaki pants. I had a green book bag in graduate school. I am a
company man. I buy my cars from Volvo or Saab, not because I like
these cars—I don't. They are built to be ugly and are no fun. But they
are part of the uniform. They are from Sweden, for goodness' sake, the
Valhalla of academic liberalism.[4] If I bought the Miata I was not just going to lose my affiliation with my PRIZM group, I was going over to a different group, to a group I abhorred. If I bought this car I was going to
become . . . a yuppie!

At the time I was making my decision, yuppies were the group du
jour of marketers and the group de résistance for all the rest of us. Yuppies were disgusting. What made them disgusting was their lack of reti-
cence in the displaying of commercial badges. More interesting still
was that no one ever would admit to being one of them. In fact, in retrospect, the real sign of being a yuppie was that you tried hard to disas-
sociate from them while all along displaying their badges.[5]

---

4. Professor Stanley Fish (who wants you to know he drives a V-12 Jaguar) has
   written a wonderfully mocking article about why professors drive Volvos
   ("The Unbearable Ugliness of Volvos") in which he attributes the attraction of the ungainliness of Volvos to aspects of "professorial self-loathing."
   Actually, the academic badge is not just the car but rather a sticker you put
   in the back window. This decal shows affiliation not with where you teach,
   but rather with where you send your kids to college. In my experience,
   there is no more important academic consumable than this school. Colleagues will borrow to the hilt, sacrifice daily, postpone their own retirement, if they can just get this badge in place. To be sure, they value education, but they also know that the "money costs" do not logically warrant the
   deprivation. When you think about it, however, the choice becomes clear.
   To a group that must professionally spurn consumption for financial and
   ethical reasons, there must be something to sacrifice for, as well as something to use to show success. Those innocuous-seeming, but really quite
   aggressive, school decals are badges the size of billboards. They are what
   we have in place of personal jets. They do not just say "My kid is an honor
   student (sorry about yours)" but "I have succeeded (what about you?)."

5. The original definition was a young urban professional, but at some point
   this became corrupted to young upwardly mobile professional. From there
   meaning spread to define an entire generation of affluent and selfish

A Cough is a Social Blunder

People who know have no hesitation in avoiding the cougher. They know that he is a public menace. They know that his cough is a proof of his lack of consideration of others.

And they know that he knows it too, so they are not afraid of hurting his feelings.

For there is no excuse for coughing. It is just as unnecessary as any other bad habit. For it can be prevented or relieved by the simplest of precautions—the use of S. B. Cough Drops.

S. B. Cough Drops are not a cure for colds. They are a preventive of coughing. True, they often keep a cough from developing into a sore throat or cold. And they are a protection to the public because they keep people who already have influenza, colds and other throat troubles from spreading them through unnecessary coughing. Have a box with you always.

Pure. No Drugs. Just enough charcoal to sweeten the stomach.

One placed in the mouth at bedtime will keep the breathing passages clear.

Drop that Cough
SMITH BROTHERS of Poughkeepsie
FAMOUS SINCE 1847

SMITH BROTHERS'
S. B.
COUGH DROPS.
S. B.
Stamped on each Drop
POUGHKEEPSIE,
N.Y., U.S.A.
Reg. U.S. Pat. Off.
TRADE   MARK
S. B. COUGH DROPS

[1919]

> Times change, tastes change, values change. Ads do too.

Again She Orders —
"A Chicken Salad, Please"

FOR him she is wearing her new frock. For him she is trying to look her prettiest. If only she can impress him—make him like her—just a little.

Across the table he smiles at her, proud of her prettiness, glad to notice that others admire. And she smiles back, a bit timidly, a bit self-consciously.

What wonderful poise he has! What complete self-possession! If only she could be so thoroughly at ease.

She pats the folds of her new frock nervously, hoping that he will not notice how embarrassed she is, how uncomfortable. He doesn't—until the waiter comes to their table and stands, with pencil poised, to take the order.

"A chicken salad, please." She hears herself give the order as in a daze. She hears him repeat the order to the waiter, in a rather surprised tone. Why had she ordered that again! This was the third time she had ordered chicken salad while dining with him.

He would think she didn't know how to order a dinner. Well, did she? No. She didn't know how to pronounce those French words on the menu. And she didn't know how to use the table appointment as gracefully as she would have liked; found that she couldn't create conversation—and was actually tongue-tied; was conscious of little crudities which she just knew he must be noticing. She wasn't sure of herself, she didn't know. And she discovered, as we all do, that there is only one way to have complete poise and ease of manner, and that is to know definitely what to do and say on every occasion.

Are You Conscious of Your Crudities?

It is not, perhaps, so serious a fault to be unable to order a correct dinner. But it is just such little things as these that betray us—that reveal our crudities to others.

Are you sure of yourself? Do you know precisely what to do and say wherever you happen to be? Or are you always hesitant and ill at ease, never quite sure that you haven't blundered?

Every day in our contact with men and women we meet little unexpected problems of conduct. Unless we are prepared to meet them, it is inevitable that we suffer embarrassment and keen humiliation.

Etiquette is the armor that protects us from these embarrassments. It makes us aware instantly of the little crudities that are robbing us of our poise and ease. It tells us how to smooth away these crudities and achieve a manner of confidence and self-possession. It eliminates doubt and uncertainty, tells us exactly what we want to know.

There is an old proverb which says "Good manners make good mixers." We all know how true this is. No one likes to associate with a person who is self-conscious and embarrassed; whose crudities are obvious to all.

Do You Make Friends Easily?

By telling you exactly what is expected of you on all occasions, by giving you a wonderful new ease and dignity of manner, the Book of Etiquette will help make you more popular—a "better mixer." This famous two-volume set of books is the recognized social authority—is a silent social secretary in half a million homes.

Let us pretend that you have received an invitation. Would you know exactly how to acknowledge it? Would you know what sort of gift to send, what to write on the card that accompanies it? Perhaps it is an invitation to a formal wedding. Would you know what to wear? Would you know what to say to the host and hostess upon arrival?

If a Dinner Follows the Wedding—

Would you know exactly how to proceed to the dining room, when to seat yourself, how to create conversation, how to conduct yourself with ease and dignity?

Would you use a fork for your fruit salad, or a spoon? Would you cut your roll with a knife, or break it with your fingers? Would you take olives with a fork? How would you take celery—asparagus—radishes? Unless you are absolutely sure of yourself, you will be embarrassed. And embarrassment *cannot be concealed.*

Book of Etiquette Gives Lifelong Advice

Hundreds of thousands of men and women know and use the Book of Etiquette and find it increasingly helpful. Every time an occasion of importance arises—every time expert help, advice and suggestion is required—they find what they seek in the Book of Etiquette. It solves all problems, answers all questions, tells you exactly what to do, say, write and wear on every occasion.

If you want always to be sure of yourself, to have ease and poise, to avoid embarrassment and humiliation, send for the Book of Etiquette at once. Take advantage of the special bargain offer explained in the panel. Let the Book of Etiquette give you complete self-possession; let it banish the crudities that are perhaps making you self-conscious and uncomfortable when you should be thoroughly at ease.

Mail this coupon *now* while you are thinking of it. The Book of Etiquette will be sent to you in a plain carton with no identifying marks. Be among those who will take advantage of the special offer. Nelson Doubleday, Inc., Dept. 3911, Garden City, New York.

"Can he really play?" a girl whispered. "Heavens, no!" Arthur exclaimed. "He never played a note in his life."

They Laughed When I Sat Down At the Piano But When I Started to Play!—

ARTHUR had just played "The Rosary." The room rang with applause. I decided that this would be a dramatic moment for me to make my debut. To the amazement of all my friends I strode confidently over to the piano and sat down.

"Jack is up to his old tricks," somebody chuckled. The crowd laughed. They were all certain that I couldn't play a single note.

"Can he really play?" I heard a girl whisper to Arthur. "Heavens, no!" Arthur exclaimed. "He never played a note in all his life...But just you watch him. This is going to be good."

I decided to make the most of the situation. With mock dignity I drew out a silk handkerchief and lightly dusted off the keys. Then I rose and gave the revolving piano stool a quarter of a turn, just as I had seen an imitator of Paderewski do in a vaudeville sketch.

"What do you think of his execution?" called a voice from the rear.

"We're in favor of it!" came back the answer, and the crowd rocked with laughter.

Then I Started to Play

Instantly a tense silence fell on the guests. The laughter died on their lips as if by magic. I played through the first bars of Liszt's immortal Liebesträume. I heard gasps of amazement. My friends sat breathless—spellbound.

I played on and as I played I forgot the people around me. I forgot the hour, the place, the breathless listeners. The little world I lived in seemed to fade—seemed to grow dim—unreal. Only the music was real. Only the music and the visions it brought me. Visions as beautiful and as changing as the wind-blown clouds and drifting moonlight, that long ago inspired the master composer. It seemed as if the master musician himself were speaking to me—speaking through the medium of music—not in words but in chords. Not in sentences but in exquisite melodies.

A Complete Triumph!

As the last notes of the Liebesträume died away, the room resounded with a sudden roar of applause. I found myself surrounded by excited faces. How my friends carried on! Men shook my hand—wildly congratulated me—pounded me on the back in their enthusiasm! Everybody was exclaiming with delight—plying me with rapid questions.... "Jack! Why didn't you tell us you could play like that?" ..."Where *did* you learn?"—"How long have you studied?"—"Who *was* your teacher?"

"I have never even *seen* my teacher," I replied. "And just a short while ago I couldn't play a note."

"Quit your kidding," laughed Arthur, himself an accomplished pianist. "You've been studying for years. I can tell."

"I have been studying only a short while," I insisted. "I decided to keep it a secret so that I could surprise all you folks."

Then I told them the whole story.

"Have you ever heard of the U. S. School of Music?" I asked. A few of my friends nodded. "That's a correspondence school, isn't it?" they exclaimed.

"Exactly," I replied. "They have a new simplified method that can teach you to play any instrument *by note* in just a few months."

How I Learned to Play Without a Teacher

And then I explained how for years I had longed to play the piano.

"It seems just a short while ago," I continued, "that I saw an interesting ad of the U. S. School of Music mentioning a new method of learning to play which only cost a few cents a day! The ad told how a woman had mastered the piano in her spare time at home—and *without a teacher!* Best of all, the wonderful new method she used required no laborious scales—no heartless exercises—no tiresome practising. It sounded so convincing that I filled out the coupon requesting the Free Demonstration Lesson.

"The free book arrived promptly and I started in that very night to study the Demonstration Lesson. I was amazed to see how easy it was to play this new way. Then I sent for the course.

"When the course arrived I found it was just as the ad said—as easy as A. B. C.! And as the lessons continued they got easier and easier. Before I knew it I was playing all the pieces I liked best. Nothing stopped me. I could play ballads or classical numbers or jazz, all with equal ease. And I never did have any special talent for music."

*   *   *   *

Play Any Instrument

You, too, can now *teach yourself* to be an accomplished musician—right at home—in half the usual time. You can't go wrong with this simple new method which has already shown almost half a million people how to play their favorite instruments *by note*. Forget that old-fashioned idea that you need special "talent." Just read the list of instruments in the panel, decide which one you want to play and the U. S. School will do the rest. And bear in mind no matter which instrument you choose, the cost in each case will be the same—just a few cents a day. No matter whether you are a mere beginner or already a good performer, you will be interested in learning about this new and wonderful method.

Send for Our Free Booklet and Demonstration Lesson

Thousands of successful students never dreamed they possessed musical ability until it was revealed to them by a remarkable "Musical Ability Test" which we send entirely without cost with our interesting free booklet.

If you are in earnest about wanting to play your favorite instrument—if you really want to gain happiness and increase your popularity—send at once for the free booklet and Demonstration Lesson. No cost—no obligation. Sign and send the convenient coupon now. Instruments supplied when needed, cash or credit. U. S. School of Music, 812 Brunswick Bldg., New York City.

Yuppies were unique in that they were the first consumption community that I can think of known *only* by their badges. No one came forward like Marlon Brando, Abbie Hoffman, John Wayne, or Elton John to personify the group. Richard Gere laying out his clothes on the bed in the movie *American Gigolo* might have been the yuppie archetype, but he seemed a little too moody about his stuff. Still, rather like Eagle Scouts, yuppies had no distinct personality other than their merit (or demerit, it's up to you) badges worn almost Pancho Villa style around their vacuous lifestyles.

Here are just a few of the yuppie badges: yellow ties and red suspenders, Merlot, marinated salmon steaks, green-bottle beer, Club Med vacations, stuff with ducks on it, Gaggenau stoves, Sub-Zero refrigerators, latte, clothing from Ann Taylor or Ralph Lauren, designer water, Filofax binders, Cuisinarts, kiwi fruit, Ben & Jerry's ice cream, ventless Italian suits, pasta makers, bread makers, espresso-cappuccino makers, cellphones, home fax machines, air and water cleaners, laptop computers, exercise machines, massage tables, and remote controls for the television, the VCR, the CD player, the stereo receiver, the garage door, the child. More than anything, of course, the car—especially the BMW, the infamous beemer—was the yuppie badge nonpareil.

The yuppie and his German or Japanese car were academic anathema. If a colleague were to see me in such a car he would surely think I had gone over to the other side. My cousin with the pricy condo, the Jenn-Air gas grill, Biggest Bertha Ever golf club, and the Suburban could be a yuppie. But not me. I only bought just the things I absolutely needed . . . like a red Miata? And that, of course, was precisely my problem. When I bought this car, I became one of them.

I dilate on my Miata decision because it shows the dynamic of pressures in the commercial world. Two generations ago maybe choosing what denomination of the Congregational church to attend would have

---

5. (*cont'd*) twenty-somethings who were hot on the heels of us baby boomers. Demographically, yuppies were part of the 76 million people born between 1946 and 1964. Their number was small (the only definitive estimate of the yuppie population found just four million of them, representing a mere 5 percent of late baby boomers [see "The Big Chill Revisited," an entire issue of *American Demographics*, September 1985]), but their impact on the rest of us was huge—reverse magnetism.

caused me such distress. Do I dare be seen with Unitarians? At the turn of this century what musical instrument you played would have been important. "They laughed when I sat down at the piano, but when I started to play!" describes a Horatio Alger experience we have trouble understanding. Maybe status would have been derived from what I read. Could I be seen reading Walt Whitman? What about what I ate? Our grandparents read etiquette books detailing the shame you should feel if you ordered the same meal too often. "Again she orders—A chicken salad, please!" is the headline of an ad for such an etiquette book. It is presumably spoken by an exasperated young man about his date. What if I coughed? Would that be a social blunder? Perhaps what I wore. Could I be seen wearing a gold stickpin in my tie? The way we live now, I worry that I might be mistaken for a yuppie.

✳ THE TRIUMPH OF STUFF

While I certainly went through the modern version of the "agonies of the damned" buying a Japanese internal-combustion engine advertised through nostalgia and wrapped in red plastic, I never once was duped, misled, waylaid, or reified. In fact, I loved the process. They offered me my dream and I gladly bought it. I never liked that dreary Volvo to begin with. Now I'm wondering about a Jaguar, perhaps something from the early '80s, not too ostentatious but still flashy, if you know what I mean.

Let's face it, the idea that consumerism creates artificial desires rests on a wistful ignorance of history and human nature, on the hazy, romantic feeling that there existed some halcyon era of noble savages with purely natural needs. Once fed and sheltered, our needs have always been cultural, not natural. Until there is some other system to codify and satisfy those needs and yearnings, capitalism—and the culture it carries with it—will continue not just to thrive but to triumph.

In the way we live now, it is simply impossible to consume objects without consuming meaning. Meaning is pumped *and* drawn everywhere throughout the modern commercial world, into the farthest reaches of space and into the smallest divisions of time. Commercialism is the water we all swim in, the air we breath, our sunlight and shade. Currents of desire flow around objects like smoke in a wind tunnel. The complications of my Miata purchase are the norm.

By no means am I sanguine about such a material culture. It has many problems that I have glossed over. Consumerism is wasteful, it is devoid of otherworldly concerns, it lives for today and celebrates the body. It overindulges and spoils the young with impossible promises. It encourages recklessness, living beyond one's means, gambling. Consumer culture is always new, always without a past. Like religion, which it has displaced, it afflicts the comfortable and comforts the afflicted. It is heedless of the truly poor who cannot gain access to the loop of meaningful information that is carried through its ceaseless exchanges. It is a one-dimensional world, a wafer-thin world, a world low on significance and high on glitz, a world without yesterdays.

On a more personal level, I struggle daily it keep it at bay. For instance, I am offended by billboards (how do they externalize costs?); I fight to keep Chris Whittle's Channel One TV and all place-based advertising from entering the classroom; political advertising makes me sick, especially the last-minute negative ads; I contribute to PBS in hopes they will stop slipping down the slope of commercialism although I know better; I am annoyed that Coke has bought all the "pouring rights" at my school and is now trying to do the same to the world; I think it's bad enough that the state now sponsors gambling, do they also have to support deceptive advertising about it?; I despise the way that amateur athletics has become a venue for shoe companies (why not just replace the football with the Nike swoosh and be done with it?); and I just go nuts at Christmas.

But I also realize that while you don't have to like it, it doesn't hurt to understand it and our part in it. We have not been led astray. Henry Luce was not far off when he claimed in a February 1941 editorial in *Life* magazine that the next era was to be the American Century: "The Greeks, the Romans, the English and the French had their eras, and now it was ours" (in Turner 2). Not only that, but we may well commandeer much of the next century as well.

Almost a decade ago, Francis Fukuyama, a State Department official, contended in his controversial essay (and later book), "The End of History?" that "the ineluctable spread of consumerist Western culture" presages "not just the end of the Cold War, or the passing of a particular period of postwar history, but the end of history as such: that is, the end point of mankind's ideological evolution" (3–4). Okay, such predictions are not new. "The End of History" (as we know it), and the "end point of mankind's ideological evolution" have been predicted before by philosophers. Hegel claimed it had already happened in 1806 when Napoleon embodied the ideals of the French Revolution, and Marx said the end was coming soon with world communism. What legitimizes this modern claim is that it is demonstrably true. For better or for worse, American commercial culture is well on its way to becoming world culture. The Soviets have fallen. Only quixotic French intellectuals and anxious Islamic fundamentalists are trying to stand up to it.

To some degree, the triumph of consumerism is the triumph of the popular will. You may not like what is manufactured, advertised, packaged, branded, and broadcast, but it is far closer to what most people want most of the time than at any other period of modern history.

To return briefly to the two fictional characters who personify to me the great divide: Anthony Trollope's Augustus Melmotte and Steve Martin's Navin R. Johnson. In the Victorian world, meaning was generated through such social conventions as the abstract concept of bloodline, the value of patina, your club, owning land, acceptable in-laws, your accent, the seating chart for dinner, the proper church pew—all things Melmotte could never master. It was a stultifying system, a real old-boy network perhaps, but one that to Trollope, still worked. It was a system presided over by chummy squires, comfortable gentlemen, and twinkling clerics.

In a consumerist culture, the value-making ligatures that hold our world together come from such conventions as advertising, packaging, branding, fashion, and even shopping itself. It is a system presided over by marketers who deliver the goods and all that is carried in their wake. It is a more democratic world, a more egalitarian world, and, I think, a more interesting world. But commercialism is a stultifying system too, and wasteful.

Remember, Augustus Melmotte, certified world-class financier, is forever kept at bay. He never achieves his goal and finally commits suicide. Navin J. Johnson, certified consumer jerk, achieves (if only for a while) the objects of his heart's desire. He finally becomes a bum on Skid Row, true, but a bum who at least can try it all over again.

It would be nice to think that this eternally encouraging market will result in the cosmopolitanism envisioned by the Enlightenment philosophers, that a "universalism of goods" will end in a crescendo of hosannas. It would be nice to think that more and more of the poor and disenfranchised will find their ways into the cycle of increased affluence without contracting affluenza. It would be nice to think that materialism could be heroic, self-abnegating, and redemptive. It would be nice to think that greater material comforts will release us from racism, sexism, and ethnocentricism, and that the apocalypse will come as it did at the end of romanticism in Shelley's *Prometheus Unbound*, leaving us "Sceptreless, free, uncircumscribed . . . Equal, unclassed, tribeless, and nationless . . . Pinnacled dim in the intense inane."

But it is more likely that the globalization of capitalism will result in the banalities of an ever-increasing, worldwide consumerist culture. Recall that Athens ceased to be a world power around 400 B.C., yet for the next three hundred years Greek culture was the culture of the world. The Age of European Exposition ended in the mid-twentieth century; the Age of American Markets—Yankee imperialism—is just starting to gather force. The French don't stand a chance. The Middle East is collapsing under the weight of dish antennas and Golden Arches. The untranscendent, repetitive, sensational, democratic, immediate, tribalizing, and unifying force of what Irving Kristol calls the American Imperium need not result in a Bronze Age of culture, however. In fact, who knows what this Pax Americana will result in? But it certainly will not produce what Shelley had in mind.

We have been in the global marketplace a short time, and it is an often scary and melancholy place. A butterfly flapping its wings in China may not cause storm clouds over Miami, but a few lines of computer code written by some kid in Palo Alto may indeed change the lives of all the inhabitants of Shanghai.

We have not been led into this world of material closeness against our better judgment. For many of us, especially when young, consumerism *is* our better judgment. And this is true regardless of class or culture. We have not just asked to go this way, we have demanded. Now most of the world is lining up, pushing and shoving, eager to elbow into the mall. Woe to the government or religion that says no.

Getting and spending has been the most passionate, and often the most imaginative, endeavor of modern life. We have done more than acknowledge that the good life starts with the material life, as the ancients did. We have made stuff the dominant prerequisite of organized society. Things "R" Us. Consumption has become production. While this is dreary and depressing to some, as doubtless it should be, it is liberating and democratic to many more.

References

This bibliography is by no means complete, but virtually all works cited in the text are included. It does reflect, however, the bias of *Lead Us Into Temptation*. The uncited one-line comments from pundits about consumption, advertising, and materialism that are sprinkled throughout the text were gleaned from standard collections of popular quotations as well as from the Advertising World Wide Web site (http://advertising.utexas.edu/research/quotes).

Abelson, Elaine. *When Ladies Go A-Thieving: Middle-Class Shoppers in the Victorian Department Store*. New York: Oxford University Press, 1989.

Andrews, Peter. "Peddling Prime Time." *Saturday Review*, June 7, 1980, pp. 64–65.

Appadurai, Arjun. *The Social Life of Things*. New York: Cambridge University Press, 1986.

Applebrome, Peter. "Children Place Low in Adult's Esteem." *New York Times*, June 26, 1997, p. A25.

Archer, Gleason L. *History of Radio to 1926*. New York: American Historical Society, 1928.

Armstrong, Stephen. "Catch 'em Young." *Sunday Times* (London), May 12, 1996, features.

Babin, Barry J., William R. Darden, and Mitch Griffin. "Work and/or Fun: Measuring Hedonic and Utilitarian Shopping Value." *Journal of Consumer Research* 20, 4 (1994): 644–68.

References

Bailey, Jeff. "Curbside Recycling Comforts the Soul, but Benefits Are Scant." *Wall Street Journal*, January 19, 1995, p. A1.

Barnouw, Erik. *The Sponsor: Notes on a Modern Potentate*. New York: Oxford University Press, 1978.

Barthelme, Frederick. "Cleo." In *Chroma Stories*, 28–41. New York: Penguin, 1987.

Barton, Bruce. *The Man Nobody Knows: A Discovery of the Real Jesus*. Indianapolis: Bobbs-Merrill, 1926.

Baudrillard, Jean. *The Mirror of Production*. Translated by Mark Poster. Saint Louis, Mo.: Telos Press, 1983.

——. *Simulacra and Simulation*. Translated by Sheila Glaser. Ann Arbor: University of Michigan Press, 1994.

Baum, L. Frank. *The Wizard of Oz*. Reprint, New York: Oxford University Press, 1997.

Bell, Daniel. *The Cultural Contradictions of Capitalism*. New York: Basic Books, 1976.

Bennett, William J. National Press Club Luncheon Address. Federal Information Systems, 1996.

Berber, John. *The Moment of Cubism, and Other Essays*. New York: Pantheon, 1969.

Berenstain, Stan and Jan Berenstain. *The Berenstain Bears and Too Much Junk Food*. New York: Random House, 1985.

Berger, John. *Ways of Seeing*. New York: Penguin, 1977.

Boorstin, Daniel J. "Advertising and American Civilization." In Yale Brozen, ed., *Advertising and Society*, 11–23. New York: New York University Press, 1974.

——. *The Americans: The Democratic Experience*. New York: Random House, 1973.

——. *The Decline of Radicalism: Reflections on America Today*. New York: Random House, 1996.

——. *The Image: A Guide to Pseudo-Events in America*. New York: Atheneum, 1961.

Bourdieu, Pierre. *Distinction: A Social Critique of the Judgment of Taste*. Translated by Richard Nice. Cambridge: Harvard University Press, 1984.

Brant, John. "Rethinking the Fast Lane: Simple Life; Materialism Fails to Ensure Happiness." *Buffalo News*, September 17, 1995, p. 6F.

Breathnach, Sarah. *Simple Abundance: A Daybook of Comfort and Joy*. New York: Warner Books, 1995.

Brewer, John and Roy Porter, eds. *Consumption and the World of Goods*. New York: Routledge, 1994.

Bronner, Simon J., ed. *Consuming Visions: Accumulation and Display of Goods in America, 1880–1920.* New York: Norton, 1989.

Brown, Les. *Television: The Business Behind the Box.* New York: Harcourt, Brace, 1971.

Brunvand, Jan Harold. *The Choking Doberman and Other "New" Urban Legends.* New York: Norton, 1984.

———. *The Vanishing Hitchhiker: American Urban Legends and Their Meanings.* New York: Norton, 1981.

Calder, Lendol. *Financing the American Dream: A Cultural History of Consumer Credit in America.* Princeton, N.J.: Princeton University Press, 1999.

Calkins, Earnest Elmo. *And Hearing Not.* New York: Scribner's, 1946.

———. "Beauty in the Machine Age: The New Concern with Esthetics." *Printers' Ink,* September 25, 1930, pp. 72–83.

———. *Modern Advertising.* 1905. Reprint, New York: Garland Publishers, 1985.

Campbell, Colin. *The Romantic Ethic and the Spirit of Modern Consumerism.* New York: Blackwell, 1987.

Canfield, Jack and Mark Hansen. *Chicken Soup for the Soul: 101 Stories to Open the Heart.* Deerfield Beach, Fla.: Health Communications, 1993.

Chopra, Deepak. *The Seven Spiritual Laws of Success.* New York: Harmony Books, 1997.

Clark, Eric. *The Want Makers: The World of Advertising.* New York: Viking, 1988.

Cowan, Tyler. *In Praise of Commercial Culture.* Cambridge: Harvard University Press, 1998.

Csikszentmihalyi, Mihalay and Eugene Rochberg-Halton. *The Meaning of Things: Domestic Symbols and the Self.* New York: Cambridge University Press, 1981.

De Witt, Karen. "So, What is the Leather Bustier Saying?" *New York Times,* January 1, 1995, sect. 4, p. 2.

Diderot, Denis. "Regrets on Parting With My Old Dressing Gown." In *Rameau's Nephew and Other Works by Denis Diderot,* 309–317. Translated by Jacques Barzun. New York: Bobbs-Merrill, 1964.

Dominguez, Joseph and Vicki Robin. *Your Money or Your Life.* New York: Viking, 1992.

Douglas, Mary and Baron Isherwood. *The World of Goods: Towards an Anthropology of Consumption.* New York: Basic Books, 1979.

Drucker, Peter F. *The Age of Discontinuity: Guidelines to Our Changing Society.* New York: Harper & Row, 1969.

Dubois, Bernard and Claire Paternault. "Observations: Understanding the

World of International Luxury Brands: The 'Dream Formula.'" *Journal of Advertising Research*, August 1995, pp. 69–76.

Duff, Christine. "Retail Giant Faces a New Generation Gap." *Houston Chronicle*, February 19, 1995, p. 6.

Dunkel, Tom. "Big Bucks, Tough Tactics." *New York Times Magazine*, September 17, 1989, p. 56 ff.

Durning, Alan. *How Much Is Enough: The Consumer Society and the Future of the Earth*. New York: Norton, 1992.

Elgin, Duane. *Voluntary Simplicity*. New York: Morrow, 1981.

Elliott, Stuart. "The Spot on the Cutting Room Floor." *New York Times*, February 7, 1997, p. C1.

Englis, Basil and Michael Solomon. "To Be and Not to Be: Lifestyle Imagery, Reference Groups, and the Clustering of America." *Journal of Advertising*, March 22, 1955, pp. 13–27.

Featherstone, Mike. *Consumer Culture and Postmodernism*. Newberry Park, Calif.: Sage Publications, 1991.

Fine, Ben. *The World of Consumption*. New York: Routledge, 1993.

Firat, A. Fuat and Alladi Venkatesh. "Liberatory Postmodernism and the Reenchantment of Shopping." *Journal of Consumer Research* 22 (1995): 239–267.

Fish, Stanley. *There's No Such Thing as Free Speech*. New York: Oxford University Press, 1994.

Fleming, Ian. *Live and Let Die*. London: Jonathan Cape, 1972.

Forty, Adrian. *Objects of Desire: Design and Society from Wedgwood to IBM*. New York: Pantheon, 1986.

Fox, Richard Wightman and T. J. Jackson Lears, eds. *The Culture of Consumption: Critical Essays in American History, 1880–1980*. New York: Pantheon, 1983.

Frank, Robert. *The Winner-Take-All Society: How More and More Americans Compete for Ever Fewer and Bigger Prizes, Encouraging Economic Waste, Inequality and an Impoverished Cultural Life*. New York: Free Press, 1995.

Frank, Thomas. *The Conquest of Cool: Business Culture, Counterculture, and the Rise of Hip Consumerism*. Chicago: University of Chicago Press, 1997.

Frazer, James. *The Golden Bough: A Study of Magic and Religion*. New York: Macmillan, 1922.

Friedman, Monroe. *A "Brand" New Language: Commercial Influences in Literature and Culture*. New York: Greenwood Press, 1991.

Fukuyama, Francis. "The End of History?" *The National Interest* 16 (1989): 3–18.

Galbraith, John Kenneth. *The Affluent Society.* New York: Houghton Mifflin, 1958.

———. *A Contemporary Guide to Economics, Peace, and Laughter.* Edited by Andrea Williams. Boston: Houghton Mifflin, 1971.

Gershman, Suzy. *Born-to-Shop: Mexico.* New York: Macmillian, 1996.

Gladwell, Malcolm. "Annals of Style: The Coolhunt." *The New Yorker,* March 17, 1997, pp. 78–88.

Glazer, Nathan. *Faces in the Crowd: Individual Studies in Character and Politics.* New Haven: Yale University Press, 1965.

Goldrich, Robert. "Go West, Creatives. . . . " *Back Stage,* August 11, 1989, p. 6B.

Goodman, Walter. "Seeing Money as the Ruler, More Despotic Than Kind." *New York Times,* September 13, 1997, p. A22.

Green, Barbara. "Retail Space Excess the Root of Decline for Mall Glory Days." *Richmond Times Dispatch,* January 24, 1996, p. L6.

Greider, William. *The Trouble with Money.* Knoxville: Whittle Direct Books, 1989.

Hambleton, Ronald. *The Branding of America: From Levi Strauss to Chrysler.* Camden, Maine: Yankee Books, 1987.

Harmetz, Aljean. "'Amazing Stories' Tries New Tactics." *New York Times,* June 2, 1986, p. 21.

Harrington, Walt. "How Wonder Bread Survived the Whole-Grain Revolution." *Washington Post,* November 25, 1984, p. 12.

Harris, Alice. *The White T.* Introduction by Giorgio Armani. New York: HarperStyle, 1966.

Harrison, Molly. *People and Shopping: A Social Background.* Totowa, N.J.: Rowman and Littlefield, 1975.

Hebdige, Dick. *Subculture: The Meaning of Style.* London: Methuen, 1979.

Heilbroner, Robert. *Limits of American Capitalism.* New York: Harper & Row, 1966.

Hine, Thomas. *The Total Package: The Evolution and Secret Meanings of Boxes, Bottles, Cans and Tubes.* New York: Little, Brown and Company, 1995.

Hirsch, E. D. *Cultural Literacy: What Every American Needs to Know.* New York: Houghton Mifflin, 1987.

Holbrook, Morris. *Daytime Television Shows and the Celebration of Merchandise: "The Price is Right".* Bowling Green, Ohio: Popular Culture Press, 1993.

Jardine, Lisa. *Worldly Goods: A New History of the Renaissance.* New York: Doubleday, 1996.

Kakutani, Michiko. "Common Threads." *New York Times Magazine,* February 16, 1997, p. 18.

References

Key, Brian. *Media Sexploitation*. Englewood Cliffs, N.J.: Prentice Hall, 1976.
———. *Subliminal Seduction*. New York: New American Library, 1973.
King, Stephen. "Apt Pupil." In *Different Seasons*, 109–285. New York: New American Library, 1983.
Kowinski, William Severini. *The Malling of America: An Insider Look at the Great Consumer Paradise*. New York: Morrow, 1985.
Krier, Beth Ann. "Hot to Shop: Can Retail Therapy Cure the Blues." *Los Angeles Times*, November 1, 1991, p. 1.
Kristol, Irving. "The Emerging American Imperium." *Wall Street Journal*, August 18, 1997, p. A14.
Kron, Joan. "It's Not Chic. It's Not Plain. It's Homey." *New York Times*, July 26, 1990, p. C1.
Lasch, Christopher. *Culture of Narcissism: American Life in an Age of Diminishing Expectations*. New York: Norton, 1979.
Laurence, Charles. "Move Over Generation X." *Daily Telegraph*, June 19, 1966, p. 21.
Lavin, Marilyn. "Creating Consumers in the 1930s: Irna Phillips and the Radio Soap Opera." *Journal of Consumer Research* 22 (1995): 75–89.
Leach, William. *Land of Desire: Merchants, Power, and the Rise of a New American Culture*. New York: Random House, 1993.
Lears, T. J. Jackson. *Fables of Abundance: A Cultural History of Advertising in America*. New York: Basic Books, 1994.
———. "From Salvation to Self-Realization: Advertising and the Therapeutic Roots of the Consumer Culture, 1880–1930." In Richard Fox and T. J. Jackson Lears, eds., *The Culture of Consumption: Critical Essays in American History*, 3–38. New York: Pantheon Books, 1983.
———. "Some Versions of Fantasy: Toward a Cultural History of American Advertising, 1880–1930." In Jack Salzman, ed., *Prospects: The Annual of American Cultural Studies*, pp. 349–405. New York: Cambridge University Press, 1984.
Lebergott, Stanley. *Pursuing Happiness: American Consumers in the Twentieth Century*. Princeton: Princeton University Press, 1993.
Leiss, William. *The Limits to Satisfaction: An Essay on the Problem of Needs and Commodities*. Toronto: University of Toronto Press, 1976.
Levy, Sidney. *Marketing, Society and Conflict*. Englewood Cliffs, N.J.: Prentice-Hall, 1975.
Lewis, Paul. "In Buying We Trust: The Foundation of U.S. Consumerism Was Laid in the 18th Century." *New York Times*, May 30, 1998, p. A13.
Lewis, Richard. *Absolut Book*. Boston: Journey Editions, 1996.

Lindbergh, Anne Morrow. *Gift from the Sea.* New York: Pantheon, 1955.

Linden, Eugene, *Affluence and Discontent: The Anatomy of Consumer Societies.* New York: Viking, 1979.

Lobrano, Alexander. "The Fine Art of Shopping." *International Herald Tribune,* February, 28 1995, feature.

Lopiano-Misdom, Janine and Joanne De Luca. *Street Trends: How Today's Alternative Youth Cultures are Creating Tomorrow's Mainstream Markets.* New York: HarperBusiness, 1997.

Lynd, Helen and Robert. *Middletown: A Study in American Culture.* New York: Harcourt, Brace, 1929.

Malloy, John. *Dress for Success.* New York: Warner Books, 1975.

Marcel, Gabriel. *Being and Having.* New York: Harper & Row, 1965.

Marks, Marjorie. "Stopping the Shopping Juggernaut." *Los Angeles Times,* December 3, 1987, part 5, p. 1.

Marx, Karl, and Friedrich Engels. *The Communist Manifesto.* 1872. Reprint, New York: Oxford University Press, 1992.

Mason, Bobbie Ann. *Shiloh and Other Stories.* New York: Harper & Row, 1982.

Mason, Roger. *Conspicuous Consumption: A Study of Exceptional Consumer Behavior.* New York: St. Martin's Press, 1981.

McAleavy, Teresa. "Home Shopping Addiction." *Bergen Record,* November 29, 1993, p. B1.

McCracken, Grant. *Culture and Consumption: New Approaches to the Symbolic Character of Consumer Goods and Activities.* Bloomington: Indiana University Press, 1988.

McDonald, William J. "Time Use in Shopping: The Role of Personal Characteristics." *Journal of Retailing* 70, 4 (1994): 345–72.

McDowell, Colin. "Spend, Spend, Spend." Review of *Fashioning the Bourgeoisie. Sunday Times* (London), July 17, 1994, p. 12.

McLaughlin, Patricia. "Chain Reaction." *Chicago Tribune,* September 24, 1989, p. 5.

Meredith, Robin. "Big Mall's Curfew Raises Questions of Rights and Bias." *New York Times,* December 4, 1996, p, A1.

Meyers, Mike. "Cosmetics Purchases Provide an Insight Into Shopping for Status." *Minneapolis Star Tribune,* January, 27, 1995, p. 2D.

Mifflin, Margot. "Youth Cultures Forecast a Future of Back to the 80s." *New York Times,* September, 15 1996, sect. 1, p. 53.

Miller, Arthur. *The Price: A Play.* New York: Penguin, 1968.

Miller, Daniel. *Acknowledging Consumption: A Review of New Studies.* New York: Routledge, 1996.

References

————. *A Theory of Shopping*. Ithaca: Cornell University Press, 1998.

Moore, Thomas. *Care of the Soul: A Guide for Cultivating Depth and Sacredness in Everyday Life*. New York: HarperCollins, 1992.

Morin, Richard. "Hot Facts and Hot Stats from the Social Sciences." *Washington Post*, June 12, 1994, p. C5.

Morley, David. *Television, Audiences, and Cultural Studies*. New York: Routledge, 1992.

Mukerji, Chandra. *From Graven Images: Patterns of Modern Materialism*. New York: Columbia University Press, 1983.

Nader, Ralph. *The Big Boys: Power and Position in American Business*. New York: Pantheon, 1986.

Nelson, Emily. "90s Getaway: Drive to Hotel, Shop." *Wall Street Journal*, November 14, 1997, p. B1.

Nemy, Enid. "Metropolitan Diary." *New York Times*, December 29, 1996, p. A27.

Nickerson, Camilla. *Fashion: Photography of the Nineties*. New York: Scalo, 1996.

Oates, Joyce Carol. *Wonderland*. New York: Vanguard Press, 1971.

Ode, Kim. "It's a Mall, Mall World: But is it a Shopper's Safe Haven." *Minneapolis Star Tribune*, August 2, 1992, p. 6.

Ogilvy, David. *Confessions of an Advertising Man*. New York: Atheneum, 1963.

Packard, Vance. *The Hidden Persuaders*. New York: D. McKay, 1957.

————. *The Status Seekers*. New York: D. McKay, 1959.

Patten, Simon Nelson. *The Theory of Prosperity*. 1902; reprint, New York: Garland, 1974.

Perec, George. *Things: A Story of the Sixties*. Translated by David Bellos. Boston: David Godine, 1965.

Peterman, J. *J. Peterman Gift Book* (winter catalog). Lexington, Ky.: The J. Peterman Co., 1997.

Quimby, Ian, ed. *Material Culture and the Study of Material Life*. New York: Norton, 1978.

Randazzo, Sal. *Mythmaking on Madison Avenue: How Advertisers Apply the Power to Myth & Symbolism to Create Leadership Brands*. Chicago: Probus, 1993.

Rathje, William. "Rubbish!" *The Atlantic*, December 1989, pp. 99–109.

Rathje, William and Cullen Murphy. *Rubbish!: The Archaeology of Garbage*. New York: HarperCollins, 1992.

Reeves, Rosser. *Reality in Advertising*. New York: Knopf, 1961.

Reisman, David in collaboration with Reuel Denney and Nathan Glazer. *The*

Lonely Crowd: A Study of the Changing American Character. New Haven: Yale University Press, 1950.

Rogers, Stuart. "How a Publicity Blitz Created the Myth of Subliminal Advertising." *Public Relations Quarterly* 34, 4 (1992): 1–12.

Rorty, James. *Our Master's Voice: Advertising*. New York: John Day, 1934.

Rosene, John. "Letter to Editor." *Advertising Age*, August 11, 1997, p. 15.

Rugoff, Ralph. "The Can's the Thing." Review of *The Complete Package*. *Los Angeles Times Book Review*, May 21, 1995, p. 1.

St. James, Elaine. *Inner Simplicity: 100 Ways to Regain Peace and Nourish Your Soul*. New York: Hyperion, 1995.

——. *Living the Simple Life: A Guide to Scaling Down and Enjoying More*. New York: Hyperion, 1996.

——. *Simplify Your Life: 100 Ways to Slow Down and Enjoy the Things That Really Matter*. New York: Hyperion, 1994.

Schama, Simon. *Embarrassment of Riches: An Interpretation of Dutch Culture in the Golden Age*. New York: Knopf, 1987.

Schor, Juliet B. *The Overspent American*. New York: Basic Books, 1998.

——. *The Overworked American: The Unexpected Decline of Leisure*. New York: Basic Books, 1991.

Schudson, Michael. *Advertising, the Uneasy Profession: Its Dubious Impact on American Society*. New York: Basic Books, 1984.

——. "Delectable Materialism: Were the Critics of Consumer Culture Wrong All Along?" *The American Prospect* 3 (1991): 26–35.

Scitovsky, Tibor. *The Joyless Economy: An Inquiry into Human Satisfaction and Consumer Dissatisfaction*. New York: Oxford University Press, 1976.

Sebastian, Pamela. "Business Bulletin: A Special Background Report on Trends in Industry and Finance." *Wall Street Journal*, July 24, 1997, p. A1.

Sheldon, Charles Monroe. *In His Steps*. New York: Grosset & Dunlap, 1935.

"Shootout at the Checkout." *The Economist*, June 5, 1993, p. 69.

Simon, Richard. "Advertising as Literature: The Utopian Fiction of the American Marketplace." *Texas Studies in Language and Literature* 22, 2 (1980): 154–74.

Simpson, James B. *Contemporary Quotations*. New York: Crowell, 1964.

Steinberg, Leo. *The Sexuality of Christ in Renaissance Art and in Modern Oblivion*. New York: Pantheon, 1983.

Tierney, John. "Recycling is Garbage." *New York Times Magazine*, June 30, 1996, pp. 24 ff.

Trollope, Anthony. *The Way We Live Now*. 1874–75; reprint, Lindon: Oxford University Press, 1941.

References

Trollope, Frances. *Domestic Manners of the Americans.* 1832; reprint, New York: Knopf, 1949.

Turner, Allen. "It's Over: WW II Forever Altered America's Face." *Houston Chronicle,* August 13, 1995, sect. 2, p. 2.

Twain, Mark. *"The Man That Corrupted Hadleyburg" and Other Stories and Essays.* New York: Oxford University Press, 1996.

Twitchell, James B. *Adcult USA: The Triumph of Advertising in American Culture.* New York: Columbia University Press, 1996.

———. *Carnival Culture: The Trashing of Taste in America.* New York: Columbia University Press, 1992.

Vasari, Giorgio. *Lives of the Most Eminent Architects, Painters, & Sculptors.* Translated by George Bull. 1550; reprint, New York: Dutton, 1963.

Veblen, Thorstein. *The Theory of the Leisure Class.* 1899; reprint, Boston: Houghton Mifflin, 1973.

Wagner, Charles. *The Simple Life.* New York: McClure, Phillips, 1901.

Wasserstein, Wendy. *The Sisters Rosensweig.* New York: Harcourt Brace Jovanovich, 1993.

Weber, Max. *The Protestant Ethic and the Spirit of Capitalism.* 1905; reprint, New York: Scribner's, 1958.

Wharton, Edith. *The Decoration of Houses.* 1899; reprint, New York: Norton, 1997.

Whyte, William H. *The Organization Man.* New York: Simon & Schuster, 1956.

Williams, Raymond. "The Magic System." *New Left Review* 4 (1960): 27–32.

Wilson, Sloan. *The Man in the Gray Flannel Suit.* New York: Simon & Schuster, 1955.

Wolfe, Tom. "Stalking the Billion-Footed Beast: A Literary Manifesto for the New Social Order." *Harper's,* November, 1989, pp. 45–57.

Zepp, Ira. *The New Religious Image of Urban America: The Mall as Ceremonial Center.* Westminster, Md.: Christian Classics, 1986.

⇧

Index

Page numbers in *italics* refer to illustrations.

Index

Index

Index

Fashion photography, 206–7; as art, 206; in *Fashion: Photography of the Nineties,* 207; in *New York Times,* 207

Fast Moving Consumer Goods (FMCG), 90, 113, 124, 128, 153

Federal Trade Commission (FTC), 115, 135

Ferrari (as brand), 179–80

Field, Marshall, 257

Filmation Associates, 115

Fish, Stanley, 278*n*

Fitzgerald, F. Scott, 217

Fleming, Ian, 161–63; and James Bond, 108

Fleming, Victor, 258

Food service (as fashion), 210–12; and beer, 212; and branding, 210; and cigarettes, 212

Forestall, 245

Fowler, Marc, 115

Fox channel, 102

Fox, Simon, 102*n*

Francis, Saint, 8

Frank, Robert, 33

Frank, Thomas, 229

Frankfurt School (of criticism), 41–42; argument of, 41; examples of, 42*n,* failure of, 41

Frazer, James, 59

Friedman, Monroe, 164–65

Fukuyama, Francis, 284–85

Gable, Clark, 218

Galbraith, John Kenneth, 34, 36, 55, 58*n*

Gallup poll, 2

Gamble, James, 170

Gandhi, Mahatma, 8

Gannett Corp., 95

Garbage, 3–6; amounts generated, 4; anxiety over, 3–5; examples of concern, 4–5; euphemisms for, 4; meaning of, 3; reported on, 5; and shame, 3–5; and recycling, 3–4, scholarship on, 5*n*

General Electric Co., 91

General Foods Corp., 130

General Motors Co., 52

Gershman, Suzy, 248–49

Gillette Corp., 189

Gissing, George, 160

Glazer, Nathan, 174

Godfrey, Arthur, 108

Goldman, Sylvan, 125

Gramsci, Antonio, 42*n*

Greider, William, 94

Grocer, 130–31, *131;* and concerns about measurement, 130*n*

Gruen, Victor, 258, 263

Gucci Group, 167, 187, 188*n,* 205, 210

Guggenheim, Peggy, 250

Hardy, Thomas, 160

Harper, Marion, Jr., 63*n*

Hatfield, Henry, 98

Hawthorne Court (housing development), 98

Hazel Bishop Corp., 100

He-Man and the Masters of the Universe (televison show and game), 115–16

Hearst, William Randolph, 250

Heath Anthology of American Literature, 55*n*

Hebdige, Dick, 43*n,* 225

Hegel, Friedrich, 285

Heilbroner, Robert, 33

Heinz, H. J. Co., 190, 230

Index

O'Neal, Shaquille, 53
Oates, Joyce Carol, 160, 266*n*
"Objects of Desire" (MOMA show, 1977), 43*n*
Ogilvy & Mather (ad agency), 82–83
Ogilvy, David, 177, 178, 274
Oldenburg, Claes, 157
Omnicom (advertising holding company), 91
Onassis, Jacqueline Kennedy, 218–19, 250
Oreos (as brand extension), *180*
Orkin Pest Control Co., 51
Orwell, George, 42

Packaging, 123–58; and advertising agencies, 148; as art, 151–58; cans, 147; clothing as, 144; color important in, 129; cost of, 128–29; criticism of, 143–44; design of, 127; designers for, 146*n*; desire for, 143; FDA regulations, 131*n*; and generics, 146*n*; role of grocer, 131; history of, 147–49; innovations in, 147; role of magazines, 147–48; metaphysics of, 143–45; Nabisco example, 148; ontology of, 145–47; influence of patent medicine, 147; plastics in, 149; and religion, 149–52, 150*n*; and safety, 130; shame of, 145; shopping bags as, 145–46; current simplicity of, 149; impact of television, 149; as trash, 145; tubes, 147–48; for vodkas, 129*n*; *see also* Pop art; Trade dress
Packard, Vance, 36
Parish, "Sister," 210
Paternault, Claire, 184
Pathmark (supermarket), 126

Patten, Simon Nelson, 36*n*
Pears' soap, 169–72, *171*
Pecuniary emulation, 37
Penn, Irving, 206
"People and Their Stuff" (ad campaign), 82–88, *84*, *87*
Pepsi, 52, 53, 83, 128, 130, 214; and advertising, 142; and Coke, 141; food division, 142*n*; and packaging of, 141
Perec, George, 46*n*
Peters, Bernadette, 1
Peters, Tom, 237
Pfahler, Kembra, 200
Philip Morris, 52, 188–89, 214; and "Marlboro Friday," 189
Philips, Irna, 107
Piggly Wiggly (supermarket), 124
Pop art, 151–58; as art, 153; and branding, 154; criticism of, 151–52; and FMCGs, 153; and grocery store, 151; importance of, 151–52; subjects of, 152; and packaging, 158; in retrospect, 156; *see also* Andy Warhol; Joseph Cornell; Christo
Popcorn, Faith, 229
Porsche (as brand), 179
Poster, Mark, 61
Pot O' Gold (television show), 110
Potter, Charles, 73*n*
Prell (shampoo), 191–93; container, 192*n*, meaning of hair, 192; and hairstyle, 191; and packaging, 192–93; other shampoos, 191–92
Price Is Right, 111–14, audience for, 112; contestants on, 112; history of, 111; how it works, 111–13; and television shows, 110; variations,

⌂